365 DEVOTIONAL READINGS FROM

MARTIN LUTHER

THROUGH FAITH ALONE

CONCORDIA PUBLISHING HOUSE · SAINT LOUIS

Through Faith Alone
365 Devotional Readings from Martin Luther

Copyright ® 1999 Concordia Publishing House
3558 S. Jefferson Avenue, St. Louis, MO 63118-3968

Copyright © 1998 by World Publishing

General Editor: James C. Galvin, Ed. D.

Translators: Ric Gudgeon, D. Min., Trudy Krucke Zimmerman, and Gerhard Meske

English Stylists: Jonathan Farrar, Kristine A. Luber

Based on GOD'S WORD, Copyright © 1995 by God's Word to the Nations Bible Society

Printed in the United States

3   4   5   6   7   8   9   10   11 10   09   08   07   06   05   04

INTRODUCTION

Martin Luther is one of the most important figures in church history because God used him to reform the Christian church. Born in Germany in 1483, Luther studied law at the University of Erfurt. During a violent thunderstorm, he made a dramatic vow to become a monk and soon after entered the Augustinian order. After rigorous academic study and intense, personal struggle to find God's approval, he was ordained and sent to the University of Wittenburg to teach theology. He became the leading figure and focal point of the Reformation.

Luther was a professor, theologian, former monk, scholar, author, Bible translator, and defender of the faith. But he was also a pastor, husband, father, and good friend to many. Luther was prolific. Besides writing commentaries, theological papers, and letters to friends, he spoke often in public, and his students and followers took careful notes of his university lectures, sermons, and later in life, even his dinner conversations.

Faith emerges as a central theme throughout Luther's writings. He loved God and wanted people to believe in Christ and to grow in their faith. He forcefully preached and defended the doctrine that we are justified through faith alone.

Through Faith Alone, then, fits well as a title for a devotional based on Luther's writings. Freshly translated from the original German into today's English, this edition is conveniently divided into daily readings for personal use. May this book point you to the Gospel of God's grace in Christ and help you understand the importance of faith, appreciate the mystery of faith, and encourage you to grow in faith.

James C. Galvin, Ed.D.

PREFACE

The selections in this devotional, originally written by Martin Luther between 1513 and 1546, have been freshly translated from German into today's English for this edition. God's Word to the Nations Bible Society, translators of the GOD'S WORD Bible translation, established the translation philosophy and process. My goal was to make this edition both accurate and easy to understand for modern readers. I wanted to provide short selections for daily devotional reading.

I excerpted these selections from Luther's commentaries, sermons, and other devotional writings. Luther tended to weave several themes into his writings and to touch on many subjects. In the German, sentences tend to be long and to include archaic terms, so most of the selections required careful editing to fit on one page and still make sense. The translators and editors worked hard to remain faithful to Luther's intent and to retain the images and voice of the original. Luther often used everyday language and life experiences to communicate God's truth to his students and common people.

You'll notice brackets and ellipses in the Bible verses quoted. GOD'S WORD uses half brackets (⌊ ⌋) to mark the occurrence of words that are used to assist in translation but that are not translations of words in the original languages. These half brackets are preserved in this edition. The full brackets ([ ]) and ellipses (. . .) indicate alterations made by the editors of this book for clarity as they excerpted the verses.

The verse at the beginning of each reading is usually the one that Luther was writing about or preaching on. At times I attached a different verse that better fit the theme of the devotional thought and the purposes of this edition. You can locate each selection and the work from which it is excerpted by using the index to the other editions in the back of this volume.

FAITH COMES FIRST

*God has made us what we are. He has created us in
Christ Jesus to live lives filled with good works that
he has prepared for us to do.*

EPHESIANS 2:10

❖

OU HAVE OFTEN HEARD me say that the
Christian life has two dimensions: the first is
faith, and the second is good works. A
believer should live a devout life and always do what is
right. But the first dimension of the Christian life, faith,
is more essential. The second dimension, good works,
is never as valuable as faith. However, people of the
world adore good works. They regard them to be far
higher than faith.

Good works have always been valued more highly
than faith. Of course, it's true that we should do good
works and respect the importance of them. But we should
be careful that we don't elevate good works to such an
extent that faith and Christ become secondary. If we
esteem them too highly, good works can become the
greatest idolatry. This has occurred both inside and outside of Christianity. Some people value good works so
much that they overlook faith in Christ. They preach
about and praise their own works instead of God's works.

Faith should be first. After faith is preached, then we
should teach about good works. It is faith—*without*
good works and *prior to* good works—that takes us to
heaven. We come to God through faith alone.

WE LIVE BY FAITH

God's approval is revealed in this Good News. This approval begins and ends with faith as Scripture says, "The person who has God's approval will live by faith."

ROMANS 1:17

❖

HEN I WAS A MONK, I didn't accomplish anything through fasting and prayer. This is because neither I, nor any of the other monks, acknowledged our sin and lack of reverence for God. We didn't understand original sin, and we didn't realize that unbelief was also sin. We believed and taught that no matter what a person did, he could never be certain of God's kindness and mercy. As a result, the more I ran after and looked for Christ, the more he eluded me.

When I realized that it was only through God's undeserved kindness that I would be enlightened and receive eternal life, I worked diligently to understand what Paul said in Romans 1:17—the righteousness of God is revealed in the gospel. I searched for a long time and tried to understand it again and again. But the Latin words for "the righteousness of God" were in my way. God's righteousness was usually defined as the characteristic by which he was sinless and condemns the sinner. All the teachers except Augustine interpreted *God's righteousness* as *God's anger*. So every time I read it, I wished that God had never revealed the gospel. Who could love a God who is angry and who judges and condemns us?

Finally, with the help of the Holy Spirit, I took a closer look at what the prophet Habakkuk said, "The righteous person will live because of his faithfulness" (Habakkuk 2:4). From this I concluded that life must come from faith. I, therefore, took the abstract to the concrete level, as we say in school. I related the concept of righteousness to a person becoming righteous. In other words, a person receives God's approval by faith. That opened the whole Bible—even heaven itself—to me!

WHAT IT MEANS TO BELIEVE

Then Jesus said loudly, "Whoever believes in me believes not only in me but also in the one who sent me."

JOHN 12:44

❖

HERE ARE TWO WAYS to believe. The first way is to believe *about God*, meaning that we believe what is taught about God is really true. It's similar to believing that what is taught about the devil or hell is true. This type of belief is more a statement of knowledge than an expression of faith.

The second way is to believe *in God.* This not only includes believing what is taught about God is true but also includes trusting him and daring to be in relationship with him. It means believing without any doubt that he really is who he says he is, and he will do all he says he will do. I wouldn't believe any person to this same degree, no matter how highly others might praise him. It's easy to believe that someone is godly, but it's another matter to completely rely on him.

A person who believes in God believes everything written about God in Scripture. He dares to believe this in life and in death. This faith makes a person a true Christian and gives him everything he desires from God. A person with an evil, hypocritical heart can't have this type of faith, for it's a living faith, as described in the first commandment: "I am the LORD your God . . . Never have any other god" (Exodus 20:2–3).

Therefore, the little word *in* is well placed and should be carefully noted. We don't say I believe God the Father, or I believe about God the Father, but I believe *in* God the Father, *in* Jesus Christ, *in* the Holy Spirit. Only God can give us this type of faith.

FAITH IN CHRIST ALONE

So we also believed in Jesus Christ in order
to receive God's approval by faith in Christ
and not because of our own efforts.

GALATIANS 2:16

❖

E RECEIVE GOD'S APPROVAL through faith in
Christ, not through our own efforts. You
shouldn't let anyone confuse you by saying
that faith only justifies people when love and good
works are added to it.

If a person hears that he must believe in Christ and
that faith alone doesn't justify unless love is added to it,
he immediately falls from faith and thinks, "If faith
without love doesn't justify, then faith is empty and useless. Love alone justifies. For if faith is not formed and
enhanced by love, then it's nothing." In order to prove
their damaging comments, my opponents point to
1 Corinthians 13:1–2: "I may speak in the languages of
humans and of angels. . . . But if I don't have love, I am
nothing." They think these verses are an impenetrable
wall. But they don't understand Paul's teachings. You
should avoid these comments as if they were poison
from hell.

Instead, you should conclude with Paul that we are
justified by faith alone, not through faith formed by
love. So we shouldn't attribute the power of justification to something formed in us that makes us pleasing
to God. We must attribute it to faith, which takes hold
of Christ the Savior and keeps him in our hearts. This
faith justifies us apart from love and prior to love. We
concede that we must also teach about good works and
love. But we only teach these at the proper time and
place—when the question deals with how we should
live, not how we are justified. But the question here is:
How do we become justified and receive eternal life?
We answer with Paul that we receive God's approval
through faith in Christ alone, not by our own efforts.

UNWORTHY TO PRAY

But the tax collector was standing at a distance. He wouldn't
even look up to heaven. Instead, he became very upset, and
he said, "God, be merciful to me, a sinner!"

LUKE 18:13

❖

OME SAY, "I would feel better about God
hearing my prayer if I were more worthy and
lived a better life." I simply answer: If you
don't want to pray before you feel that you are worthy
or qualified, then you will never pray again. Prayer
must not be based on or depend on your personal worthiness or the quality of the prayer itself but on the
unchanging truth of God's promise. If the prayer is
based on itself, or on anything else besides God's
promise, then it's a false prayer that deceives you—even
if your heart was breaking with intense devotion, and
you were weeping drops of blood.

We pray because we are unworthy to pray. Our
prayers are heard precisely because we believe that we
are unworthy. We become worthy to pray when we risk
everything on God's faithfulness alone.

So go ahead and feel unworthy. But know in your
heart that it's a thousand times more important to
honor God's truthfulness. Yes, everything depends on
this alone. Don't turn his faithful promise into a lie by
your doubts. For your worthiness doesn't help you and
neither does your unworthiness hinder you. A lack of
faith is what condemns you, but confidence in God is
what makes you worthy.

ASKING GOD FOR FAITH

The child's father cried out at once,
"I believe! Help my lack of faith."

MARK 9:24

❖

 F YOU HAVE DIFFICULTY believing, you should ask God for faith. For the ability to believe is in God's hands alone. God sometimes gives faith openly and sometimes secretly.

But you can spur yourself on to believe. To begin, you shouldn't continually focus on the suffering of Christ. This has already done its work and frightened you. Rather, move beyond that and look at Christ's caring heart. See how full of love it is towards you, so that it drives him to lift the heavy load of your sin. Then your heart will be filled with love towards him, and your faith will be strengthened.

After this, move beyond Christ's heart to God's heart. You will see that Christ wouldn't have shown you love unless God in his eternal love had wanted him to. Christ is being obedient to God when he loves you. You will discover the good heart of the Father, and, as Christ says, you will be drawn to the Father through Christ. Then you will better understand what Christ says in John 3:16, "God loved the world this way: He gave his only Son." We recognize the nature of God best, not by thinking about his power or wisdom, which are terrifying, but by thinking about his goodness and love. Then we are truly born anew in God, and we can grow in faith.

POUR YOUR SINS ON CHRIST

God had Christ, who was sinless, take our sin
so that we might receive God's approval through him.

2 CORINTHIANS 5:21

❖

WHEN WE BECOME AWARE of our sin and frightened by it, we must not allow the sin to remain on our conscience. This would only lead to despair. Rather, just as our awareness of sin flowed to us from Christ, so we must pour our sin back on him to free our conscience.

So be careful you don't become like the misguided people who allow their sin to bite at them and eat at their hearts. They strive to rid themselves of this sin by running around doing good works. But you have a way to get rid of your sins. You throw your sins on Christ when you firmly believe that Christ's wounds and suffering carried and paid for your sins. As Isaiah said, "The LORD has laid all our sins on him" (Isaiah 53:6). Peter said, "Christ carried our sins in his body on the cross" (1 Peter 2:24). And Paul said, "God had Christ, who was sinless, take our sin" (2 Corinthians 5:21).

You must rely on these and similar verses with your whole heart. The more your conscience torments you, the more you must rely on them. For if you don't do this and try to quiet your conscience through your own sorrow and penance, you will never find peace of mind and will finally despair in the end. If you try to deal with sin in your conscience, let it remain there, and continue to look at it in your heart, your sins will become too strong for you. They will seem to live forever. But when you think of your sins as being on Christ and boldly believe that he conquered them through his resurrection, then they are dead and gone. Sin can't remain on Christ. His resurrection swallowed sin up.

UNDER HIS WINGS

Jerusalem, Jerusalem, you kill the prophets and stone to death those sent to you! How often I wanted to gather your children together the way a hen gathers her chicks under her wings!

MATTHEW 23:37

❖

N THIS PASSAGE, Christ gives us a beautiful illustration of faith. The Lord tenderly says to the Israelites that he would have gladly been their mother hen if they were only willing to be his chicks. Note carefully his words and illustration. Christ pours this out with his whole heart and with great seriousness. In this picture, we see how we should act towards Christ. It shows us how he can help us, how we should make use of him and enjoy him. If we watch how a hen behaves with her chicks, then we will see Christ and ourselves depicted better than any artist can paint.

Our souls are the chicks, and the devil and evil spirits are the hawks in the air. Except, we aren't as clever as the chicks who flee under their mother hen. Also, demons are more skillful in attacking us than are the hawks in grabbing chicks. I previously taught how it isn't enough to be devout, do good works, and live in grace. For not even our righteousness, let alone our unrighteousness, will endure before God's eyes and his judgment. I have said that faith, if it is genuine faith, doesn't rely on its own ability to believe but holds on to Christ and places itself under his righteousness. Just as chicks don't rely on themselves and their own quickness but simply flee under the hen's body and wings, so we must run to Christ and let him be our shield and protection.

TEMPORARY RESIDENTS

So if you call God your Father, live your time as temporary residents on earth in fear. He is the God who judges all people by what they have done, and he doesn't play favorites.

1 PETER 1:17

❖

ETER IS SAYING, "Because you have a Father who doesn't play favorites, live your life during the time of your pilgrimage on earth in fear." In other words, you should fear the Father. You should not fear him because he will punish you, which is the way unbelievers and even the devil fear him. But fear that he will leave you and take away his protecting hand, just as a pious child would be afraid of making his father angry and doing something to displease him. God wants us to have that kind of fear so that we will guard ourselves from sin and serve our neighbor while we live here on earth.

If a Christian is a sincere believer, he has all of God's treasures and is God's child. The rest of his life on earth is merely a pilgrimage. God allows him to live in this body and walk on this earth so that he can help other people and bring them to heaven. Therefore, we must use all things on earth in no other way than as a guest who travels across the country and comes to an inn. He spends the night there and takes only food and lodging from the innkeeper. He doesn't claim that the innkeeper's property now belongs to him. This is how we must deal with material possessions, as if they did not belong to us. We should enjoy only as much as is necessary for us to maintain the body and use the rest to help our neighbors. Similarly, the Christian life is like being an overnight guest. For "we don't have a permanent city here on earth" (Hebrews 13:14), but we must go to our Father in heaven. This is why Peter says we shouldn't behave wildly but live in fear.

THE SPIRIT CRIES OUT

*Because you are God's children, God has sent the
Spirit of his Son into us to call out, "Abba! Father!"*

GALATIANS 4:6

❖

AUL COULD HAVE SAID: "God has sent the Spirit
of his Son into us to *pray:* 'Abba, Father.' " But
he purposely says "call out" to indicate the
anguish of the Christian who is still weak and needs to
grow in the faith. In Romans 8:26, he describes this calling out as "groans that cannot be expressed in words."

But in the middle of trials and conflicts, it's difficult
to call out to God, and it takes a lot of effort to cling to
God's Word. At those times, we cannot perceive Christ.
We do not see him. Our heart doesn't feel his presence
and his help during the attack. Christ appears to be
angry with us and to have left us. Then during the
attack, we feel the power of sin, the weakness of our
bodies, and our doubt. We experience the flaming
arrows of the devil (Ephesians 6:16) and the terrors of
death. We feel the wrath and judgment of God. All this
raises very powerful and horrible shouts against us so
that there does not appear to be anything left but
despair and eternal death. However, in the middle of
these terrors of the law, the thundering of sin, the shaking of death, and the roar of the devil, the Holy Spirit
in our hearts begins to call out, "Abba! Father!" And his
cry is much stronger and drowns out the powerful and
horrible shouts of the law, sin, death, and the devil. It
penetrates through the clouds and heaven and reaches
up to the ears of God.

TENDING THE VINEYARD

[Then Jesus said,] "I am the true vine,
and my Father takes care of the vineyard."

JOHN 15:1

❖

HIS PASSAGE PRESENTS a very comforting picture. Christ understood all the suffering that he and his followers would experience as nothing else but the work of a diligent gardener. Grapevines can only grow and produce much fruit with careful tending by the gardener. Christ wants to teach us that we should look at trials and suffering very differently than the way it appears and feels to us in this world. Suffering doesn't occur apart from God's will. It's not a sign of his anger, but of his mercy and of his fatherly love. It will serve for the best.

It's an art to believe that what hurts and distresses us doesn't occur to harm us, but to make us improve. What if the vine were aware of this, could talk, and could see the gardener cutting around its roots with a hoe? What if it could see the gardener pruning its branches with his pruning knife? After seeing and feeling all of this, it might say, "Oh! What are you doing? Now I will wither and spoil because you are working on me, taking the soil away from me, and scraping me with those iron teeth. You are tearing and pinching me everywhere, leaving me to stand here half-naked. You are more cruel to me than you are to other trees or plants."

But the gardener would reply, "You just don't understand. If I cut off a branch, it's because it's a useless branch, which takes strength and sap away from you. The other branches won't be able to produce fruit and will also begin to fail. So, off it goes. It's for your own good. I am doing it so you will yield more fruit and will be able to produce good wine."

OUR FATHER IN HEAVEN

This is how you should pray: Our Father in heaven,
let your name be kept holy.

MATTHEW 6:9

❖

OW SHOULD WE ADDRESS GOD? How should we honor the one we pray to? And how should we present ourselves so that he will be gracious and willing to listen to us? No name anywhere makes a more favorable impression on God than the name "Father." Calling him Father is a friendly, affectionate, deep, and heartfelt way to address him. It wouldn't comfort us nearly so much if we were to call him Lord, or God, or Judge. For the name Father is instinctive and naturally affectionate. That is why hearing us call him Father pleases God the most and moves him to listen to us. By doing so, we acknowledge ourselves as children of God, which again stirs God's heart. For there is no voice more dear to a father than his own child's voice.

It also helps when we say, "in heaven." These words express distressing need and misery because we are on earth and God is in heaven. Whoever prays, "Our Father in heaven," and does so out of the depths of his heart, acknowledges that he has a Father and that his Father is in heaven. Moreover, he acknowledges that he is abandoned on earth and is in misery. Anyone who prays this way soon feels a heartfelt yearning, like a child who lives far from his father's land in misery and distress among strangers. It's as if he were saying, "O Father, you are in heaven. I am your poor child far from you on earth, in misery, in peril, in distress, and in need. I am surrounded by devils, great enemies, and many kinds of danger." Anyone who prays in this way stands with a pure, uplifted heart towards God. He is able to pray and move God to mercy.

COMFORT FOR TROUBLING TIMES

Don't be troubled. Believe in God,
and believe in me.

JOHN 14:1

❖

 HENEVER WE FEEL DISTRESSED and anxious, let us believe Christ and strengthen ourselves with his words. We should receive the comfort Christ offers in this passage. It's as if Christ were saying to us, "What are you doing? Why are you cringing? Are you scared to death? Be encouraged and take heart. All is not lost, even if the devil, the world, or your conscience plagues and terrifies you. You're not ruined if you don't feel my presence. Don't you remember that I told you about this long ago and left these comforting words to strengthen and preserve you?"

From these and other words of Christ, we should begin to know the Lord Christ in the right way. We should develop a more loving confidence in him. And we should pay more attention to his Word than to anything that may come before our eyes, ears, and senses. For if we are Christians and stay close to him, we know that he speaks to us. We learn in this passage and elsewhere that he wants to comfort us with his words. Everything that he says or does is nothing but friendly and comforting words and actions.

We can be sure of this: A sorrowful, timid, and frightened heart doesn't come from Christ. Christ doesn't frighten hearts or make them depressed. He came to this earth, did everything, and ascended into heaven to take away sorrow and fearfulness from our hearts and replace them with a cheerful heart, conscience, and mind. That's why he promises to send the Holy Spirit to his followers. Through the Spirit, he wants to strengthen and preserve his followers after he has left. Whoever can trust in what Christ says in this passage will be in good shape and will have won more than half the battle.

The Heart of an Angel

Suddenly, a large army of angels appeared with the angel.
They were praising God by saying, "Glory to God in the highest
heaven, and on earth peace to those who have his good will!"

LUKE 2:13–14

✤

ROM THIS ANGELIC SONG, we can learn what the angels are really like. Forget what the worldly-wise teachers speculate about angels. This passage portrays angels so clearly that we can discern their thoughts and hearts. First of all, by joyfully singing about the honor of God, they show how full of light and fire they are. They recognize how everything belongs to God. They don't take credit for anything. They enthusiastically give honor to God, the one to whom it belongs. If you wonder what a humble, pure, obedient, and happy heart in God is like, then think of the angels praising God. This is their first priority as they live in God's presence.

The second characteristic is that they love us, just as we are taught to love other people. Here you see what wonderful, great friends they are to us. They love us as much as themselves, and they celebrate our salvation as if it were their own. They give us good reason to regard them as highly as we would our best friends. This is the right way to try to understand angels. It's no use trying to understand them according to their essence as the worldly-wise teachers do, whose pursuits are futile anyway. The right way to understand angels is according to their inner heart, attitude, and mind. We might not know what they're made of, but we do know what their highest desire is and what they're continually doing. In this way, we see into their hearts.

LIVING IN CHRIST

Now, dear children, live in Christ.
Then, when he appears we will have confidence,
and when he comes we won't turn from him in shame.

1 JOHN 2:28

❖

HAT SHOULD YOU DO when the thought of death frightens you and your conscience bothers you? Live in Christ. You must believe you can accomplish nothing by your own works, but the only way is through Christ's righteousness. John 6:29 says that the work of God is believing in the one he has sent. So when Nathan corrected David, and David confessed his sin, Nathan replied, "The LORD has taken away your sin; you will not die" (2 Samuel 12:13). David simply lived in grace. He didn't even think about trying to satisfy God with his works. When Nathan said, "The LORD has taken away your sin," he was proclaiming the message of grace. And David believed it.

After Adam sinned, he could do nothing that would bring him into a state of grace. But God said that one of his descendants would "crush [the serpent's] head" (Genesis 3:15). It was by this promise he was made alive. Because he believed in this word, he was saved and justified without any works. Our nature struggles fiercely against being saved without our works and tries to deceive us with a grand illusion of our own righteousness. So we may find ourselves attracted to a life that merely appears to be righteous. Or because we know we aren't righteous, we may be frightened by death or sin. Therefore, we must learn that we should have nothing to do with any other way of becoming righteous, except through Christ alone.

TESTED BY FIRE

*Don't be surprised by the fiery troubles that are coming in order
to test you. Don't feel as though something strange is happening
to you, but be happy as you share Christ's sufferings.*

1 PETER 4:12–13

❖

ETER USES UNUSUAL IMAGERY to remind us what
Scripture says about suffering. Throughout
the Bible, suffering is described as a hot, fiery
oven. Elsewhere, Peter says, "The purpose of these troubles is to test your faith as fire tests how genuine gold is"
(1 Peter 1:7). In the book of Isaiah, God says, "I have
tested you in the furnace of suffering" (Isaiah 48:10). In
Psalms, David says of God, "You have tested me like
silver" (Psalm 17:3). And regarding Israel, the psalmist
says, "We went through fire and water" (Psalm 66:12).
So the Bible speaks of suffering as being engulfed in fire
or tested by fire. Peter says that we shouldn't become
upset or think it's strange when we experience this fire.
We are tested by fire, just as gold is refined by fire.

When we begin to believe, God doesn't abandon us
but lays a holy cross upon our backs to strengthen faith.
The gospel is a powerful Word, but it cannot do its
work without trials. No one will discover its power
unless he experiences it. The gospel can only show its
power where there is a cross and where there is suffering. Because it's a Word of life, it must exercise all its
power in death. If dying and death are absent, then it
can do nothing. No one would discover that it's
stronger than sin and death.

Peter says fiery troubles "are coming in order to test
you." This fire or heat is the cross and suffering which
makes you burn. God inflicts this fire for no other reason except to test you, to see whether you're depending
on his Word. That's why God imposes the cross on all
believers. He wants them to experience and demonstrate God's power.

RESURRECTION BODIES

But someone will ask, "How do the dead come back to life?
With what kind of body will they come back?" You fool!
The seed you plant doesn't come to life unless it dies first.

1 CORINTHIANS 15:35–36

❖

PAUL IS A TRUE MASTER to present this subject so well and with such charm. For no one else could have painted such a portrait. He took what the world considers dead and created a picture of life. He uses such ordinary and small objects—seeds and kernels in a field—to portray it. So when a person dies, we should not look at it any other way than as a seed planted in the ground. If the seed could see and feel what was happening, it would fear that it was ruined forever. But the farmer, if he could talk to the seed, would paint a much different picture. He would portray the seed as if it were already a growing plant with a beautiful stalk and tiny ears of grain.

So we must picture in our own hearts that when we are buried under the ground, we will come up again and grow into a new existence and everlasting life. We don't have to think of ourselves as dead and decaying, but rather as planted. We must learn a new way of speaking about death and the grave. When we die, it doesn't mean we are dead, but instead we are seeds planted for the coming summer. The cemetery is not a mound for the dead, but a field full of little seeds, which are called God's seeds. They will one day blossom again and become more beautiful than anyone can imagine.

THE BRONZE SNAKE

You are all God's children by believing in Christ Jesus.
Clearly, all of you who were baptized in Christ's name
have clothed yourselves with Christ.

GALATIANS 3:26–27

❖

OME PEOPLE IMAGINE that faith is a quality that sticks to the heart on its own, with or without Christ. This is a dangerous error. Christ should be placed directly before our eyes so that we see and hear nothing apart from him and believe that nothing is closer to us than Christ. For he doesn't sit idly in heaven but is continually present in us. He is working and living in us, for Paul says, "I no longer live, but Christ lives in me" (Galatians 2:20). He also says that you "have clothed yourselves with Christ" (Galatians 3:27). Therefore, faith is an unswerving gaze that looks on Christ alone. He is the conqueror of sin and death and the one who gives us righteousness, salvation, and eternal life.

This is beautifully illustrated by the story of the bronze snake, which points to Christ (John 3:14). Moses commanded the Israelites, who had been bitten in the desert by poisonous snakes, to look at this bronze snake with an unswerving gaze. Those who did so were healed, simply by steadily gazing at the snake alone. In contrast, others, who didn't obey Moses, looked at their wounds instead of the snake and died. So if you want to be comforted when your conscience plagues you or when you are in dire distress, then you must do nothing but grasp Christ in faith and say, "I believe in Jesus Christ, God's Son, who suffered, was crucified, and died for me. In his wounds and death, I see my sin. In his resurrection, I see the victory over sin, death, and the devil. I see righteousness and eternal life as well. I want to see and hear nothing except him." This is the true faith in Christ and the right way to believe.

No Other Way

Jesus answered him, "I am the way, the truth, and the life.
No one goes to the Father except through me."

JOHN 14:6

❖

UNDERSTAND WHAT JESUS is saying here in the simplest manner, so that it all applies to this one person, Christ. Jesus is called "the way" because he is the beginning, "the truth" because he is the one who helps us continue, and also "the life" because he is the end. For he must be everything—the beginning, the middle, and the end of our salvation. That is why we place him as the foundation stone on which the other stones are set and on which the entire roof is built. He is the first, middle, and last rung on the ladder to heaven (Genesis 28:12). For through him we must begin, continue, and finally reach the life beyond. So there is only one Christ, but he assumes different roles in our salvation experience.

In the beginning it's hard to find the way. Then life becomes more difficult as we continue to walk along the way. It becomes extremely tough when we have traveled on the way for a long time and are about to reach our final shelter—heaven.

So if you hold on to Christ in faith, then you have started in the right place. If you remain with him, then you will be walking on the right path. If you persevere until the end, then you will be saved. Christ wants to pry our hearts away from trusting anything else. There is no other way, highway, bridge, or path for us than Christ alone.

Don't Wait to Pray

Have pity on me, O God, in keeping with your mercy.
In keeping with your unlimited compassion,
wipe out my rebellious acts.

PSALM 51:1

❖

YOU MUST PRAY when you are in the heat of temptation—when your mind is preoccupied with thoughts of lust or revenge. If someone urges you to pray under these circumstances, your mind often insists that it's too impure—as if your dirty thoughts leave no room for prayer. But you must not wait for temptation to end or the thoughts of lust and other sins to totally disappear from your mind before you pray.

At precisely the moment when you feel the strongest temptation and are least prepared to pray, go to a place where you can be alone. Pray the Lord's Prayer or any other prayer you can think of to defend against the devil and his temptations. Then, you will feel the temptation decrease, and Satan will run away. Those who think that you should wait until your mind is free from impure thoughts to pray only help Satan, who is already far too strong. Waiting to pray is an unchristian approach to prayer. It's a teaching that comes from the devil.

In order to keep yourself from believing these kinds of wrong ideas, you must follow David's example in this psalm. Even after David admitted his terrible sin with Bathsheba, he didn't run away from God. He didn't say what Peter foolishly said while in the boat, "Leave me, Lord! I'm a sinful person" (Luke 5:8). Instead, David trusted in God's mercy and began to pray, "Lord, even though I am a sinner, have pity on me." The time when you feel your sins the most is exactly the time when you most need to pray to God.

INFINITELY MORE THAN WE ASK

When the children inside her were struggling with each other, [Rebekah] said, "If it's like this now, what will become of me?" So she went to ask the LORD.

GENESIS 25:22

❖

EBEKAH'S PRAYER WAS FOR her own life and that of her babies. Yet her prayer resulted in giving birth to two great leaders and all their descendants. She asked God for only a penny, but obtained a mountain of gold—something she hadn't hoped for or dared to believe. She kept her prayer modest and reasonable, and she was willing to be satisfied with small favors.

We, too, are in the habit of praying for trivial and insignificant things. When we pray, we don't take into account the great majesty of God. If God wanted to give us only petty and superficial things, he wouldn't have given us such a magnificent model for prayer: "Our Father in heaven, let your name be kept holy. Let your kingdom come. . . ." God has plenty of resources, and he's not a tightwad. He generously offers us the best gifts available in heaven and on earth. He expects that we will ask him for many things and that we will sincerely believe that we will get what we request. When we receive what we ask for in the Lord's Prayer, we are, in effect, receiving heaven and earth and everything they contain. For when we ask for God's name to be kept holy, for his kingdom to come, and for his will to be done, we are overpowering countless devils and engulfing the whole world with one prayer.

Because we are so narrow-minded and have such weak faith, we should carefully note how God answered Rebekah's prayer. God isn't content to provide us with a small amount even if we only ask for a little. He prefers to give us "infinitely more than we can ask or imagine" (Ephesians 3:20).

RESPOND WITH GENTLENESS

But dedicate your lives to Christ as Lord. Always be ready to defend your confidence ₍in God₎ when anyone asks you to explain it. However, make your defense with gentleness and respect.

1 PETER 3:15

❖

HEN YOU'RE CHALLENGED or asked about your faith, you shouldn't respond arrogantly. You shouldn't be defiant or forceful, as if you were tearing trees out of the ground. Rather, you should respond with fear and humility, as if you were standing before God and answering him. If you were summoned before kings and princes and had prepared yourself well in advance with Scripture, you might think, "Just wait, I'll answer correctly." But the devil will grab the sword out of your hands and give you a shove. You will be disgraced and find out you put your armor on in vain. He can even take your best verses from your hands so that you can't use them, even though you have them memorized. God allows this to happen to subdue your arrogance and make you humble.

So if you don't want this to happen, you must stand in fear and not rely on your own power. Rely instead on what Christ promised: "When they hand you over ₍to the authorities₎, don't worry about what to say or how to say it. When the time comes, you will be given what to say. Indeed, you're not the ones who will be speaking. The Spirit of your Father will be speaking through you" (Matthew 10:19–20). When you have to give an answer, you ought to arm yourself with Scripture. But don't pound it home with a proud spirit. Otherwise, God will tear the verse from your mouth and from your memory even if you were armed with all the verses beforehand. Therefore, caution is needed here. But if you are prepared, you can answer princes, leaders, and even the devil himself. Just make sure you aren't speaking insignificant human words, but the Word of God.

WHEN WE SIN

If anyone does sin, we have Jesus Christ,
who has God's full approval. He speaks on our behalf
when we come into the presence of the Father.

1 JOHN 2:1

❖

HO DOESN'T GO ASTRAY at times? I and everyone else have a need for praise. But when we
sin, we shouldn't despair of not finding
God's mercy. Whoever imagines that his achievements
are worth something mistrusts God's mercy and sins in
the same way.

Don't despair after you have sinned, but lift your
eyes upward, where Christ intercedes for you. For he is
your Advocate and Intercessor. He pleads for you,
saying, "Father, for this person I have suffered. I am
looking after him." This prayer is never useless because
Christ is our Chief Priest (Hebrews 5:10).

Even though we have Christ, our Chief Priest,
Advocate, Mediator, Reconciler, and Comforter, we have
turned instead to dead saints and considered Christ as
our judge. That's why we should write this passage from
the apostle John in gold letters and inscribe it on our
hearts. So reach out to him and say, "Lord Christ, I know
of no other Advocate, Comforter, and Mediator than
you alone. I do not doubt that you are all this to me. I
cling firmly to it, and I believe it." Christ was born for
us. He suffered for us. He ascended into heaven for our
sake, sits at the right hand of the Father, and prays for us.
Satan tries with all his might to blind our hearts so we
will not believe what the Holy Spirit says in this passage.
A Christian's condition is wonderful! For a Christian is
both sinful and righteous. He's a sinful person because
of the corrupt nature he carries with him that is contaminated by sin. He's a righteous person because the
Spirit pulls him back from sin. With our reason, we can
never understand the wonder of this condition.

GOD'S MERCY AND KINDNESS

Wash me thoroughly from my guilt,
and cleanse me from my sin.

PSALM 51:2

❖

FTER A CHRISTIAN has received God's approval through faith and knows that his sins are forgiven, he shouldn't become overconfident and start thinking he's immune from sinning. He will still face a constant struggle with what sin remains in him, just as David did.

David had received God's approval and had been made holy by a righteousness completely outside of himself. It was only because of God's mercy and kindness that he had received this. God's mercy and kindness aren't human emotions or attitudes. Rather, they're a divine blessing we receive by believing that our sins have been forgiven in Christ. Because of Christ, we can expect mercy and compassion, as David did in Psalm 51. So the righteousness we receive comes completely outside of us. It's a genuine gift from God, who is compassionate and merciful to us because of Christ.

Suppose a person deserving the death penalty was brought to a prince's court. But the prince released him out of compassion, even though he deserved nothing but death. Wouldn't you say that this person's guilt was forgiven, not because of anything he had done, but because of the kindness of the merciful prince? Yet, it's not enough for this person to be forgiven for the crime he committed. He must also be released from jail, must be given clothes to wear, and must find a job so that he can live. The same happens to us when we receive God's approval. After God in his mercy frees us from guilt, we still need the gift of the Holy Spirit to clean away what sin remains in us. We need the Spirit to strengthen us so that we are not overpowered by sin and our corrupt desires.

THE GREAT PHYSICIAN

But now Christ has brought you back to God by dying
in his physical body. He did this so that you could come
into God's presence without sin, fault, or blame.

COLOSSIANS 1:22

❖

CHRISTIAN IS RIGHTEOUS and a sinner at the same time—both a friend and an enemy of God. The philosophers will not admit this paradox because they don't accept the right way of becoming justified. That's why they demanded that people keep on doing good works until they don't feel sin anymore. This caused many people to become very distraught because they were striving as much as they could to become completely righteous but could never achieve it. Even among those who spread this godless teaching, countless numbers of them have fallen into despair in their hour of death. This would have happened to me if Christ hadn't mercifully looked upon me and freed me from this error.

In contrast, we teach and comfort troubled sinners this way: Dear brothers and sisters, it's impossible for you to become so righteous in this life that you won't feel sin anymore. It's impossible for your body to become as bright and spotless as the sun. Though you still have wrinkles and spots, in spite of this, you are holy. But you may wonder, "How can I be holy since I sin and feel sinful?" Recognizing and feeling your sin is good. Thank God, and don't despair. It's a step toward health whenever a sick person recognizes his disease. "But how can I be freed from sin?" Run to Christ, the Physician, who heals the brokenhearted (Psalm 147:3). He makes sinners holy.

PRAY WITHOUT DOUBTING

Have faith that you will receive
whatever you ask for in prayer.

MATTHEW 21:22

❖

EFORE YOU PRAY, check to see whether you believe or doubt that you will be heard. If you are doubting or uncertain, or if you are merely trying a prayer to see what happens, your prayer won't be worth anything. For you aren't keeping your heart steady, but letting it wobble back and forth. As a result, God cannot give anything to this kind of heart, just as you cannot give something to a person who doesn't hold his hand still.

Imagine how you would feel if a person had earnestly asked you for something but then said to you, "I don't really believe you will give it to me," even though you had promised that you would beforehand. You would think he was mocking you by his request. You would take back everything you had promised and perhaps even punish him on top of it.

How can it please God when we do the same to him when we pray? God assures us that when we ask him for something, he will give it to us. By doubting him, we call him a liar and contradict our own prayer. By not believing him, we insult God's truthfulness, the same truthfulness we rely on when we pray. This is why we say the little word *Amen* at the end of our prayers. We use it to express our firm, heartfelt faith. It's like saying, "O God, I have no doubt that you will give me what I ask for in prayer."

RESIST THE DEVIL

Keep your mind clear, and be alert. Your opponent the devil is prowling around like a roaring lion as he looks for someone to devour. Be firm in the faith and resist him.

1 PETER 5:8–9

❖

OU SHOULD KEEP your mind clear and be alert. Then your body will be prepared. But the devil isn't defeated through this alone. By keeping your mind clear and alert, you merely give your body less reason to sin. Your true sword is remaining strong and firm in the faith. If you grasp hold of God's Word in your heart and cling to it with faith, the devil cannot win. He has to flee. If you can say, "My God has said this, and I stand upon it," you will find that the devil will quickly leave. Then apathy, evil desire, anger, greed, despair, and doubt will soon go away. But the devil is crafty and doesn't want to let you get to that point. He tries to snatch the sword out of your hand. If he makes you lazy so that your body becomes unfit and out of control, he can tear your sword out of your hand. This is what he did to Eve. She had God's Word. If she had clung to it, she would not have fallen. But when the devil saw that she held the Word loosely, he tore it from her heart. She let it go, and the devil won (Genesis 3:4, 13; 2 Corinthians 11:3).

So Peter has instructed us on how we should fight against the devil. It doesn't require a lot of running around or doing special kinds of works. Rather, it calls for nothing more than clinging to the Word through faith. If the devil wants to drive you to despair because of your sin, just grab the Word of God. It promises forgiveness of sins. Rely on God's Word, and the devil will quickly leave you alone.

WHEN NOTHING MAKES SENSE

They said to each other, "Look, here comes that master dreamer! Let's kill him, throw him into one of the cisterns, and say that a wild animal has eaten him."

GENESIS 37:19–20

❖

OD PROMISED TO CARE for his people. But when Joseph's brothers said a wild animal had killed Joseph, Jacob and Joseph were both put through a severe test. This appeared to go totally against God's promise. You would think that God would pay some attention to them and show some concern. But God didn't send an angel, or even so much as the leaf of a tree, to stop the devil or force him away. Instead, he opened all the doors and windows to let the devil rant and rave, attacking both father and son in horrible ways.

God had given Jacob an important promise. In his twelve sons, Jacob had living proof that the promise would be fulfilled. Still, many problems came his way, as if he had no God and no promise. But despite all these problems, God hadn't deserted him.

We can be certain that God's promises will always remain: "Can a woman forget her nursing child? Will she have no compassion on the child from her womb? Although mothers may forget, I will not forget you. I have engraved you on the palms of my hands" (Isaiah 49:15–16).

So why do our own flesh and blood—our children and family members—cause us so many terrible problems? This is a part of God's plan. It's the way God works in the lives of his people in this world. So we desperately need wisdom that is above our natural reason. On the basis of that wisdom, we can say, "God won't lie to me or deceive me, though at times, nothing in life will seem to make sense."

FAITH COMES FROM GOD

The people asked Jesus, "What does God want us to do?"
Jesus replied to them, "God wants to do something for you
so that you believe in the one whom he has sent."

JOHN 6:28–29

❖

 HE ENTIRE BIBLE AGREES on what it means to serve God. Scripture firmly establishes that if you want to serve him, you must believe in the one whom the Father has sent. If you want to know how to receive God's kindness, how to approach him, how to satisfy the penalty for your sins, how to receive forgiveness of sin and escape death, then you must do what God wants and believe in Christ. Here, Christ is plainly telling you what you should do—believe.

Faith is the work we must do. Yet faith is also called God's work. Later, Christ tells us how we are able to believe, for no one can believe on his own. "People cannot come to me unless the Father who sent me brings them to me" (John 6:44). He also says, "people cannot come to me unless the Father provides the way" (John 6:65). For faith is a divine work that God asks us to do. But at the same time, God must give us faith, for we can't believe on our own.

What an excellent passage this is! Like a lightening bolt, it strikes down all wisdom and righteousness, every law and commandment, even the law of Moses. It lays before us a different work—a work that is above and beyond us. We cannot grasp Christ with our thoughts or our reason. Therefore, faith cannot be our own work. We are drawn to Christ, even though we can neither feel him nor see him.

ENRICHED WITH SCRIPTURE

Take these words of mine to heart and keep them in mind.
⌊*Write them down,*⌋ *tie them around your wrist, and wear them*
as headbands as a reminder. Teach them to your children.

DEUTERONOMY 11:18–19

❖

HEN CHILDREN ARE OLD enough to begin grasping the concepts of faith, they should make a habit of bringing home verses of Scripture from church. They should recite these verses to their parents at mealtime. Then they should write the verses down and put them in little pouches or pockets, just as they put pennies and other coins in a purse. Let the pouch of faith be a golden one. Verses about coming to faith, such as Psalm 51:5; John 1:29; Romans 4:25; and Romans 5:12, are like gold coins for that little pouch. Let the pouch of love be a silver one. The verses about doing good, such as Matthew 5:11; Matthew 25:40; Galatians 5:13; and Hebrews 12:6, are like silver coins for this one.

No one should think he's too smart for this game and look down on this kind of child's play. Christ had to become a man in order to train us. If we want to train children, then we must become children with them. I wish that this kind of child's play were more widespread. In a short time, we would see an abundance of Christian people rich in Scripture and in the knowledge of God. They would make more of these pouches, and by using them, they would learn all of Scripture.

As it is now, people go to hear a sermon and leave again unchanged. They act like a sermon is only worth the time that it takes to hear it. No one thinks about learning anything from it or remembering it. Some people listen to sermons for three or four years and still don't learn enough to respond to a single question about faith. More than enough has been written in books, but not nearly enough has been driven into our hearts.

WHEN WE FEEL FORGOTTEN

Nevertheless, the chief cupbearer didn't
remember Joseph. He forgot all about him.

GENESIS 40:23

❖

FTER BEING FORGOTTEN by the cupbearer, Joseph struggled with the temptation of becoming impatient and complaining. When the devil saw this, he attacked Joseph with even more fiery arrows. Christ himself felt these arrows when the devil tempted him: "If you are the Son of God, tell these stones to become loaves of bread" (Matthew 4:3). In the same way, the devil might have said to Joseph, "Go ahead and continue your miserable struggle. Your know that your prayers are useless. You cry to God and believe in him—but all for nothing. You had hoped that God would free you and restore your honor because you interpreted the chief cupbearer's dream. Well, let God save you if he feels like it!" The devil continued to torment Joseph with his fiery arrows, even though Joseph was already weak and wounded.

When faithful people are happy and when they sing, "The LORD is my strength and my song" (Psalm 118:14), the devil stays far away from them. All complaining and impatience soon end. As long as believers praise and thank God, then temptation, sadness, and unbelief disappear. Heaven is opened wide and hell is shut with words like these: "I will thank the LORD at all times. My mouth will always praise him" (Psalm 34:1).

But as soon as we stop praising God, miserable, lonely, sad thoughts return. That's what happened to Joseph when he remembered how his brothers had sold him. They were at home having a good time while he was lying in prison, tied up and miserable. This is how the devil works. When the water becomes troubled, he likes to fish. He uses these opportunities to tempt people to abandon their faith and give up in despair.

THE GOLDEN RULE

*Always do for other people everything
you want them to do for you.*

MATTHEW 7:12

❖

WHAT COULD BE MORE CLEAR and concise than the truth stated in this verse? But the world won't let us reflect on these words. Our corrupt nature won't let us measure our lives against this standard. We let this verse go in one ear and out the other. If we would continually compare our lives and actions against this standard, we wouldn't live so carelessly. We would have more than enough to do and wouldn't need to pursue other works we consider holy. We would become our own teachers and begin teaching ourselves how we should live. We wouldn't need so many lawyers and law books, for this standard is concise and easy to learn. If only we were diligent and serious enough to live according to it!

Let me give a rough illustration. No one would like to be robbed. If you ask yourself, you would have to admit that you certainly wouldn't enjoy it. So, why don't you conclude that everyone else feels the same way? At the market, you see that everyone charges as much as he wishes for what he's selling, so that it costs three times what it's worth. If you were to ask a vendor, "Excuse me, would you like this done to you?" he would have difficulty replying. If he were honest and thinking sensibly, he would have to say, "I want to pay the market value—what is just and fair. I don't want to be overcharged." So do you see the point? Your heart tells you how you would like to be treated, and your conscience tells you that you should treat others the same way.

FAITH AND WORKS ARE NECESSARY

If you obey my commandments, you will live in my love.
I have obeyed my Father's commandments,
and in that way I live in his love.

JOHN 15:10

❖

 ESUS IS SAYING, "You are in me and remain in me, so make sure you keep my commandments. For I must give each of you a task as a sign to others that you are my true branches. That task is to love each other. I keep this command myself, so I can be an example and model to you. And I remain in my Father's love because I keep this command. Therefore, if you keep my commandments, you will remain in my love." Earlier in this book, Christ also says, "Everyone will know that you are my disciples because of your love for each other" (John 13:35).

So there are two parts of Christian teaching that we must emphasize for Christians daily. Neither faith nor works can be ignored. For when faith isn't preached—when no one explains how we are joined to Christ and become branches in him—then everyone resorts to their own works. On the other hand, if we teach only about faith, it leads to false Christians. These people praise faith, are baptized, and even call themselves Christians, but they don't show any fruit or power.

That's why it's so difficult to preach. No matter how I preach, something goes wrong. Someone always goes off on a tangent. If I don't preach about faith, the result will be useless and hypocritical works. If I only emphasize faith, no one does any good works. The result is either useless, faithless do-gooders or believers who don't do any good works. So we must preach the message to those who accept both faith and works. We must preach to those who want to remain in the vine, put their trust in Christ, and put their faith into action in their everyday lives.

Relying on Our Own Strength

*[Peter] was afraid of those who insisted that circumcision
was necessary. The other Jewish Christians also joined him in
this hypocrisy. Even Barnabas was swept along with them.*

GALATIANS 2:12–13

❖

AUL DOESN'T CHALLENGE Peter over a minor
matter, but the most important teaching of
Christianity, which Peter practically ruined
with his hypocrisy. Barnabas and the other Jewish
Christians were acting like hypocrites. They all sinned,
not out of ignorance and malice, but out of fear of the
Jewish leaders. These leaders had blinded their hearts so
much they didn't even know they were sinning. It's truly
astonishing that great men, such as Peter, Barnabas, and
others, were so easily tripped up. That's why Staupitz
warned that it was very dangerous to rely on our own
strength—no matter how holy and educated we are or
how well we have understood a truth. For even in matters that we know well, we can fall into error and end up
harming ourselves as well as other people.

If God isn't with us, we are nothing at all, no matter
how great our gifts may be. If he removes his hand from
us, our wisdom and our knowledge are nothing. If he
doesn't constantly uphold us, the greatest amount of
knowledge will be useless, even if we are experts in theology. For in the hour of temptation, the devil can tear
away all the comforting Bible verses from us and leave
us with threatening ones that crush our spirits. So we
should learn from this passage that we can easily fall if
God were to withdraw his hand from us. Let's not boast
in our righteousness and in our gifts. But let's humble
ourselves and pray with the apostles, "Give us more
faith" (Luke 17:5).

COMPLETE IN CHRIST

All of God lives in Christ's body, and God
has made you complete in Christ.

COLOSSIANS 2:9–10

❖

N PAUL'S LETTERS, such as Romans, Galatians, and Colossians, there are many passages that say God has fulfilled all the requirements of the law in Christ (Romans 10:4). Christ is the fulfillment of the law, of time, and of all things. Christ is all and has all. The person who holds on to Jesus in faith will receive forgiveness of sins. God's laws will be fulfilled, death will be conquered, and the devil will be overcome. That person will receive the gift of eternal life. For in this one man, Jesus, all is settled. He has fulfilled everything. Whoever accepts him has everything. As Paul says here, "God has made you complete in Christ."

When I feel anxious about sin and hell, I remind myself that when I have Christ, I have all that is necessary. Neither death, sin, nor the devil can hurt me. If I believe in Christ, I have fulfilled the law; it cannot accuse me. I have conquered hell; it cannot hold me. Everything that Christ has is mine. Through him, we obtain all his possessions and eternal life. Even if I am weak in faith, I still have the same treasure and the same Christ that others have. There's no difference: we are all made perfect through faith in him, not by what we do.

For example, imagine that two people each have a hundred dollars. One person carries it in a paper bag. The other keeps it in an iron chest. Both have the same treasure no matter where they put it. Similarly, we all have the same Christ. It doesn't matter if one person has a stronger or weaker faith than another. Both of them still believe in the same Christ and have everything through him.

HOLDING TIGHTLY TO THE PROMISE

God said, "Take your son, your only son Isaac, whom you
love, and go to Moriah. Sacrifice him there as a burnt
offering on one of the mountains that I will show you."

GENESIS 22:2

❖

HENEVER TROUBLES COME into our lives, we naturally assume that we are being punished
for something we've done wrong. With the
help of the devil, our consciences remind us of past
sins. We scrutinize our lives and wonder what offended
God. This can even lead to blaming God for our problems. Eventually, we can end up hating him.

Perhaps Abraham had similar thoughts when God
asked him to sacrifice Isaac: "God kept his promise to
me. He gave me a son, and this made me extremely
happy. Perhaps I've become proud because God gave
me a son. Perhaps I wasn't as thankful as I should have
been. Maybe the Lord regrets making his promise to
me." It's difficult to silence anxious thoughts like these
when we can't understand what God is doing. People
can't comprehend how an unchanging God can change
his mind. Inevitably, we come to one of two conclu-
sions: either God is a liar, or God has become our
enemy. Thinking of God as a liar is blasphemy.
Thinking of God as our enemy leads to despair.

Often, serious doubts arise, such as: "What if God
doesn't want me to be saved?" But when our consciences are troubled in this way, we have to continue
to believe the promise of salvation—a promise we can
trust in and depend on. When we doubt God's promise,
we must pray sincerely and persistently. We must hang
on to God's promise because if Satan can prevent us
from believing it, then we have nowhere else to turn.
We must hold tightly to the promise and be ready for
the times when God will test us, as he did Abraham.
God doesn't test us because he enjoys it. He tests us to
find out whether we love him above all things.

Don't Put God to the Test

Jesus said to him, "Again, Scripture says,
'Never tempt the Lord your God.' "

MATTHEW 4:7

❖

F WE DON'T USE THE RESOURCES available to us, but instead want other resources we don't have, then we're tempting, or testing, God. This is what Satan wanted Christ to do. Satan told Jesus to throw himself from the temple when there were steps he could've used to climb down. Someone who doesn't wear proper clothing in cold weather but expects God to miraculously keep him from freezing is also testing God. This is like the Jewish leaders who ignored the signs they had been given and waited for a different one from heaven. In the same way, the person who sleeps when he should be working is testing God. Because God promised to take care of him, he assumes that God will find a way. But in Proverbs, God told him to work: "Lazy hands bring poverty, but hard-working hands bring riches" (Proverbs 10:4).

God's work is accomplished when we use the resources given to us. He wants us to use our resources but not put our trust in them. While it's true that hard-working hands bring riches, it's also true that only the Lord's blessing brings riches, as Solomon says, "hard work adds nothing to it" (Proverbs 10:22). When people use weapons to defend themselves, God is still delivering them. Without God's help, a person who attempts to deliver himself will fail. As David said, "I do not rely on my bow, and my sword will never save me. But you saved us from our enemies" (Psalm 44:6–7). God will use weapons to deliver people if weapons are available, but he can still deliver people even if they aren't available. Therefore, we should make use of what we have but not rely on those things. We must trust in God alone, whether we have the resources we need or not.

GOD LISTENS TO US

We are confident that God listens to us if we ask for anything
that has his approval. We know that he listens to our requests.
So we know that we already have what we ask him for.

1 JOHN 5:14–15

❖

HIS PASSAGE IS AN ENCOURAGEMENT to Christians who have been instructed on how they should believe and love. They must remember that their godliness comes from the Word that has been proclaimed, and they must not live any other way than in faith and love. John anticipates an objection from these people: "What if my heart is cold, and I feel that I lack faith?" "Here is the remedy," says John, "Ask and pray. He will hear you."

James says, "If any of you needs wisdom to know what you should do, you should ask God, and he will give it to you. God is generous to everyone and doesn't find fault with them" (James 1:5). Your best course of action is to rely on prayer. Paul says, "Never worry about anything. But in every situation let God know what you need in prayers and requests while giving thanks" (Philippians 4:6). Likewise Augustine says, "Lord, give me what you are commanding." So we also should pray, "Lord, give us faith."

This verse is an encouragement to pray, and John describes how to pray in an excellent way. First, he reminds us to be "confident," which is the soul of prayer. Next, he instructs us what to ask for: "ask for anything that has his approval." Finally, we must also believe that "he listens to our requests." James supports this, "A person who has doubts . . . can't make up his mind about anything" (James 1:8). "When you ask for something, don't have any doubts" (James 1:6).

Great Answers from a Great God

Then Esau ran to meet Jacob. Esau hugged him,
threw his arms around him, and kissed him.
They both cried.

GENESIS 33:4

❖

 ACOB'S ANGUISHED PRAYER accomplished more than he dared to ask. He hadn't expected so much comfort from God or from his brother. All he had asked for was that his brother would leave him and his family unharmed. He never thought he would receive so much kindness from his brother. Esau even ran to meet Jacob. With tears streaming from his eyes, he hugged and kissed him.

We should pray with confidence, knowing that God will answer our requests without delay. It's impossible for sincere, persistent prayer to remain unheard. But because we don't believe, we aren't persistent enough and don't experience God's goodness and help. So we must become more enthusiastic about faith and prayer, knowing that God is pleased when we persevere. In fact, God ordered us to be persistent in prayer: "Ask, and you will receive. Search, and you will find. Knock, and the door will be opened for you" (Matthew 7:7).

Our prayers are answered much differently—actually more generously—than we could ever ask for or imagine (Ephesians 3:20). Paul says, "we don't know how to pray for what we need. But the Spirit intercedes along with our groans that cannot be expressed in words. The one who searches our hearts knows what the Spirit has in mind" (Romans 8:26–27).

We always ask for less than we should and don't even think God is willing to give us what we ask for. We don't ask the right way. We don't understand that what we pray about is more important than we can comprehend. We think small, but the Lord is great and powerful. He expects us to ask for great things. He wants to give them to us to demonstrate his almighty power.

LOVING YOURSELF

All of Moses' Teachings are summarized in a single
statement, "Love your neighbor as you love yourself."
GALATIANS 5:14

❖

OME OF THE EARLY CHURCH fathers concluded
from this passage that love begins with loving
yourself. They said this because loving yourself was given as the measure for how much you should
love your neighbor. I used to consider this from all sides
to try to understand it. I understand this commandment
to mean that only love towards your neighbor is being
commanded, not love of yourself.

First, self-love is already present in all people.
Second, if God had wanted to command you to love
yourself, he would have said, "You should love yourself
and your neighbor as yourself." But he said instead,
"Love your neighbor as you love yourself." In other
words, "as you love yourself" means the way you
already love yourself, without a commandment to do
so. When describing love in 1 Corinthians 13:5, Paul
teaches that love doesn't seek its own. It completely
rejects self-love. In Mark 8:34, Christ commands that
we should deny ourselves. Philippians 2:4 clearly says,
"Don't be concerned only about your own interests, but
also be concerned about the interests of others." This
commandment presupposes that a person already loves
himself, just as when Christ says in Matthew 7:12,
"Always do for other people everything you want them
to do for you." Clearly he isn't commanding you to love
yourself here either.

So it seems to me the part of this commandment
that says "as you love yourself" is referring to the wrong
kind of love—the kind where you forget your neighbor
and seek only your own interests. But this can become
the right kind of love if you forget yourself and only
think about serving your neighbor.

FAITH IS MORE IMPORTANT THAN WORKS

We conclude that a person has God's approval by faith, not by his own efforts.

ROMANS 3:28

❖

UR OPPONENTS INSIST that good works are necessary for salvation, and the world enthusiastically agrees with them. Certainly, what the saints did was admirable, and they did many great works. But even if you were to show me the most holy saint of all, would that person have done enough good works to earn God's approval?

We also recognize that love is an essential aspect of the Christian life and that all believers need to restrain their corrupt desires and practice self-denial. "But you don't do that," our opponents protest. Our reply is, "Even if we could do all that, would we have done enough for God's approval?" The only reason we think so highly of what we do is that we don't want God to receive any of the credit. We readily admit that good works are necessary. But they're not more important than what we already have: God's approval, which comes through faith. We must understand the difference between what is priceless and what is cheap, what is important and what is trivial. This distinction is important in all of life, but especially in this doctrine. Even animals understand the difference between good and bad food. A dog knows that meat is better than bread.

Therefore, we should value good works and remember doing them is still necessary. But we should value God's Word and his promises even more highly. We will live in God's presence because we believe in what he says, not because we do good works that make us holy. We have to make a clear distinction between our good works and our faith in God's Word. Believing in God's Word defeats the devil and makes us holy children of God.

THE BREAD OF LIFE

Jesus told them, "I am the bread of life.
Whoever comes to me will never become hungry,
and whoever believes in me will never become thirsty."

JOHN 6:35

❖

HESE ARE UNUSUALLY direct words: Christ is bread. He is food given by God. Whoever eats this bread will be satisfied, will not hunger or thirst, and will live forever. Furthermore, this bread from heaven was standing right in front of the Israelites.

Jesus began his sermon gently enough, "Whoever comes to me." The further he proceeded, the more pointed and direct he became. He could have easily said, "whoever eats of me," instead of "whoever comes to me." But that would have been premature. He wanted the people to understand him, so he used the words, "whoever comes to me," and then explained that it meant, "whoever believes in me." This is a profound statement: To come to Christ is to believe in Christ. It means having the bread and eating it. Jesus, however, wasn't talking about eating in a church or at a wedding. He wasn't talking about eating beef or veal, as his listeners might have thought. He was speaking of bread in the sense of people coming to Christ—in other words, believing in Christ. For "eating" and "coming to Christ" and "believing in Christ" all mean the same.

Christ comes to us, and the Father gives us manna from heaven. All that is missing is for us to come to him. This may offend you. You can't come to Christ—even if you are his closest relative—unless you believe in him. Through his Word, Christ is closer to you than a child with his arms wrapped around your neck. When you believe in him, then he is with you and close to you. He is right in front of you, before your eyes and ears, so that you can almost see and hear him. Simply believe in him.

STANDING UP AGAIN

Those who live sinful lives are disobeying God.
Sin is disobedience.

1 JOHN 3:4

❖

E ARE ALL SINNERS, and at times we all fall into sin. But when a true Christian falls, he soon comes back, turns around, and struggles against the sin so that he won't offend his neighbor. To illustrate, it's difficult to avoid being wounded in times of war. Yet it's an honor if one stands up to fight again. But it's a disgrace if someone retreats. Similarly, even if a Christian were completely surrounded by sin, he should still fight against it. Some people think they're Christians because they've been baptized. These people give their desires free rein and don't care about conquering their sins. They merely follow their own cravings.

Committing sin comes from following the enticement and desire to sin. Many give these sinful desires free rein. They don't want to repent or stand up to fight again. Today they commit adultery, tomorrow they want to live purely. It's impossible for these people to avoid offending their neighbor. If they don't offend him by something they do, then they certainly will by neglecting what they ought to do for their neighbor.

An important part of Christianity is love, and love doesn't insist on its own way (1 Corinthians 13:5). Insisting on our own way is not loving our neighbor, but following our own desires. So not showing love is the same as being disobedient. Whoever isn't pure, whoever doesn't struggle daily against himself, will give in to sin and do wrong. Whoever doesn't have the fruit on the inside won't show it on the outside towards his neighbor. If you have not died to yourself so that you can disregard your own desires, how can you seek what's best for others?

WAITING FOR THE LORD

Nevertheless, the chief cupbearer didn't remember Joseph.
He forgot all about him.

GENESIS 40:23

❖

O OTHER MODEL we can think of compares to Joseph. He had so many unbearable tortures heaped on him, and he didn't have any help or hope. In contrast, martyrs for the faith usually suffer for only a short time. But Joseph had to suffer for a long time. You won't find many people who, when abandoned like Joseph, wouldn't complain, become angry, and become impatient. Yes, Joseph had his weak moments, too. At times, he felt depressed and wanted to complain, cry, and give up.

Joseph's example illustrates the importance of waiting for the Lord. In Psalms, we read, "Wait with hope for the LORD. Be strong, and let your heart be courageous" (Psalm 27:14). Habakkuk says, "The vision will still happen at the appointed time. It hurries toward its goal. It won't be a lie. If it's delayed, wait for it. It will certainly happen. It won't be late" (Habakkuk 2:3). Isaiah encourages us, "Then you will know that I am the LORD. Those who wait with hope for me will not be put to shame" (Isaiah 49:23).

But our human weakness tells us, "It's been too long. I've been waiting for help for five, ten, or twenty years, and there's no end in sight." But remember that God made these promises to you. He is your friend and father. Because of his kindness and mercy, God has promised to take care of you like a father cares for his little child. He is your father, and you are his dear child. Does your sinful nature still tell you that hoping in God is foolish? Don't worry. Continue to wait with all believers. What Christ promises in Matthew 24:13 will come to pass: "The person who endures to the end will be saved."

CALLED BY GOD

From Paul—an apostle ₍chosen₎ not by any group or indi-
vidual but by Jesus Christ and God the Father who brought
him back to life—and all the believers who are with me.

GALATIANS 1:1–2

❖

ELIGIOUS LEADERS FACE a very foolish yet strong
temptation. Some claim they must teach
because they have a talent from the Lord and
feel compelled to teach because of the command of the
gospel. Confused by a foolish conscience, they think
that if they don't teach they're burying the gold of their
Lord and will be condemned for it. The devil does this
to make them neglect the responsibilities to which they
are called.

My dear friend, with one word Christ frees you from
this notion. Look at the parable in Matthew, "He called
his servants and entrusted some money to them"
(Matthew 25:14). It says, "He called them." But who
has called you? Wait for God to call you. In the meantime, don't be concerned about it. Even if you were
wiser than Solomon and Daniel, unless you are called
to spread the Word, avoid that calling even more than
hell. If God needs you, he will call you. If he doesn't
call you, you won't burst from the wisdom inside of
you. In fact, it isn't even true wisdom. It only appears
that way to you. And it's very foolish for you to imagine
that you could produce fruit. The only one who produces fruit by the Word is one who is called to teach
without wishing for it. For Jesus Christ is our leader
(Matthew 23:10). He alone teaches and produces fruit
through his servants, whom he calls. But whoever
teaches without being called endangers both himself
and his hearers, for Christ is not with him.

LOVE FROM A PURE HEART

*My goal in giving you this order is for love
to flow from a pure heart, from a clear conscience,
and from a sincere faith.*

1 TIMOTHY 1:5

❖

OVE, AS EVERYONE already knows, is simply being kind to someone, showing that person goodness, and offering friendship. Now, there are some who preach and sermonize about love, but they slant it to their own point of view and to their own advantage. They are like the heretics, the godless, and evil scoundrels who also have love—but only for themselves and others like them. Meanwhile, they hate and persecute all good Christians and would murder them if they could. Choosing a couple of people who are pleasing to you, who do what you want, and then being friendly to those people is a long way from love. This is a soiled love that doesn't come from a pure heart. It's nothing more than dirt.

For love that flows "from a pure heart" thinks this way: "God has commanded me to direct my love to my neighbor. My heavenly Father wants me to be favorable to everyone, whether friends or enemies, just as he is. He lets the sun rise and shine on both good and evil people." God shows goodness to those who continually dishonor him and misuse what he has provided through their disobedience, blasphemy, sin, and shameful behavior. In the same way, he lets rain fall on both the thankful and the unthankful. He gives money, property, and all types of things from the earth to the very worst scoundrels. Why does he do this? He does it out of genuine, pure love. His heart is full and overflowing with love. He pours his love over everyone, leaving no one out, whether good or bad, worthy or unworthy. This love is righteous, godly, whole, and complete. It doesn't single out certain people or separate people into groups. He freely gives his love to all.

THE MARRIAGE PARTNERSHIP

*The man said, "This is now bone of my bones
and flesh of my flesh. She will be named* woman
because she was taken from man."

GENESIS 2:23

 HE WORD *WOMAN* PRESENTS an amazing and lovely picture of the institution of marriage. Everything the husband has also belongs to his wife. Not only do they share their assets, but also their children, income, food, drink, bed, and home. Besides that, they are to be one in mind and spirit. The only difference between a husband and wife is in their anatomy. Otherwise, they are the same. Because of this, whatever the husband has or owns also belongs to his wife.

Compared to the very first marriage, our marriages today are only pathetic copies of the original design. If a married woman is honorable, moral, devout, and God-fearing, she and her husband will equally share the cares, duties, and responsibilities of their household. This is why she was created and why she is called *woman*.

Even though a wife today doesn't come from her husband's flesh and bone as Eve did, she is still a head of the household the same as her husband because she is the wife. This doesn't invalidate the law, given after the fall into sin, which places the wife under the authority of her husband. This punishment, like the others, clouds the glorious life humans enjoyed in paradise. This passage reminds us that Moses wasn't describing the miserable life of married people today, but the innocence humans enjoyed in paradise. Back then, the authority of the husband and wife were equal. Now, men are obligated to work by the sweat of their brows, and wives are commanded to place themselves under their husbands' authority. Nevertheless, we still see a remnant of the original design in marriage because the wife is called *woman* and because she owns property and possessions jointly with her husband.

OBSTACLES TO PRAYER

So far you haven't asked for anything in my name.
Ask and you will receive so that you
can be completely happy.

JOHN 16:24

❖

HERE ARE TWO MAJOR obstacles to prayer. The first obstacle arises when the devil prompts you to think, "I am not yet prepared to pray. I should wait for another half-hour or another day until I have become more prepared or until I have finished taking care of this or that." Meanwhile, the devil distracts you for half an hour, so that you no longer think about prayer for the rest of the day. From one day to the next, you are hindered and rushed with other business. This common obstacle shows us how maliciously the devil tries to trick us. He often tries this on me. The devil also has an influence over our bodies, which are so lazy and cold that we can't pray the way we want to. Even if we do begin to pray, we become distracted by useless thoughts and lose our concentration in prayer.

The second obstacle arises when we ask ourselves, "How can you pray to God and say the Lord's Prayer? You are too unworthy and sin every day. Wait until you are more devout. You might be in the mood to pray now, but wait until you have confessed your sin and taken the Lord's Supper so that you can pray more fervently and approach God with confidence. Only then can you really pray the Lord's Prayer from your heart." This serious obstacle crushes us like a heavy stone. Despite our feelings of unworthiness, our hearts must struggle to remove this obstacle so that we can freely approach God and call upon him.

SURRENDERING OUR WILL

Let your kingdom come.
Let your will be done
on earth as it is done in heaven.

MATTHEW 6:10

❖

OD'S WILL IS DONE when our will is broken. It pleases him when our will is hindered and defeated. So when someone talks about you as if you were a fool, you shouldn't disagree. Instead, agree and let the criticism appear correct, for it's certainly correct before God. If a person wants to take something from you and harm you, you should allow it to happen as if it were all right with you. For undoubtedly it's right before God. Even if the person were wronging you, it still wouldn't be unjust. For it's God's will either way, whether he uses a wicked person or good person to take something away from you. Instead of resisting, you should simply say, "Your will be done." This is true in both physical and spiritual matters. For Christ said, "If someone wants to sue you in order to take your shirt, let him have your coat too" (Matthew 5:40).

Someone might ask, "If that's what it means for God's will to be done, who can be saved? Who can keep this difficult command to surrender everything and not have his own will in anything?" My reply is that we should learn how great this prayer is, why we need it, and how earnestly we should pray it. It's crucial that we allow our will to be totally defeated so that only God's will is done.

Notice that in the garden, Jesus said, "Your will must be done, not mine" (Luke 22:42). Undoubtedly, Christ's will was good—in fact, the best one of all time. If Christ had to surrender his will so that God's will could be done, why do we poor, little worms want to make such a fuss over our own wills?

CHRIST IN US

*On that day you will know that I am in my Father and
that you are in me and that I am in you.*

JOHN 14:20

❖

E ARE IN CHRIST, and Christ is in us. The first
truth points upward, the second points
downward. We must first be in him with all
our being—with our sin and weakness, and even with
death. We know that in God's eyes we are freed,
redeemed, and saved from these through Christ.

Then, we must swing above and beyond ourselves to
Christ. Yes, we must be totally one with Christ and his
people—those who are baptized in him and receive the
Lord's Supper. Consequently, sin, death, the devil, and
struggles with a bad conscience disappear. We can then
say, "I'm not sure about death or hell. If there is death,
let it consume my Lord Christ first. If there is hell, let it
devour my Savior. If sin, the law, or my conscience condemn me, let them accuse the Son of God. If that happens, then let me be condemned, consumed, and
devoured with my Lord. But because the Father and
Christ live, I will also live. Because Christ remains unde-
feated by sin and death, so I will also remain undefeat-
ed. For I know that Christ is in the Father; therefore, I
also am in Christ." This is how we soar above and
beyond ourselves to Christ.

After that, Christ comes down to us from above. If
we are in Christ, then Christ is in us. We have received
him and crept into him. We have left sin, death, and the
devil behind. So Jesus shows himself to us and says,
"Go. Preach, comfort, and baptize. Serve your neighbor.
Be obedient and patient. I will be in you, and I will do
all this through you. Whatever you do will be accomplished by me. Be happy. Be bold and courageous.
Remain in me, then I will certainly remain in you."

Training Ground for Spirituality

[Sarah said,] "Get rid of this slave and her son, because this slave's son must never share the inheritance with my son Isaac." Abraham was upset by this because of his son Ishmael.

GENESIS 21:10–11

❖

AMILY LIFE IS A TRAINING ground for faith, hope, love, patience, and prayer. Sarah and Abraham were arguing about God's promises, but they were doing so out of fear and respect for God. Some people give up their homes and leave their families, thinking they are devoting themselves to God. They dismiss the kind of obedience and devotion we see in this story as the mere efforts of amateurs—something any married couple could do.

This story should reassure married couples. They shouldn't assume that they'll never have disagreements and arguments. Even the most loving and godly spouses will sometimes disagree. We should remember that these disputes are opportunities for practicing godliness and love.

Abraham was the natural and legal father of Ishmael. Yet Sarah asked him to give up both Ishmael and Hagar. Because Abraham was emotionally attached to both of them, this was a difficult decision. Besides, God commands that a husband should protect his wife and support his children. But Sarah was insistent that Hagar and her son should be thrown out. They weren't being thrown out because they were disrespectful to Abraham. I'm sure they treated him with the proper respect. They were being thrown out for mocking Isaac.

These are the kinds of problems our opponents know nothing about. They regard marriage as a secular institution. Yet we should recognize marriage for what it is—a training ground for spirituality. The greatest passions, both towards God and one another, are challenged and expressed within marriage.

Faith Shows Itself in Love

*Love each other. This is what I'm
commanding you to do.*

JOHN 15:17

❖

N THIS PASSAGE, Christ repeats the command
to love each other. By love, believers are held
together, and love is the mark of true believers. Jesus emphasized this command because he knew
how many false Christians would arise—how many
would praise faith with elegant words and a great show
but wouldn't back up their words. Just as God's holy
name is dishonored and used for evil, and just as
Christianity, the church, and everything that is holy is
misused, so also the names of faith, love, and good
works will also be used for a false show and mask. For
the devil doesn't want to be as dark as he is painted, but
he wants to shine in the fine clothes of God's Word, the
Christian church, faith, and love.

So Christ teaches us that it's not enough to praise
faith and Christ, but we also need to produce Christian
fruit. For where these fruits aren't evident, or where the
opposite appears, Christ is certainly not present. In that
case, only a false name exists. That's why we must say to
these types of people, "I hear that beautiful and glorious name, which is noble and worthy of honor. But
what about you?" Similarly, the evil spirit said to the
sons of Sceva, "I know Jesus, and I'm acquainted with
Paul, but who are you?" (Acts 19:15).

But some may object, "Doesn't faith justify and save
us without works?" Yes, that's true. But where's your
faith? How does it show itself? Faith must never be useless, deaf, dead, or in a state of decay. But it must be a
living tree that bursts forth with fruit. That's the difference between genuine faith and false faith. Where
there's true faith, it will show itself in a person's life.

STRUGGLING WITH OUR WEAKNESSES

So Jacob named that place Peniel [Face of God],
because he said, "I have seen God face to face,
but my life was saved."

GENESIS 32:30

❖

ACOB PROVIDED THE CHURCH with a beautiful example of faith struggling in weakness. This helps us to see that the Hebrew ancestors and prophets weren't like rocks that showed no signs of weakness. If that were the case, we would have to despair because of the weaknesses we feel in ourselves. Our bodies often complain that we're being treated unfairly. We don't want to suffer and be mistreated by others. But the example of the Hebrew ancestors can comfort us because they, too, were not always firm and strong in their faith.

Jacob was comforted by showers of blessings from God. He also received the benefits of the blessings that were given to his father, Isaac, and grandfather, Abraham. Nevertheless, he struggled with his weaknesses.

You should say to yourself, "I am not alone when I'm afraid of God's anger, when I wonder if God has chosen me, and when I worry about losing my faith. I am not alone!" All believers—every believer past and present who has ever believed in God's Son—experience the same struggle. God uses these experiences to refine us. Eventually, like Jacob, you'll be able to stand up and joyfully proclaim, "I have seen God face to face, but my life was saved" (Genesis 32:30).

SINFUL DESIRES

What your spiritual nature wants is contrary to what your corrupt nature wants. They are opposed to each other.

GALATIANS 5:17

❖

HEN I WAS A MONK, I thought that my salvation was immediately lost if I experienced a sinful desire of the corrupt nature—for example, an evil emotion, sexual desire, anger, hatred, or envy towards any brother. I tried many spiritual exercises, such as confessing daily, but I made no headway. The desires of the corrupt nature always returned so that I couldn't find rest. I was constantly tormented by thoughts such as these: "You committed this and that sin, and you are guilty of envy, impatience, and more. As a result, you have entered this monastic order in vain, and all your good works are useless." If I had at that time better understood Paul's statements about the corrupt nature battling against the Spirit and that "they are opposed to each other," I would not have tortured myself so much.

I would have thought the way I do today, "Martin, you cannot be completely without sin because you are still in this body. As a result, you will experience the conflict with the corrupt nature. The corrupt nature battles against the Spirit, just as Paul teaches. Therefore, don't give up, but fight against it so that you do not gratify these evil desires. Then you will no longer be under the law."

PLACES OF HONOR

Then Jesus noticed how the guests always chose the places
of honor. . . . "When someone invites you to a wedding,
don't take the place of honor."

LUKE 14:7–8

❖

OW CAN SITTING in a place of honor be right and not right? It's not prohibited to sit in a place of honor. In fact, Christ himself says, "When your host comes, he will tell you, 'Friend, move to a more honorable place.' Then all the other guests will see how you are honored" (Luke 14:10). Why does he tell us not to sit in a place of honor but also say that it's appropriate to be seated in an honorable place? The answer is found by noting the word *chose* in the verse: "Jesus noticed how the guests always chose the places of honor."

Some people must sit in higher places and some in lower places. For we cannot set aside a special place, spot, time, or chapel for every person in the congregation. Accordingly, we cannot all be princes, counts, preachers, noblemen, townspeople, men, women, masters, or servants. Every person has enough to do in his own position. So we should not and cannot all sit at a higher place and at a lower place at the same time. But God has arranged matters so that the person in a higher position should rightly sit higher than the others. A count shouldn't set himself above the prince or a servant set himself over the master. So there must also be distinctions between other positions in life.

It's important that you correctly understand what Christ is saying here. If you are in a higher position or above others in some way, realize that God has given it to you. Don't make the mistake of bragging about it and lording it over others as if you were better than them in God's sight. Rather, God has commanded that you should humble yourself and use your position to serve your neighbor.

AS YOU LOVE YOURSELF

*All of Moses' Teachings are summarized in a single
statement, "Love your neighbor as you love yourself."*

GALATIANS 5:14

❖

HIS STATEMENT IS EXPRESSED in a beautiful and
powerful way: "Love your neighbor as you
love yourself." There is no attitude more
outstanding, respected, and virtuous than love. No one
can show you a model that is better, more certain, and
more real than yourself. There is no better object to
whom you can direct your love than your neighbor. So
the attitude, model, and object are all superior.

If you want to know how to love your neighbor and
want to have a clear example of it, then pay careful
attention to how you love yourself. In times of need
and danger, you certainly would want to be loved and
helped with all of the advice, resources, and power of
everyone everywhere. So you don't need a book to
teach and admonish you how to love your neighbor.
For you have the best and the most lovely book about
all laws right in your heart. You don't need a teacher,
just consult your own heart. It will thoroughly teach
you that your neighbor should be loved the way you
love yourself. Further, love is the highest virtue. It's not
only prepared to serve with words, hands, money, and
possessions, but also with the body and even life itself.
It's not motivated by reward or anything else. It's not
slowed down by any unworthiness or ungratefulness of
a neighbor. We should serve our neighbor out of love,
just as a mother cherishes and cares for her child simply out of love.

BITTEN BY SIN

If we say, "We have never sinned,"
we turn God into a liar and his Word is not in us.

1 JOHN 1:10

❖

OT ONLY HAVE WE SINNED, but we also continue to sin. Because of the weakness of our
sinful, corrupt nature, which we will have as
long as we have these bodies, there is an ongoing battle
between the corrupt nature and the Spirit. Paul talks
about this: "I know that nothing good lives in me; that
is, nothing good lives in my corrupt nature. Although I
have the desire to do what is right, I don't do it"
(Romans 7:18). Certainly, it's not just the immoral sexual desire of a man towards a woman or a woman
towards a man that is sin. In the legends of the saints,
there are also many sins that take on the form and the
appearance of holiness and are passed on as good conduct. For the church fathers usually looked at outward
sins and not at inner ones—such as envy, jealousy, a
hostile heart, and falling from faith and hope.

We still have sin that bites and entices us, but it
doesn't rule over us. The sin within us is like a person
who is tied up and is being led away to his death. The
weapons he might use to harm others have all been
taken away from him. But he isn't dead yet. Similarly,
the sin in our bodies surges up, rages and rants, and
doesn't let up. For we always love what is ours and
depend on our own strength. We don't put our trust in
the Word and don't believe God. Our corrupt nature
doesn't want it any other way. But the best remedy
against this is meditating diligently on God's Word.

UNAFRAID OF DEATH

Certainly, if the dead don't come back to life, then Christ hasn't come back to life either. If Christ hasn't come back to life, your faith is worthless and sin still has you in its power.

1 CORINTHIANS 15:16–17

❖

T HAS WISELY BEEN SAID, "He who fears death is a fool, for by doing this he loses his own life." This would be a good saying if anyone could do it. Everyone knows that people won't get anywhere by fearing death. They will only ruin their lives and never be happy. We see this with people who are in deep sadness. They wouldn't be comforted or feel joyful even if you wrapped them with golden robes, filled them with the best food and drink, and offered them all kinds of entertainment, even music on stringed instruments. They don't feel alive. They walk around with morbid thoughts of death, and they are practically dead already. So people tell us that the best thing to do is to throw off this fear, force it out of our minds, and say to ourselves, "Why should we worry? When we are dead, we are dead." Just as the Corinthians said, "Let's eat and drink because tomorrow we're going to die" (1 Corinthians 15:32). However, this is a shortcut because it pretends God's wrath, hell, and damnation don't even exist.

But Christians can't do that. They can't just toss this fear out of a heart that wants to believe. In fact, they only feel this fear even more as their faith struggles to grow. We should comfort them by saying, "Dear friend, if you are continually distressed by living, if you feel poor and miserable, then take care and understand this is happening because you are a Christian. Otherwise, you wouldn't be tormented by this fear of death and hell. But you must guard yourself against this fear and hold firmly to the fact that your Christ has risen from the dead."

THE GREATEST PRAYER

This is how you should pray: Our Father in heaven,
let your name be kept holy.

MATTHEW 6:9

❖

ECAUSE JESUS IS THE AUTHOR of the prayer in this passage, it's undoubtedly the greatest and best prayer. For if this good, faithful teacher had known a better one, he certainly would have taught it to us. This doesn't mean a prayer that doesn't use these exact words is worthless. For prior to Christ's birth, many believers who had never heard these words also prayed. But we should be cautious about other prayers that don't convey the meaning of this prayer. The psalms are good prayers, and they express the same thoughts as the Lord's Prayer but don't express them as clearly.

So it's a mistake to prefer other prayers over this one. Watch out especially for those written out with titles decorated in red ink, in the hope that God will give us health and long life, possessions and honor, indulgences to free us from punishment, and so on. Through these kinds of prayers, we pursue our will and our honor more than God's will and his honor. Many people have begun regarding these other prayers more highly than the Lord's Prayer. Not that I completely disregard these prayers, but people put too much confidence in them. Subsequently, the true Lord's Prayer, which is inner and spiritual, is despised. All forgiveness, all blessings, all that is useful, and everything else that a person needs for his body and soul on earth and in heaven overflow from this prayer.

It would be better if you prayed one Lord's Prayer—praying it with all your heart, really thinking about the words, and letting it change your life for the better—than for you to recite all other prayers combined.

FORGET ABOUT GOOD WORKS

Listen, daughter! Look closely!
Turn your ear ₍toward me₎.
Forget your people, and forget your father's house.

PSALM 45:10

 AITH IS VERY FRAGILE and needs to hear the command: "Forget your father's house." Something inside of us strongly compels us to keep trying to earn God's approval. We look for good works, in which we can place our trust and which will bring us praise. We want to show God what we have done and say, "See, I have done this or that. Therefore, you must give me your approval."

None of us should be overconfident when it comes to forgetting our own good works. Each one of us carries in our heart a horrible, religious fanatic. We would all like to be able to do something so spectacular that we could brag, "Look what I've done! With all my prayers and good works, I've done enough for God today that I can feel at peace." This happens to me, too, after I have accomplished something in my ministry. I'm much happier than if I hadn't done it. Being happy isn't wrong in itself. But this joy is impure because it isn't based on faith. It's the kind of happiness that can make your conscience confused. Consciences are delicate. We need to guard them against the sin of arrogance. So, we can't be overconfident. We who confess Christ should always walk in fear and grow in faith. We should realize that we all carry in our heart a horrible, religious fanatic, who will destroy our faith with foolish delusions of good works.

The Holy Spirit provides us with a way to counter this godless delusion. We need to hold tightly to what we have received through the undeserved kindness of God. God's approval doesn't come to us by what we do. Rather, it comes through the holiness of Christ, who suffered for us and rose again from the dead.

BLESSINGS FOLLOW TESTING

Isaac planted ₍crops₎ in that land. In that same year he harvested a hundred times as much as he had planted because the Lord had blessed him. He continued to be successful.

GENESIS 26:12–13

❖

 E MUST LEARN FROM Isaac's example to be firm in our faith so that we don't doubt or waver when hardships come our way. After Isaac had sinned, God lovingly forgave him and even blessed him. We learn from this that God doesn't remain angry forever. If we rely on his promises, we can remain faithful when things go wrong and say, "The Lord who asked me to believe in him will keep his promises. Meanwhile, I will cling to him and trust him." The Psalms remind us: "Wait with hope for the Lord. Be strong, and let your heart be courageous" (Psalm 27:14). "Be strong, all who wait with hope for the Lord, and let your heart be courageous" (Psalm 31:24). Believers can remain confident even in the worst dangers and hardships because God has promised to take care of them: "Turn all your anxiety over to God because he cares for you" (1 Peter 5:7).

It's important for believers to be tested by trials. Without these tests, their faith would grow cold and weak. It could eventually disappear completely. But if they are tested with hardships, believers will discover what faith is and will be strengthened in their knowledge of Christ. They will become so strong that even when they have troubles and anxieties, they can be just as happy as they are in good times. They can look at each hardship as if it were a cloud or a fog that will soon vanish.

Refusing God's Help

This is why people are condemned: The light came into the world. Yet, people loved the dark rather than the light because their actions were evil.

JOHN 3:19

❖

 O US, GOD MAY APPEAR to be angry. He seems to be an unjust, harsh, and stern judge. But God is saying here, "Now then, I will cancel the charges against you. You will no longer have to mourn. To be sure, you have sinned and earned the judgment of God. But your sin will be pardoned. The death penalty will be removed. I will no longer remember the sinfulness of the world—the sin in which people were born and in which they lived. Everything is settled. I will no longer look at your sin. Simply believe in my Son."

What's missing? Why does judgment still hang over us if the Son has removed our sins? This judgment remains because people reject Christ, the Son of God.

Suppose a physician were treating a sick person whom he definitely knew he could help. Suppose he had promised to get rid of his patient's pain. The physician suggests a remedy for his patient's illness or an antidote to counteract the poison his patient had ingested. Suppose further that the sick person knew without a doubt that the physician was capable of helping him. In spite of all this, the patient says, "Get out of here. I don't need your advice. You're not a physician. You're a fraud. I'm not sick. I didn't eat any poison. And besides, it probably won't hurt me." Then what if the patient tried to choke and even kill his doctor? Wouldn't you say that person was not only sick but also stark raving mad? The spiritual madness of refusing the help God's Son wants to give us is ten times worse than this.

GOD NEVER SLEEPS

You know with all your heart and soul that not one single promise which the LORD your God has given you has ever failed to come true. Every single word has come true.

JOSHUA 23:14

❖

HRISTIANS ARE WISE when they accept what God has planned and persevere in believing the promises they have from him. His promises are dependable and lasting. The Lord's own pledge is permanent, as we read in the Psalms: "Indeed, the Guardian of Israel never rests or sleeps" (Psalm 121:4).

But human reason responds, "That's all fine and good. It even sounds nice. But I'm experiencing the exact opposite. God not only sleeps, he snores! In reality, there isn't a God who takes care of me or watches over me."

Jacob was certain of God's promises. He knew that God's pledge was permanent. Yet, when Joseph's brothers were angry at Joseph, God didn't spare either Jacob or his son Joseph. It was as if they had no protection at all from the holy angels. Nobody resisted the anger of Joseph's brothers (Genesis 37:12–28). God and the angels remained dead silent. Even today, they appear to let the devil wreak havoc on the church and believers. Where is God in all of this?

Examples like these remind us that we must believe God's promises and never doubt his words. Because God can't lie, he won't stop constantly watching over us, especially if we believe his promise. Because he is faithful, God can't abandon us when we hang on to what he has promised. God may allow us to be attacked, led to the edge of hell, or even killed. It's during those times we need to remember that God promised to be our guardian—one who never rests or sleeps.

THE SPIRIT OF TRUTH

That helper is the Spirit of Truth. The world cannot accept
him, because it doesn't see or know him. You know him,
because he lives with you and will be in you.

JOHN 14:17

❖

 HRISTIANS CAN DEPEND on nothing except
Christ, their Lord and God. For the sake of
Christ, they surrender everything and declare,
"Before I deny or leave my Christ, I will abandon food
and drink, honor and possessions, house and property,
wife and child—everything." A Christian's courage cannot be fake or weak. It must be genuine and certain. For
a Christian cannot encourage himself with any temporary thing on this earth. Instead, he clings only to the
Lord Jesus Christ, who was crucified and died for us. So
Christ will say, as he promises in this passage, "Because
you acknowledge me, you have this advantage and this
comfort. Your courage won't mislead you, for your
helper is the Spirit of Truth." All other courage comes
from the spirit of lies—a false spirit that cannot please
God. But whatever a Christian does, or suffers, for his
faith in the Lord Christ is done for the truth. He has
done what is proper and right. He can boast truthfully
and joyfully that what he has done is pleasing to God
and the angels. A Christian can feel so confident that he
doesn't have to fear the devil or the world. He doesn't
have to be afraid of any threat or terror.

Let this encourage you, for nothing on earth can
comfort you more during times of need than a confident heart. As long as your heart is plagued with uncertainty and doubts, you cannot be courageous. But if
you live in truth, you can be sure that any suffering you
experience isn't caused by your own sin. You're not suffering because you tried to attain possessions, honor, or
praise for yourself. The only charge against you is that
you believe in the Lord Christ and trust in his Word.

THE HIDDEN KINGDOM

Then the end will come.
Christ will hand over the kingdom to God the Father
as he destroys every ruler, authority, and power.

1 CORINTHIANS 15:24

❖

AUL SAYS CHRIST WILL hand over the kingdom to God the Father. How can that be? Everywhere else the Scripture says he will remain king forever, and his kingdom will never end. But Paul says in this verse that Christ will hand over the kingdom and lay in his Father's lap his crown, scepter, and everything else. How can we resolve this? Here is the answer: In this verse, Paul is speaking about Christ's kingdom on earth. This is a kingdom of faith. Instead of reigning in a visible, public way, he reigns through the Word. To us, it's like looking at the sun through a cloud. We see the light, but we don't see the sun itself. But when the clouds leave, we see both the light and the sun at the same time in the same object. Similarly, Christ now reigns undivided with the Father. It's one and the same kingdom. But to us, it appears dark, hidden, concealed, and covered.

He wants to reign secretly and invisibly in our hearts, by the Word alone. Through the Word, he protects and upholds us in our weakness against the world's might and power. Though the kingdom is now here on earth, it will later be in heaven. It will not be covered and hidden as it appears now. A gold coin remains a gold coin whether I hide it in my pocket or pull it out and hold it in my hand. In the same way, Christ will present and publicly display before the eyes of the whole world the treasure that is now concealed from us.

Watch Out for Selfish Ambition

Examine me, O Lord, and test me.
Look closely into my heart and mind.

PSALM 26:2

❖

N THIS PASSAGE, David is saying, "If the doctrine is pure and nothing is lacking in the Word and preaching, then the heart should also be pure. At the same time, I still feel the sinfulness of my corrupt nature. I feel a tendency toward pride, lust, hate, and envy. In particular, the subtle poison of selfish ambition is always beneath the surface. Even people who understand God's Word very well often stumble over this sin."

This sin causes all heresies. As the saying goes, "Ambition is the mother of heresies and sects." Some people always want to be special. They're never content being like everyone else. This is how they wander off the path without even realizing it. People must pray every day that God would keep this secret rebel inside of them in check. As Paul says, "Excel in showing respect for each other" (Romans 12:10). Here, Paul acknowledges that the ego—that old idiot—always wants to be the center of attention. As soon as a person learns something and can speak about the Lord Jesus Christ, he wants to become someone special. He wants people to say, "Yes, he can get the job done. He's an educated man. He's a cut above the rest." Like a kitten adorning itself, people like to make themselves look good. But afterwards, faith and God's Word are no longer important.

We can't do enough to protect ourselves from this shameful wickedness. Other human vices are so crude that we easily perceive them, but this one sneaks up on us. It disguises itself as honoring God and doing what his Word tells us to do. However, selfish ambition lies hiding like a secret rebel behind it all.

CONTROLLING YOUR THOUGHTS

Jacob was terrified and distressed.
So he divided the people, the sheep and goats,
the cattle, and the camels into two camps.

GENESIS 32:7

❖

HILE JACOB WAS ON HIS WAY to be reunited with his brother Esau, he was plagued with doubts. He learned that his brother Esau was wealthy and had a large family. He thought, "What if God has changed his mind? Maybe God has rejected me in favor of my brother." These were Jacob's thoughts, but they remained just that—thoughts. Because of human nature and weak faith, people can't keep from having these kinds of thoughts any more than they can avoid other emotions, such as impatience, anger, and lust. You can't keep thoughts and temptations from coming into your head. Just don't let these thoughts become fixed in your mind so that they begin to affect your judgment.

You should follow the advice of a hermit who was approached by a young man complaining of having lustful thoughts and other temptations. The old man told him, "You can't stop the birds from flying over your head. But only let them fly. Don't let them nest in your hair." It's all right to have these thoughts, but let them remain just that—thoughts. Don't let them grow to the point where you have to act on these thoughts.

This was the problem that led to despair in the lives of Cain, Saul, Judas, and others. They let their thoughts grow and grow until they were saying, "My punishment is more than I can stand!" (Genesis 4:13), or "I've sinned by betraying an innocent man" (Matthew 27:4). When they did this, their temptation was turned into a judgment because they rejected the Word of God, faith, and prayer. But in spite of the many thoughts and severe temptations that Jacob experienced that night, he didn't throw his faith away.

SHORT PRAYERS

When you pray, don't ramble like heathens who think
they'll be heard if they talk a lot. Don't be like them. Your
Father knows what you need before you ask him.

MATTHEW 6:7–8

❖

E SHOULD PRAY WITH FEW WORDS but with deep, meaningful thoughts. The fewer the words, the better the prayer. The more words, the worse the prayer. Few words and deep meaning are Christian. Many words and little meaning are heathen. That's why Christ says, "When you pray, don't ramble like the heathens who think they'll be heard if they talk a lot" (Matthew 6:7). Similarly, he says to the Samaritan woman, "Those who worship him must worship in spirit and truth" (John 4:24). The Father looks for worshipers who pray this way. To pray "in spirit," or to pray spiritually, is very different from a prayer that comes from our evil desires. To pray "in truth" is very different from a fake prayer.

For the showy prayer that comes from our evil desires is pointless mumbling and babbling. It shows no respect for God. To those who are watching and listening, it looks like prayer. It may be spoken with words, but it isn't spoken in truth. The spiritual and true prayer, however, comes from within. It comes from the sighing and yearning of the depths of the heart. Unspiritual prayer produces hypocrites and a false sense of security. Spiritual prayer produces true believers and reverent children of God.

SAINTS WHO SLIP

[Lot] and his two daughters settled in the mountains . . .
The older daughter said to the younger one, ". . . Let's give
our father wine to drink. Then we'll go to bed with him."

GENESIS 19:30–32

❖

MOSES RECORDED THIS DESPICABLE SIN in Genesis for a good reason. It was horrible enough for so many people in Sodom and Gomorrah to perish. But for Lot and his daughters to fall into such a sin, after witnessing the destruction of so many people, is even more horrible. This incident was recorded in the Bible to frighten the ungodly and to keep believers from becoming smug.

You might ask, "Why did God permit his people, whom he loved, to sink so low?" We shouldn't question God's motives for what he permits. Still, in this case, we can easily find a probable explanation. God wants us to recognize our helplessness so that we don't lapse into a false sense of security. Lot and his family saw the sins of the people of Sodom and condemned them. But then what happened? Lot's devout daughters disgraced themselves by committing incest. This was so scandalous that it seldom occurred even among the people of Sodom.

So God's intent is clear. He wants us to humble ourselves and to find comfort in his mercy and kindness. As far as humans are concerned, no one is better or more holy than the next person. Thankfully, God protects us from sinning too seriously. But if he were to withdraw his hand, we might fall into the very same sins. So this story teaches us to humble ourselves in God's presence and continually pray for the Holy Spirit's guidance.

THE GREATEST LOVE

*The greatest love you can show
is to give your life for your friends.
You are my friends if you obey my commandments.*

JOHN 15:13–14

❖

HRIST USES FRIENDLY and kind words in this passage to convince his disciples of the importance of the command he was giving to them. He reminds them of his own example of how he loved them and of all that he had done for them. It would take a great and powerful love for someone to give another person in need one hundred dollars, a thousand dollars, or even to pay off that person's entire debt. But think how amazing it would be for a king to give a poor beggar an entire city—even his own kingdom, land, and people. The entire world would hold this up as an unprecedented act of love. But that would be trivial compared to Christ giving his body and life for you. This is certainly the highest expression of love a person can show to another on this earth. Someone can love and serve others with his money, his property, and even his life. But everyone would rather give up his money and property, his land and people, than to die for someone else. Even if someone did that, it still would be nothing compared to God sending his Son from heaven. It would be nothing compared to God's Son taking your place, willingly shedding his blood and dying for you, even though you were his enemy and were condemned. This love is greater and higher than heaven and earth and anything else you could name.

What will you do for Christ in return? Even if you gave your life for your neighbor, what is that compared to his life? But Christ doesn't even ask that much of you, except in emergencies, of course, when you should risk your life to save others. Christ simply asks you to show love to your neighbor in a tangible way.

WHY OUR PLANS FAIL

The LORD blocks the plans of the nations.
He frustrates the schemes of the people of the world.

PSALM 33:10

❖

E MUST DO WHAT GOD WANTS and stop think-ing and worrying about what God hasn't told us to do. Nothing is safer for us or more pleasing to God than when we trust in God's Word instead of our own ideas. In his Word, we will find enough guidance about what we are to do. God requires us to have faith, to love, and to endure suffer-ing. These three should be enough to keep us delight-fully busy. We should deal with everything else as it comes along and let God worry about how it all turns out. If we don't want to listen to what God says in his Word, he punishes us by simply letting us torment our-selves for no good reason.

When wise men and princes ignore God's Word, God doesn't let any of their intentions happen, whether good or bad. This psalm says, "The LORD blocks the plans of the nations." God will always thwart the plans of those who work the hardest by using their own wis-dom. But even this doesn't convince us to subject our plans to what God wants. So our plans and ideas only distress and torment us, even though these are not bad in themselves. As Jesus said, "Each day has enough trouble of its own" (Matthew 6:34). God doesn't send this trouble to destroy us. Rather, he sends it to us to persuade us to give up our foolish ideas and plans. He wants to show us that our wisdom is worthless. Ultimately, our wisdom isn't what makes things hap-pen, only the will of God does that. So we must learn to pray, "Let your will be done."

FLOATING ON GOD'S PROMISE

God blessed Noah and his sons and said to them,
"Be fertile, increase in number, and fill the earth."

GENESIS 9:1

❖

HE TERROR OF GOD'S ANGER had come to an end. The earth itself had been ruined, and all life had been destroyed. Now the blessing God promised to Noah and his sons was about to begin. They were going to restart the human race. No doubt they had fears as they waited for this to be accomplished. Living solely by faith is a difficult way of life. Noah and his family lived this way, with their eyes fixed on heaven. The world was covered with water. There was no dry ground to walk on. God's words were their only support as they floated on top of the water.

When people aren't in physical danger, they consider faith as something insignificant. But look at Noah. He was surrounded by water—nearly swallowed by the flood. He wasn't saved through his own efforts but through relying on God's mercy. He had confidence because he trusted what God had said.

The words, "God remembered," in Genesis 8:1, indicate just how difficult Noah's situation was. Moses points out that Noah drifted aimlessly on the water for so long that he felt as if God had forgotten him. Some people struggle with similar thoughts, feeling that they are living in darkness and without God's favor. People who feel that God has forgotten them soon find that living by God's Word alone—living by faith—is more difficult than practicing a lifestyle of rigorous spiritual discipline.

PRUNING THE BRANCHES

He removes every one of my branches that
doesn't produce fruit. He also prunes every branch
that does produce fruit to make it produce more fruit.

JOHN 15:2

❖

CHRIST SAYS HIS FATHER is the gardener, who tends and looks after his vine. God separates the wild branches from the others so that they won't spread and spoil the true vine. God singles them out to protect the true vine. He determines which ones should be cut off and tossed into the fire.

But it all appears very different to us. We see these wild branches growing and spreading. They are much stronger and thicker than the others. They look like the only true ones that will produce fruit. In contrast, we appear small, puny, and unfruitful. Yes, people want to root us out and cut us off as useless and unfit. But the false vines appear as if they will remain forever, and the entire world respects them highly.

We need spiritual understanding and vision. No matter how many scoundrels rise up against Christians, God always cuts them off and preserves a remnant of believers. From the time of the apostles until now, many heresies have challenged the teachings of Christ, of baptism, of the Lord's Supper, of justification by faith, and so on. These heresies are so pervasive that it appears they are correct teachings and the Christian church might pass away. But God has cut off all of these wild branches and preserved his true branches, so that we nevertheless hold on to right teaching, baptism, and the Lord's Supper as the apostles gave them to us. Beginning with Abel, faith has pushed forward throughout the world and will prevail as long as there are believers. Not one of them will be cut off the vine. All will remain there. So we must not look at how large and strong these wild branches are. Instead, we should look for the true branches in Christ.

THE ART OF FAITH

*We were kept under control by Moses' laws until this
faith came. We were under their control until this faith
which was about to come would be revealed.*

GALATIANS 3:23

❖

RACE IS PRESENT WHEN your heart is restored by
the promise of God's free mercy. Then your
heart can say with the author of Psalm 42,
"O my soul, why are you so troubled and restless? Do
you only see the law, sin, terror, sadness, despair, death,
hell, and the devil? Aren't grace, forgiveness of sins,
righteousness, comfort, joy, peace, life, heaven, Christ,
and God also present? Stop being troubled, my soul.
What are the law, sin, and everything evil compared to
them? Trust God. He didn't spare his own Son but
offered him up to death on a cross for your sins."

So when you are frightened by the law, you can say,
"Lady Law, you are not the only thing, and you are not
everything. Besides you there is something even greater
and better, specifically, grace, faith, and blessing. They
don't accuse, frighten, or condemn me. They comfort
me, tell me to expect the best, and assure me of my certain victory and salvation in Christ. So there's no reason
for me to despair."

Whoever truly understands this can be called a theologian. Certain leaders who are always boasting about
the Spirit believe that they understand living by faith
extremely well. I, however, and others like me, know
that we scarcely possess the fundamentals. We are diligent students in the school where the art of faith is
taught. No matter how well it's taught, as long as we
remain in these sinful bodies, we will never finish
learning.

Don't Put It Off

*When they got up in the morning, [Eleazar] said, "Let me go
back to my master. . . . Don't delay me now that the LORD
has made my trip successful. Let me go back to my master."*

GENESIS 24:54–56

❖

HIS SCRIPTURE PASSAGE provides a good example
for us. Isaac's servant was eager to take his
master's future bride to her groom. We are
reminded here that when it comes to doing God's work,
we shouldn't keep stalling and procrastinating. We
should clear away all the obstacles that keep us from
completing what we are supposed to do.

Even non-Christian writers say that after adequately
thinking over a matter, people should follow through
with their intentions quickly and bring it to pass without
delay. Sallust, the Roman statesman and historian, gave
this advice: "After thinking it over, act quickly!"
Bonaventure also made an excellent statement about this
subject, "Those who pass up great opportunities will be
passed over themselves." But worse than all of this is
when people postpone doing what God demands.

Procrastination results in serious harm. The person
who doesn't answer quickly when the Holy Spirit calls
will miss his chance. The Holy Spirit seldom asks more
than once. I've learned this from personal experience.
Whenever it was necessary to pray, read, or take Holy
Communion, the longer I put it off, the less I felt the need
to do it. The Holy Spirit doesn't give his gifts to those who
procrastinate. He prefers those who willingly obey and
gladly carry out God's commands without delay. We see
this eager attitude in Psalm 119:60: "Without any hesita-
tion I hurry to obey your commandments." The Holy
Spirit approved of this same eagerness in Rebekah when
she quickly gave Eleazar a drink of water and ran to tell
her family about Eleazar's visit. Examples like these from
the lives of God's servants should inspire us to resist the
foolishness of procrastination.

A NEW AND DIFFERENT PERSON

*Don't be surprised when I tell you
that all of you must be born from above.*

JOHN 3:7

✤

 HIS NEW BIRTH SHOWS ITSELF most clearly when trials and death draw near. Then it becomes clear whether or not a person has experienced the new birth. At that time, human reason—the old light—twists and wrestles, refusing to let go of its own thinking. It doesn't want to give up and turn to the gospel. Reason simply won't let go of its own light. But those who are born anew, or who are being born anew, surrender and follow God. They give up their old light, life, possessions, honor, and whatever else they have. They trust what John records in his Gospel and cling to it. As true children of God, they will receive their eternal inheritance.

If your old, arrogant light of reason grows dark, becomes dead, and is replaced by a new light, then your entire life will be transformed. For when your reason is changed, your will follows soon after. And when your will is changed, what you love and desire change as well. In order to become new, you must crawl into the gospel with your whole self. You must shed off the old skin, as a snake does. When its skin becomes old, a snake looks for a narrow hole in the rock. It crawls through it and sheds its skin, leaving it outside in front of the hole. Similarly, you must also go into the gospel and God's Word. You must confidently believe its promise that God does not lie. So you shed off your old skin, leaving behind your old light, arrogance, will, love, desires, and what you say and do. You become a new and different person who views everything differently than before.

LIVE IN HARMONY

Finally, everyone must live in harmony, be sympathetic,
love each other, have compassion, and be humble.

1 PETER 3:8

❖

E SHOULD STRIVE TO LIVE in harmony with each
other. Both Peter and Paul emphasize that we
all should be of one heart, one spirit, and one
mind. What seems right and good to one person should
be regarded with consideration by others also. This is a
powerful teaching that we should strive to understand.

All of us cannot do the same work. Each one of us
must pursue his own work. It's foolish to teach that we
should all do one kind of work, as some preachers have
taught. They preach about the legends of saints—that
this saint has done one work, another a different one.
Then they conclude we should also do these works.
Undoubtedly, Abraham did a precious work when he
offered his son because it was specifically commanded
by God. But then the pagans wanted to sacrifice their
children too. That was an outrage to God. Similarly,
King Solomon did well when he built the temple, and
God rewarded him for it. Now these blind fools come
along and tell us to build churches and temples when
God has commanded nothing of the sort. So it's
reversed today: They say that we should all do one
work, but there are various opinions about which one.
This is directly against the gospel.

So we must teach that there should be one mind and
many works, one heart and many hands. We all
shouldn't try to do the same work. Rather, each one
should pay attention to his own responsibilities.
Otherwise, we cannot be of one mind and one heart.
We must allow the works to be varied so that each
person can remain with what God has entrusted to
him. We should simply do the work at hand.

CAREFUL OBEDIENCE

Abraham picked up the knife and took it in his hand to sacrifice his son. But the Messenger of the LORD called to him from heaven and said, "Abraham! Abraham!"

GENESIS 22:10–11

❖

AN ANGEL FROM HEAVEN was an eyewitness to what Abraham was doing. Yes, God himself and all the angels were watching. The angel didn't come flying in at the last moment from a distant corner of the world. Instead, he was watching over Abraham and Isaac all along. He observed as Abraham tied up his son and raised the knife. The son willingly obeyed and waited for the deadly thrust. Tears were undoubtedly streaming down Abraham's cheeks, and Isaac was lying on his back looking up toward heaven. All the while, the angel was watching. Right when Abraham was raising the knife, the angel shouted to him and called him by name.

How closely the holy angels gather around those of us who follow God and live faithfully! Obedience like Abraham's gives God immense pleasure. Of all the sacrifices we can make, the one most acceptable to God is this: getting rid of sin, living a holy life, obeying God, and killing our corrupt nature. This is very painful and unpleasant for us to do. Still, we must get used to determining what "God really wants—what is good, pleasing, and perfect" (Romans 12:2).

We merely talk about these matters, but Abraham and Isaac actually lived them out. They did what God wanted. In comparison, we haven't even begun to do this. Careful obedience pleases God, but it's unpleasant and distasteful to us. Nothing is more agonizing than getting rid of sin and killing our corrupt nature. Still, we must get used to obeying God and start following Abraham's example. Abraham didn't try to get out of what he had to do. Instead, he looked forward to pleasing God with eager anticipation.

Serving God or Money

No one can serve two masters. He will hate the first master and love the second, or he will be devoted to the first and despise the second. You cannot serve God and wealth.

MATTHEW 6:24

❖

HE LITTLE WORD *serve* is key to this verse. It isn't sinful to have money and property, a spouse and children, and a house or home. But don't let these possessions control you. Rather, make them your servants and be their master.

Remember what people say about a kind and generous individual, "He is master of his money." Money doesn't control him, unlike a greedy miser who ignores God's Word and everything else God wants. A miser would rather withhold a helping hand than let go of his money. This kind of greed is the mark of a tight-fisted, childish, and insensitive individual. That type of person doesn't put his resources to good use or even enjoy them. He ignores eternal treasures for the sake of money. He pursues his own selfish goals and neglects God's Word, thinking he can get around to it at a more convenient time. Meanwhile, he scrambles to get everything he can, without a penny to spare for the work of God. If left unchecked, he will sink deeper and deeper into greed and jealousy, moving further and further away from God's Word. Eventually, his heart will be filled with cynicism, and he will become an enemy of God.

So, Christ spoke sternly when he said, "He will hate the first master and love the second, or he will be devoted to the first and despise the second." This is the same as saying, "The love of money makes people enemies of God." That's ultimately what happens when we serve wealth. Christ also said, "Your heart will be where your treasure is" (Matthew 6:21). We pursue what we love. We talk about it because that is where our heart and thoughts are. Augustine came right to the point when he said: "Whatever I love is my god."

A ROARING LION

Keep your mind clear, and be alert.
Your opponent the devil is prowling around
like a roaring lion as he looks for someone to devour.

1 PETER 5:8

❖

ETER GIVES US A WARNING and wants us to open our eyes. This is a verse worth writing in gold letters. Here you see what life is really like. It's almost enough to make us wish we were dead. We're living here on the devil's turf. Our situation is similar to a traveler who stays at an inn where he finds out that everyone in the place is a robber. If he had to stay there, he would arm himself in the best possible way and probably wouldn't get much sleep. In the same way, we now live on this earth, where the evil spirit is the prince. He controls the hearts of the people under his power, and he does whatever he wants through them. This is a horrible situation if viewed correctly.

So Peter warns us to be alert. He wants us to be like a faithful servant who is aware of what is really happening. Therefore, he says, "Keep your mind clear." For those who eat and drink too much are like stuffed pigs that are good for nothing. Therefore, we must keep this treasure with us at all times. "Be alert," he says, not only spiritually, but physically. For a lazy person who likes to sleep won't be able to resist the devil after he has gorged himself and drunk his fill. After all, it's hard enough for those who have faith and the Spirit to resist the devil.

DOWN FROM THE MOUNTAIN

Then Abraham returned to his servants,
and together they left for Beersheba.
Abraham remained in Beersheba.

GENESIS 22:19

❖

BRAHAM LEFT MOUNT MORIAH. This was the mountain where he had been asked to sacrifice Isaac—where he had heard the voice of the angel and experienced God's presence. This place was a holy mountain—a place unlike any other in the whole world. It was where Abraham had received God's promise and pledge.

This story shows how highly Abraham regarded his duty toward his family and his God-given responsibilities as head of the household. Since God gave him no further commands, he didn't start doing anything differently after this experience. Instead, he returned to his familiar household activities—overseeing his servants and guiding his wife and family. His life didn't appear to be especially religious or spiritual. Abraham left all that on Mount Moriah. He didn't even let the fact that he had seen angels on the mountain hold him there. He went back to the young men watching his donkey.

If certain overly religious people were to comment on this passage, they would question Abraham's piety and condemn him for leaving the mountain. They would think that if Abraham really were such an outstanding example for later generations, then he wouldn't have left that holy place. After all, that is where Abraham had met God and his angels. How could he return to his donkey and go back to his everyday work? What kind of piety is that? It's remarkable how much certain religious people despise honest work and everyday chores.

THE UNFORESEEABLE FUTURE

God also decided ahead of time to choose us
through Christ according to his plan,
which makes everything work the way he intends.

EPHESIANS 1:11

❖

EWARE OF THE PHILOSOPHY that leads people to say, "What can I do? What's the use of praying? What good is it to worry? If it's predestined, it must happen." Yes, it's true that what is predestined will happen. However, we aren't commanded to know what is predestined. In fact, we are forbidden to know it. We test God when we delve into unknowable matters. God has given Scripture to us so that we can know what we should and shouldn't do. He expects us to act on this knowledge. What we cannot know, we should leave to God. We should stick to our responsibilities, vocation, and position in life. God and God alone knows what is predestined. You aren't supposed to know.

Take for example the time when Joab was being attacked both in front and from behind by his enemies. He didn't say to his brother Abishai, "Wait, let's see what is predestined, and then we will act accordingly." Rather he said, "If the Arameans are too strong for my ₁troops₁, be ready to help me. And if the Ammonites are too strong for your ₁troops₁, I'll come to help you. Be strong! Let's prove ourselves strong for our people and for the cities of our God, and the LORD will do what he considers right" (2 Samuel 10:11–12).

So we should also concentrate on our duties, not whether or not something is predestined. Because we have no word or light from God on that matter, we don't know anything about it. Therefore, we should put the thought of trying to find out whether something is predestined or not out of our mind and heart. Let the future remain in darkness. Let it stay secret and hidden. In the meantime, we should do what we know we ought to. We should live by God's Word and the light he has given to us.

GOD WORKS IN SECRET

As the Midianite merchants were passing by, the brothers pulled
Joseph out of the cistern. They sold him to the Ishmaelites for
eight ounces of silver. The Ishmaelites took him to Egypt.

GENESIS 37:28

❖

OD HUMBLES HIS PEOPLE before he elevates them. He kills them in order to bring them back to life. He devastates them before honoring them. He knocks them down in order to pick them up. God's methods show the highest artistry and wisdom. We cannot understand how events like these are a part of God's plan until we see his plan completed. When these events are happening, they can't be understood, except through faith alone.

In the same way, faith in the Son of God will comfort me when I leave this earth. And yet, I will be buried in the ground, eaten by worms, rot and decay (Job 17:14). I don't see God's plan for me when I look at death. Yet, God has promised that I will come back to life. Christ said, "You will live because I live" (John 14:19). But how will I live? I will live in eternal life, in a body that is more beautiful and bright than the sun. I can't see or feel any of this yet. But I believe it, and I can tolerate the short delay. Eternal life is already prepared. As Paul says, "The prize that shows I have God's approval is now waiting for me. The Lord, who is a fair judge, will give me that prize on that day" (2 Timothy 4:8).

But God does everything in secret. We have to be patient while God hides his intentions from us. Jacob and Joseph couldn't see the future prize. But with the sale of Joseph to the Ishmaelites, the future was being prepared. God sees everything as if it has all taken place already. Everything he wants to happen will certainly happen!

THE OPPORTUNITIES AT HAND

Make the most of your opportunities because
these are evil days. So don't be foolish,
but understand what the Lord wants.

EPHESIANS 5:16–17

❖

E AREN'T SUPPOSED TO QUESTION if God in his unchangeable wisdom is willing to help us and give us what we need. Instead, we should say with conviction, "I believe that God will take care of me, but I don't know his plan. I don't know exactly how he's going to fulfill his promise."

So, we must take advantage of the opportunities we have at hand. We have to earn our money through hard work and diligence. In order to stay alive, we have to have milk, food, clothes, and so on. This means we have to cultivate the fields and harvest the crops. Providing for ourselves is a God-given responsibility. We can't use God's promise to take care of us as an excuse for not working diligently. That would be wrong. God doesn't want us to be lazy and idle. He tells us in Genesis, "By the sweat of your brow, you will produce food to eat until you return to the ground, because you were taken from it" (Genesis 3:19). He also says, "The ground will grow thorns and thistles" (Genesis 3:18).

The Lord is saying, "I promise that I will take care of you and give you food. But to the best of your ability, I want you to take advantage of the opportunities I have made available to you. Otherwise, you will be testing me. However, if you are in need and have nothing available to you, at that time I will take care of you and give you food in a miraculous way. But keep this in mind: If there are any opportunities available to you, don't forget that I am the one who gave them to you so that you would be able to take care of yourselves."

FIGHTING EVIL DESIRES

If your spiritual nature is your guide,
you are not subject to Moses' laws.

GALATIANS 5:18

❖

HEN WE ARE FIERCELY ATTACKED by anger, hatred, impatience, sexual desire, sorrow, or desires of the corrupt nature, we cannot get rid of these desires no matter how much we would like. What should we do? Should we despair? No. We ought to say, "My corrupt nature fights and rages now against the Spirit. Let it rage as long as it wants to. I won't give in to it. But I will live by the Spirit and be led by him, so I won't gratify the desires of the corrupt nature. If I do this, I am free from the law. It will accuse and frighten me but does so in vain."

When you are suffering temptation, you should not be upset that the devil can exaggerate sin. At the time, he may make your sins appear so large that you fear you will be immediately and totally overcome, so that you feel nothing but the wrath of God and despair. At that moment, don't follow your feelings but hold on to the words of Paul, "If your spiritual nature is your guide," that is, if you encourage yourself through faith in Christ, "you are not subject to Moses' laws." Then you will have the most powerful defense with which to extinguish all the flaming arrows that the devil shoots at you (Ephesians 6:16). All the agitation and raging of the corrupt nature cannot hurt or condemn you because you follow the Spirit and don't give in to the corrupt nature or gratify its desires. Therefore, this is the only remedy. When we feel the stirrings of the corrupt nature raging in us, we ought to grasp the sword of the Spirit—that is, the Word of salvation. Then we will undoubtedly be victors though we will feel the total opposite as long as the battle lasts.

TRUSTING GOD IN DIFFICULT TIMES

While Joseph was in prison, the LORD was with him.
The LORD reached out to him with his
unchanging love and gave him protection.

GENESIS 39:20–21

❖

HE STORY OF THE SUFFERING Joseph experienced when he was sold into slavery can comfort us. He suffered horribly, but God appeared unable to hear or speak. It didn't look like God knew what was happening. In spite of this, Joseph kept his faith. God encouraged Joseph and spoke to his heart: "Dear Joseph, wait. Be patient. Just believe and don't despair. Hang on to the promise you heard from your father." In this way, God talked to Joseph through the words of his father. But Joseph didn't really see or hear anything. This made God appear to be blind or dead. Yet, Joseph believed the promise God gave to Joseph's ancestors. He thought, "God promised to be with Abraham's descendants. I believe in the God of my ancestors." Later God would speak in a wonderful way when he made Joseph a ruler and rescuer in Egypt.

We were given these examples so that we would learn to have patience in suffering. Then, we will never complain about God no matter how horrible the grief, fear, or pain may be. Surely Joseph, too, experienced deep pain and depression when he was unjustly torn from his father and sold to strangers. He realized he would be a slave forever with no hope of owning any-thing or ever regaining his freedom.

Because our Lord lets such awful things happen to his children, we must patiently bear the bad things that happen to us. They aren't signs that God has aban-doned us or is angry with us. Rather, they prove we have his favor. They show us that he's testing our faith.

Following Christ's Steps

*God called you to endure suffering because
Christ suffered for you. He left you an example
so that you could follow in his footsteps.*

1 PETER 2:21

❖

S GOD'S SERVANTS, we should impress on our
hearts that we should be ready and willing
to suffer what comes our way because Christ
did so much for us. We should think along these lines,
"Though completely innocent, my Lord served me and
gave his life for me. Why should I refuse to serve him in
return? He was entirely pure and without sin. Yet he
humbled himself, shed his blood, and died, wiping out
my sin. Shouldn't I also suffer a little bit if this pleases
him?" Whoever thinks about Christ's death without
feeling moved must be made out of stone. For if a master walks ahead and steps in the mud, it's only reasonable for his servant to follow him through the mud.

So Peter says, "God called you." To what? To endure
suffering as Christ did. Peter is saying, "If you wish to
follow Christ, you must not argue and complain very
much when you are wronged. You must endure it and
even forgive it. Remember that Christ suffered everything for you, even though he was completely innocent.
He didn't appeal to justice when he stood before his
judges. In the same way, you should set justice aside
and say to yourself, "Thank you, God. I'm called to
endure injustice. Why should I complain when my
Lord didn't complain?"

ONLY ONE GOSPEL

There is one Lord, one faith, one baptism,
one God and Father of all, who is over everything,
through everything, and in everything.

EPHESIANS 4:5–6

❖

LL OF THE APOSTLES TEACH one message. So we must be careful when we talk about four evangelists and four Gospels. Everything the apostles wrote is one gospel. The word *gospel* means nothing other than an announcement about God's grace earned and purchased through Christ by his death. Actually, the gospel is not what we read in books and what is written with letters. Instead, it's a living Word, a voice that rings throughout the whole world. It is publicly proclaimed and heard everywhere. The gospel is also not a law book, which contains many good teachings, as has been thought in the past. It doesn't tell us to do good works to become virtuous but announces God's grace to us, given freely and without our merit. It tells us how Christ stood as our representative. He paid for our sins and wiped them out so that we become faithful and blessed through his work.

Whoever preaches or writes about this teaches the true gospel as all apostles have, most notably as Paul and Peter did in their letters. Although preachers teach different ways and choose different words, they only preach one gospel. It may be a shorter or longer account. It may be presented briefly or more extensively. But if the preachers teach us that Christ is our Savior, that we are justified by faith in him without works, then it's the same Word. There is only one gospel, just as there is only one faith and one baptism.

GOD'S LAWS POINT THE WAY

The Teachings were given through Moses,
but kindness and truth came into
existence through Jesus Christ.

JOHN 1:17

❖

HE TEACHINGS GIVEN THROUGH Moses are God's laws. God's laws and the Ten Commandments point you in the right direction. They show you how to live. They tell you about righteousness and eternal life. God's laws are like sermons that point you to life. You must remember these instructions, but they won't give you life.

God's laws are like a finger that points to the right road. Fingers are a useful part of the body. However, if you don't also have feet to take you there, a wagon to ride in, or even a horse to ride on, you'll never be able to get to the right road. A finger can point you in the right direction, but it can't get you there. In a similar way, God's laws tell you what God wants done and how he wants things to be done. They show you that you are unable to obey them. God's laws show you what human nature is really like—what it can do and what it can't do. God's laws were given to you in order to reveal your sins, but they don't have the power to free you from sin or help you get rid of it. God's laws hold a mirror in front of you. When you look at God's laws, you become aware that you don't have life or God's approval. What you see in the mirror forces you to cry out, "Come, Lord Jesus Christ, help me and give me your kindness so that I can do what your laws demand!"

SARAH'S FAITHFUL EXAMPLE

Sarah obeyed Abraham and spoke to him respectfully.
You became Sarah's daughters by not letting
anything make you afraid to do good.

1 PETER 3:6

❖

BRAHAM OBEYED GOD, who had called him to leave everything and wander in a new country. Yet he didn't flaunt the fact that he was giving up everything he had. And later when God blessed him, he still had to put up with being attacked and raided by unbelievers all the time. His wife, Sarah, voluntarily followed him into this life of hardship. She managed the household and the servants. Yet she was always helpful to neighbors and obedient to her husband.

Dedication to duty, obedience, and helpfulness are the highest virtues. But sadly, not everyone practices them. So treasure God's commands and give them preference over all human rules, no matter how noble these rules appear. These rules water down faith in the same way a greedy bartender might dilute wine with water.

We must pay close attention to the biblical story of Sarah. Sarah is praised for her dedication to duty—diligently taking care of her household. For if a woman desires to serve God and to please him, she shouldn't neglect her home, spending all of her time at church, fasting constantly, or praying the same prayers over and over. Rather, she should take care of her home and family, raising and teaching the children, preparing meals, and doing whatever else needs to be done. If she does all of this, believes in the Son of God, and lives in the hope that God approves of her through Jesus Christ, then she is truly blessed.

TRUSTING OR TESTING GOD

[Jacob] said to his sons, "Why do you keep looking at each other? I've heard there's grain for sale in Egypt. Go there and buy some for us so that we won't starve to death."

GENESIS 42:1-2

❖

WHY DID JACOB TELL HIS SONS, "Go, buy grain for us so that we don't starve"? Why didn't he trust God's promise to protect and take care of him? Why was Jacob afraid of dying when, up to now, he had experienced God's help and guidance throughout his life? God had protected him, his entire family, and all his servants in the foreign country of Canaan. Why did he stop trusting God's promise when it was still fresh in his mind? He had always taught his children about God's promise. Where is your faith now, Jacob? Where is the promise?

Here is how I reply to these questions: God orders us to believe and trust in his goodness, but at the same time, we should never test him. We must take advantage of opportunities that God gives us. If we don't, we aren't living according to his plan. At the same time, we must continue to maintain our faith and hope in God. That's why Jacob didn't say, "Stay here and wait. The Lord is powerful enough to make food fall right out of the sky. Maybe that's the way he will choose to feed us." No, that's not what God's promise means.

There's no doubt that God can take care of you in a miraculous way. But you must not pass up opportunities that could provide the help you need. If you don't use what is readily available to you, then you are testing God. Jacob was careful not to test God. He didn't sit idly at home, hoping to get food some other way. He sent his sons to Egypt to buy grain, saying, "What are you waiting for? Food isn't going to rain down from the clouds. Go! Believe in God and do what you can."

LOOKING BACK ON LIFE

A person may plan his own journey,
but the LORD directs his steps.

PROVERBS 16:9

❖

O ONE SEES THE HAND of God working in his life more clearly than when he reflects back on the years of his life. Augustine said that if a person had a choice of either dying or reliving his life over again, he would certainly choose death because of all the danger and evil he so narrowly escaped. In one sense, this statement is certainly true.

Looking back, a person can see how much he has accomplished and suffered without trying or thinking about it, even against his wishes and will. He gave such little thought to what he was doing before it occurred or when it was happening. Now, after everything has been carried out, he is amazed and says, "Why did these things happen to me when I never thought about them or thought something completely different would happen?" So Proverbs 16:9 is true, "A person may plan his own journey, but the LORD directs his steps," even against his plan and will. So we must agree that our own cleverness and foresight don't guide our life and actions. Instead, God's wonderful power, wisdom, and goodness guide us. Only as we look back do we fully recognize how often God was with us when we neither saw his hand nor felt his presence at the time it was happening. Accordingly, Peter said, "He cares for you" (1 Peter 5:7).

Even if there were no books or sermons to tell us about God, simply looking back on our own lives would prove that he tenderly carries us in his arms. When we look back on how God has led and brought us through so much evil, adversity, and danger, we can clearly see the ever-present goodness of God, which is far above our thoughts, mind, and perception.

EVERYONE EXPERIENCES SUFFERING

After all, if it is God's will, it's better to suffer
for doing good than for doing wrong.

1 PETER 3:17

❖

F YOU THINK BELIEVERS will only have good days on earth, while unbelievers don't get to have any—well, it doesn't work that way. Everyone experiences suffering. God said to Adam, "By the sweat of your brow, you will produce food to eat" (Genesis 3:19), and to Eve, "I will increase your pain and your labor when you give birth to children" (Genesis 3:16). Since that time, everyone shares in that tragic condition. This makes it all the more necessary for those seeking eternal life to bear the cross. Peter teaches us, "If it is God's will, it's better to suffer for doing good." Those who suffer for doing wrong also have a bad conscience. So they have a double punishment. But Christians have only half of this. Though they experience suffering outwardly, they are inwardly comforted.

Notice too that Peter has set a boundary for our suffering when he says, ". . . even though you have to suffer different kinds of trouble for a little while now" (1 Peter 1:6). In other words, God doesn't want us to look for misfortune and choose it for ourselves. So move ahead in faith and love. If the cross comes your way, accept it. If it doesn't come, don't search for it. We should take care of our bodies in such a way that we neither become self-indulgent nor destroy them (Romans 13:13–14). We should willingly suffer when someone else inflicts suffering on us, but we shouldn't bring it on ourselves. This is what it means when Peter says, "if it is God's will." If God sends suffering to us, it's better than if he didn't. We are happier and better off if we suffer for doing good.

DEEP SIGHS AND FEW WORDS

Jacob prayed . . . "I'm not worthy of all the love and faithfulness you have shown me. . . . Please save me from my brother Esau, because I'm afraid of him."

GENESIS 32:9–11

❖

HEN WE PRAY, WE SHOULDN'T "ramble like heathens who think they'll be heard if they talk a lot" (Matthew 6:7). People who ramble on when they pray aren't thinking about God's promises and commands regarding prayer or even the help they so desperately need. This isn't true prayer. I used to pray this way when I was a monk. I called out to God in times of need, but I didn't know anything about God's promise to hear me or about his command to pray. I was only mumbling words.

Real prayer, on the other hand, comes from deep down. Like Jacob's prayer in this passage, real prayer comes from a heart full of faith that realizes both the need to pray and God's command to pray. Both of these truths should inspire you to pray and to think carefully about the words being prayed. But some people routinely mumble their prayers while their thoughts are far away. They're not really praying, for they don't even know what they're saying.

A real prayer doesn't require a lot of words. Instead, it often involves long, deep sighs, without any words at all. Jacob's prayer probably wasn't limited to the words recorded by Moses here. Most likely, Jacob sighed all day and all night. Judging from this, his prayer must have been very long, with few words.

Though we should use few words in prayer, we shouldn't neglect to be thankful for how God has blessed us in the past. Remembering past examples of God's love and faithfulness kindles our faith and pleases God. Jacob showed his gratitude to God when he prayed, "I'm not worthy of all the love and faithfulness you have shown me."

MADE ALIVE THROUGH CHRIST

As everyone dies because of Adam,
so also everyone will be made alive because of Christ.

1 CORINTHIANS 15:22

❖

AUL IS SPEAKING HERE only about Christians. He wants to teach and comfort them about being made alive in Christ. Although non-Christians will also rise from the dead, it will not be a comfort or a joy to them because they will be raised to judgment, not to life. This is not a comforting or happy message to the world. Godless people don't want to hear about this. This is the way I felt when I wanted to be a holy monk and tried to be pious. I would rather have heard about all the devils in hell than about judgment day. The hair on my head stood on end when I thought about it. The whole world hates to think about leaving this life. They don't want to die, and they are terrified when we speak of death and the afterlife. Aside from that, all of us are stuck in the muck of our own holiness and think that by our life and works we can pacify God's judgment and earn a place in heaven. All we accomplish by this is that we become even worse and grow more hostile towards the judgment day.

I won't say anything about the large group of people who look for all their pleasure and comfort here in this life, despise God's Word, and won't give a penny for God and his kingdom. It's no surprise if such people are aggravated by hearing about the resurrection. But to us, this message is pure comfort and joy because we hear that our greatest treasure is already in heaven. Only a small part remains on earth, which Christ will resurrect and draw to himself, as easily as a person awakening from sleep.

PRESERVING PURITY

Each of you should know that finding a husband or wife for
yourself is to be done in a holy and honorable way, not in
the passionate, lustful way of people who don't know God.

1 THESSALONIANS 4:4–5

❖

LL YOUNG PEOPLE SHOULD avoid casual sex and preserve their purity. They should resolve to strengthen themselves against lust and sexual passions by reading and meditating on a psalm or some other portion of God's Word. When the flames of passion plague you and sexual arousal reaches unmanageable proportions, go to a psalm or any other chapter or two in the Bible and read. After the flames of passion die down, devote yourself to serious prayer.

If your sexual appetites continually tempt you, be patient. Resist them as long as necessary, even if it takes more than a year. But above all, keep praying! If you feel that you can't stand it any longer, pray that God will give you a devout spouse with whom you can live in harmony and true love.

I have known many people who, because of their crude and shameful fantasies, indulged their passions with unrestrained lust. Because of their insatiable desires, they abandoned self-control and lapsed into terrible immorality. In the end, they had to endure dreadful punishment. Blinded to the realities of married life, some of them took unsuitable mates and ended up in incompatible relationships. They got what they deserved.

You must pray diligently and strive to resist the desires of your corrupt nature. Ask God to give you a Rebekah or Isaac instead of a Delilah or Samson—or someone even worse. Finding a devoted, loyal wife or husband isn't a matter of good luck. It's not the result of good judgment, as unbelievers think. Rather, a devout spouse is a gift from God.

A New Creation

Certainly, it doesn't matter whether a person is circumcised or not. Rather, what matters is being a new creation.

GALATIANS 6:15

❖

 CHANGE IN CLOTHING or other externals doesn't make a new creation, as some imagine. It happens through the renewal of the mind by the Holy Spirit. This is subsequently followed by a change in the body, limbs, and senses. For when the heart receives new light, new judgment, and new impulses through the gospel, the external senses are also renewed. Then the ears have the desire to hear God's Word instead of human ideas and dreams. The mouth and the tongue no longer praise their own works, righteousness, and rules, but joyfully praise God's mercy, which was revealed in Christ. These are not merely changes in words, but real changes. They include a new mind, new will, new senses, and also new ways of behaving. The eyes, ears, mouth, and tongue not only see, hear, and speak differently than before, but the mind itself resolves and follows a different way of living.

Formerly, when our hearts were blinded by errors in teachings from Rome, we imagined that God was a salesman who sold his grace in exchange for our works and achievements. Now, however, since the light of the gospel has dawned, we know that we are only credited as righteous by faith in Christ. Our hearts throw out all self-chosen works and only perform the work of their calling and the works of love, which God commands. They praise God and joyfully boast in their trust in God's mercy. When enduring danger or disaster, our hearts suffer with joy and gladness, even though our corrupt nature continues to grumble. This is what Paul means by a new creation.

Courage to Trust God

*Jacob wouldn't send Joseph's brother Benjamin
with the other brothers, because he was afraid
that something would happen to him.*

GENESIS 42:4

❖

ACOB DECIDED TO KEEP Benjamin close to himself in order to prevent him from being killed, as his brother Joseph was. This was a very human, but foolish, thought—as if Benjamin couldn't die at home! Jacob seemed to be thinking that Benjamin's life and well-being were under his control. If such a great spiritual leader—one who had God's promise of protection—showed such weakness, what will we do when faced with danger and trials?

Examples like this are given to instruct and comfort us so that we may learn to always trust in God. At the same time, we have to take care of our children and jobs that God has given to us. We shouldn't think, "I'm a deacon, and I know that God takes care of his church. That means I can take it easy. I don't need to worry about my responsibilities."

Just as a father can never be lazy or indifferent, we need to be courageous and work diligently to fulfill our responsibilities. God doesn't forbid work. He doesn't want us to be lazy—even though he's in charge of everything, and everything happens the way he wants. We need to be trained and tested by danger, terrifying trials, and by the uncertain results of our own efforts. However, we must always remember God's promise and be firm in our faith. We must pray and do our daily work, but everything we do must flow from faith.

CRUCIFY THE CORRUPT NATURE

Those who belong to Christ Jesus have crucified their corrupt nature along with its passions and desires.

GALATIANS 5:24

❖

 AUL SAYS THAT ALL THOSE who belong to Christ crucify the corrupt nature, along with its shortcomings and sins. Believers have not yet completely taken off their corrupt nature, and they are still inclined to sin. They don't fear and love God enough. They are driven to anger, envy, impatience, sexual immorality, and other evil impulses as well. However, believers don't act on these impulses because, as Paul says here, they crucify their corrupt nature with its desires and sins. Suppressing wickedness, fasting, or exercising other spiritual disciplines aren't enough to crucify the corrupt nature. It only happens when believers live by the Spirit (Galatians 5:16). God's threats to punish sin also serve as a warning and frighten believers from sinning. Armed with God's Word, faith, and prayer, they refuse to give in to the desires of the corrupt nature. By resisting the corrupt nature in this way, they nail it to the cross with its lusts and cravings so that the corrupt nature—though it's still alive and moves—can't achieve what it wants, for it's fastened to the cross by its hands and feet.

In summary, believers must crucify the corrupt nature for as long as they live on the earth. This means they are aware of its desires, but they don't obey these desires. With the armor of God and with the spiritual weapons of faith, hope, and the sword of the Spirit, believers fight against the corrupt nature. With these nails, they fasten it to the cross so it is forced against its will to be subject to the Spirit. When they die, they put off the corrupt nature completely. When they are resurrected, believers will have a pure nature with no passions and cravings.

THE VALUE OF EVERYDAY WORK

Jacob saw Rachel, daughter of his uncle Laban, with his uncle Laban's sheep. He came forward and rolled the stone off the opening of the well and watered his uncle Laban's sheep.

GENESIS 29:10

❖

AS THE HEAD OF GOD'S PEOPLE and a light for the world, Jacob was an extremely important person. He had the blessing and the promise, and had even heard God speak to him. It's remarkable that he lived as if he had nothing at all. He lived like an ordinary person and did everyday work, actions for which God doesn't give any specific instructions in his Word. God didn't tell Jacob how he would help or direct him, how things would turn out, or whether there would be a good harvest in any given year.

Accordingly, we should never say, "I don't know what's going to happen, so I won't do anything." God tells us to do the best we can and leave the rest to him. He didn't promise that everything we do would be successful. We don't need to know what's going to happen or how everything is going to turn out. We should simply do our assigned work to the best of our abilities.

In the Bible, we hear about the impressive and heroic acts of our ancestors in the faith. Along with these, we also hear about the humble, unpleasant, and distasteful work they had to do. This should comfort us whenever our everyday work bogs us down. Then, we won't feel depressed or fall into despair, thinking that God will despise us. Instead, we should realize that all work is made holy through God's Word and our faith. But the world doesn't view work in this way. They think that reading stories about people in the Bible doing common, everyday tasks is a waste of time. Only believers are able to see and understand that God is at work in these ordinary activities. This work is precious, not only in our sight, but also in the sight of God.

DEFYING THE WORLD

*But you don't have anything in common
with the world. I chose you from the world,
and that's why the world hates you.*

JOHN 15:19

❖

 HRIST WARNS US HERE about the world's opposition to Christians. We must learn to despise
the world's envy and hatred and whatever
else it tries to do to us. It's inevitable that the people of
the world will hate God and Christ. And because they
hate Christ, they will also hate us. Because of this ongoing opposition, we must know how to overcome it.
We overcome it by despising the world's arrogance.

The more we let the world's arrogance bother us, the
more the devil and the world likes it. If the devil could
make us agonize and worry day and night about the
world's opposition to the gospel, he would laugh up his
sleeve and have great fun with it. The people of the
world would only rant and rave longer and louder.
They would think they were succeeding because they
were making us wail and cry. But if we defiantly ignore
them, they become angry, sad, and irritated that their
enemies are mocking them to their face—even when
their ranting and raving is at its peak.

The devil is extremely arrogant, and so is his bride,
the world. So there's nothing worse to him than being
despised and mocked. When he experiences this and
can't do anything about it, he retreats. Otherwise, he
doesn't stop until he makes us discouraged and
exhausted. He urges and pushes so long and hard that
one could die of sorrow. But when he sees that we're
determined to hold out against his hatred and that we
continue to be cheerful and even mock him on top of
it, he'll be the first one to grow tired. He's so haughty
that he can't tolerate it when we defy him.

CALLING ON GOD FOR HELP

Call on me in times of trouble.
I will rescue you, and you will honor me.

PSALM 50:15

❖

HIS PASSAGE DESCRIBES the life of faithful believers. All of the misfortunes we experience are nothing but a joyful game that God plays with us. Sometimes a father will tell his little child to do something, even though he knows the child isn't strong enough, or the task is too difficult. He may tell his little son to bring him a bucket or to take off his socks or boots. When the child tries hard to accomplish the task, even though it's much too hard for him, the father will gladly and quickly lend a hand. He will praise his child for his efforts. This will train the child to obey, and the child will also learn to love his father more and more.

These are the kinds of games that God plays with the God-fearing and faithful people who are his children and who call him Father. They don't doubt his fatherly love and good intentions in the least. They experience his tenderness firsthand when he reaches down to them and helps them in a fatherly way. God will be pleased with their efforts and will praise everything they do—even if it's small and weak. This is very similar to the way an earthly father appreciates and praises the efforts of his little children when they try to complete a task that is much too difficult for them.

TRUE CONTEMPLATION

*Always think about Jesus Christ. He was brought
back to life and is a descendant of David.
This is the Good News that I tell others.*

2 TIMOTHY 2:8

❖

ORMERLY, MANY PEOPLE wrote and taught about
the differences between contemplating God
and serving him in the world. Some people,
who had the best intentions, spent their whole lives
searching for visions and revelations. Some of them
even recorded all of their dreams. They expected to
receive personal messages from God without using the
Word of God. What else is this but trying to climb into
heaven without using the ladder God has provided?
They were being fooled by the devil's tricks.

If you want to contemplate, then contemplate the
right way. Think about your baptism. Read the Bible.
Listen to sermons on God's Word. Honor your father and
mother. Help a needy neighbor. Don't hide in a corner
like people who think their personal devotions will give
them a place on God's lap. They believe that they can be
close to God without Christ, without God's Word, and
without the sacraments. These people consider living life
and doing everyday work beneath them. I also thought
that way until God freed me of my error. The idea of
spending life in quiet contemplation is very appealing.
Human reason enjoys dabbling in miraculous signs and
supernatural matters that it cannot understand.

Don't let Satan trick you. Approach spiritual matters
in a different way. The true contemplative life is to listen to God's Word and believe it. Like Paul, decide to
"deal with only one subject—Jesus Christ, who was crucified" (1 Corinthians 2:2). Jesus, along with his Word,
is the only worthwhile object of contemplation. Don't
neglect him.

UNWAVERING FAITH

Then Israel said to Joseph, "Now I'm about to die,
but God will be with you. He will bring you
back to the land of your fathers."

GENESIS 48:21

❖

SRAEL'S WORDS GIVE US a beautiful example of true faith. When Israel died, he didn't have any doubts. Rather, because of his strong and unwavering faith, he stated, "God will be with you." His faith shows that even though he is dead, he still lives. He went to his grave trusting God and his promises. This kind of faith swallows up death. Mere knowledge of what God has done would never be enough to stand up against death and hell in times of trial. The devil himself possesses that kind of knowledge. But true faith, which believes God's Word and trusts that his promises will come true, gives glory to God and acknowledges that he is trustworthy. This kind of faith defies and conquers death, as Paul says, "Death, where is your victory? Death, where is your sting?" (1 Corinthians 15:55). Even though death swallows us up, we will return again to light and life.

When I'm talking about faith, I'm not talking about merely acknowledging that something is true. That kind of faith doesn't place any confidence in what God says. It merely states, "Christ's suffering and death are historical facts." Genuine faith, however, confesses, "I believe that Christ suffered and died *for me*. I have no doubts about this, and I rest in this faith. I can depend on God's Word to help me fight against sin and death."

We need to be reminded of Scripture passages such as these. They show us the examples of believers who, by their unwavering faith, showed us the way. We should learn to follow and imitate their faith so that we, too, may proclaim, "I am baptized and saved. I will die in this faith. Any further troubles I have won't make me abandon my faith."

TWISTING SCRIPTURE

I will ask the Father, and he will give you another
helper who will be with you forever.

❖

HEN OTHERWISE INTELLIGENT people hear these words of Christ, they cleverly reply, "Those aren't God's words, but those of a mere human. If he were God, he would say, 'I myself will send you the helper.' " These people want to instruct the Holy Spirit and make fine distinctions with grammar and logic. They insist that anyone who has to ask for something can't be God. Therefore, Christ cannot be God. They argue persuasively and even assert that the Holy Spirit doesn't know how to speak correctly. In their eyes, whatever the Holy Spirit says or does is wrong. They find fault with everything. They aren't godly enough to take the time to compare these verses with others. Instead, they take a verse here and a verse there. They pounce on a couple of words and distort them in order to obscure what the Bible means. If it were valid to tear one or two words from the text and forget about the rest, then I could also twist Scripture any way that I wanted.

But this is the correct way to approach Scripture: Look at the entire passage; look at what comes before and after the verse. In this case, you will find that Christ speaks both as God and as man. This is powerful proof that Jesus is both true man and true God, as our teaching and faith hold. How can we explain that Jesus speaks as God and as man at the same time? He can speak either way because he possesses both divine and human natures. If Jesus spoke everywhere as God, no one could prove that he was a true man. If he spoke as a man all the time, no one would know that he is also true God.

COURAGE TO FACE DEATH

[Sarah] died in . . . Canaan. Abraham went to mourn
for Sarah and to cry about her death. . . . After this,
Abraham buried his wife Sarah in the cave.

GENESIS 23:2,19

❖

THE STORIES OF PEOPLE in the Bible should instruct and inspire us. These examples are better than using the Lord Christ as an example for reaching and comforting people who have weak faith. When such people hear the stories of Abraham, Isaac, Jacob, and Sarah and how they all died, devout and God-fearing people won't be so afraid of death.

It's not their own fragile condition that bothers people with weak faith as much as the gruesome appearance of dead bodies. They say to themselves, "If my body were like the body Christ had here on earth, and if it couldn't be destroyed by death and eaten by worms, then I would wait for my last day with greater courage." Because Christ came back to life in only three days, his death doesn't seem like a good example of dying to people who are weak in faith. So it's reasonable that they are drawn to the examples of other people in the Bible whose bodies decayed, just as ours will.

In contrast, those who have stronger faith laugh at death. They fearlessly defy it: "What is death? What is hell? Christ, the Son of God, placed himself under God's laws and died. But Christ's death defeated death and gave us life." We need the strength to believe and not doubt that Christ died for our sins and was brought back to life. If we believe that Christ did this so that we could have God's approval, then we don't have to fear death. Christ's death assures us that our own death means nothing. But other examples are helpful for those who are weak in faith. For them, knowing that Sarah died and was buried helps them accept the fact that the same will one day happen to them.

TREASURES IN HEAVEN

Stop storing up treasures for yourselves on earth, where
moths and rust destroy and thieves break in and steal.
Instead, store up treasures for yourselves in heaven.

MATTHEW 6:19–20

❖

HEN CHRIST SAYS, "Store up treasures for yourselves in heaven," he is saying, "Let the
world have the earthly treasures, which dete-
riorate, rust, and are easily stolen. The pleasures these
things provide is the only happiness the world knows.
You, however, aren't citizens of this world. You are citizens of heaven bought by my blood. You are destined
to receive eternal treasures, which have been prepared
and reserved for you. Don't let your heart get caught up
in material possessions. If you must work with earthly
treasures in your job, then guard against their appeal
and don't become a slave to them. Instead, set your
sights on the treasures that are waiting for you in
heaven. Those are real treasures that moths and rust
can't touch. They can't be destroyed or stolen."

Whoever wants to be a Christian should be inspired
by the possibility of receiving eternal treasures.
Undoubtedly, a greedy miser would be overjoyed to
receive riches that can't be destroyed by rust or carried
off by thieves. Yet, the people of this world don't pay
any attention to heavenly treasures because they can't
see or touch them. By nature, people are enthralled
with love for gold and silver, even though they know
from experience that these aren't safe from corrosion
and thieves for even an hour. Preaching to these people
is useless. If someone refuses to believe what Christ
said, preferring instead to rely on his uncertain riches,
then let him go. We won't bring anyone to his senses by
dragging him by the hair. Just wait until it's time for
him to leave this world. Let him try to find comfort
from the earthly treasures he has piled up. Then, he will
realize how little these treasures can actually help him.

THE SIGNS OF FAITH

So if you call God your Father, live your time as temporary residents on earth in fear. He is the God who judges all people by what they have done, and he doesn't play favorites.

1 PETER 1:17

❖

E TEACH THAT GOD saves us only by faith, apart from our works. Why then does Peter say that God judges all people by what they have done? Here is why: What we have taught—how faith alone justifies us before God—is unquestionably true because it is so clear in Scripture that no one can deny it. What the apostle says here, that God judges according to works, is also true. We should always remember that where there is no faith, there can be no good works, and on the other hand, where there are no good works, there is no faith. Therefore, keep faith and good works connected. The entire Christian life is embodied by both. The way you live is important because God will judge you accordingly. Even though God judges us according to works, it's still true that works are only the fruits of faith. This is how we know whether or not we have faith. So God will judge you on the basis of whether you have believed or not believed. Likewise, the only way to judge a liar is by his words. Yet it's still obvious that he doesn't become a liar through his words but that he was already a liar before he ever told a lie. For the lie comes into the mouth from the heart.

Works are the fruits and signs of faith. God judges people according to these fruits. These fruits spring from faith in a way that publicly indicates whether or not someone has faith in his heart. God will not judge you by asking whether you are called a Christian or whether you have been baptized. He will ask you, "If you are a Christian, then tell me, where are the fruits that demonstrate your faith?"

A LIFELONG PURSUIT

We conclude that a person has God's
approval by faith, not by his own efforts.

ROMANS 3:28

❖

EOPLE DON'T EARN God's approval or receive
life and salvation because of anything
they've done. Rather, the only reason they
receive life and salvation is because of God's kindness
through Christ. There is no other way.

Many Christians are tired of hearing this teaching over
and over. They think that they learned it all long ago.
However, they barely understand how important it really
is. If it continues to be taught as truth, the Christian
church will remain united and pure—free from decay.
This truth alone makes and sustains Christianity. You
might hear an immature Christian brag about how well
he knows that we receive God's approval through God's
kindness and not because of anything we do to earn it.
But if he goes on to say that this is easy to put into practice, then have no doubt he doesn't know what he's talking about, and he probably never will. We can never
learn this truth completely or brag that we understand it
fully. Learning this truth is an art. We will always remain
students of it, and it will always be our teacher.

The people who truly understand that they receive
God's approval by faith and put this into practice don't
brag that they have fully mastered it. Rather, they think
of it as a pleasant taste or aroma that they are always
pursuing. These people are astonished that they can't
comprehend it as fully as they would like. They hunger
and thirst for it. They yearn for it more and more. They
never get tired of hearing about this truth. Similarly,
Paul admits in Philippians 3:12 that he has not yet
reached this goal. In Matthew 5:6, Christ says that those
who hunger and thirst for God's approval are blessed.

THE STRENGTH OF GOD'S WORD

Simon Peter answered Jesus, "Lord, to what person could we go? Your words give eternal life. Besides, we believe and know that you are the Holy One of God."

JOHN 6:68-69

❖

ES, PETER, YOU SPEAK THE TRUTH! This is written as a comfort and example to us. Though one of the twelve would fall, which in itself is an important lesson to us all, God upheld Peter. Everything rests on God's kindness, power, and word to such a degree that we can't even trust the apostles. Though one of them claimed he was so strong that he would never fall, he couldn't make it unless God blessed him and said, "I have chosen you." The reason the apostles were able to prevail was because Christ said, "I have chosen you." Though Judas would fall and remain fallen, Peter, in contrast, was held so tightly by God's Word that he wouldn't stay down. When he stumbled and fell, he stood up again.

You must realize that God allows people to stumble, so they will despair of trusting in themselves. God is the one who stamps out inborn arrogance. Moses, Aaron, David, and others fell, yet they found their way again. Scripture says that though people fall, God's Word will remain firm and never fall. Anyone who falls will be able to stand up again on the strength of God's Word.

Judas, the one who betrayed the Lord, was the first to defect. He was the one who brought harm to God's kingdom, even though he ranked above the other apostles as overseer of the finances. If I, or someone greater, should fall—may God protect me from that—it would certainly be scandalous. But we should stand firm and rest on the foundation of the Word. Jesus said, "I chose all twelve of you. Yet, one of you is a devil" (John 6:70). This example shows that we can't rely on people, but we must learn to depend on God's Word.

WHEN LIFE DOESN'T WORK OUT

Isaac sent Jacob to Paddan Aram.
Jacob went to live with Laban,
son of Bethuel the Aramean and brother of Rebekah.

GENESIS 28:5

 ACOB WAITED MANY YEARS for the promised blessing and after receiving it, he had to go into exile. He was forced to leave his dear parents, and they were separated from their beloved son for a long, long time. On the surface, one might think this wasn't so bad. But it's very difficult for anyone to leave father and mother, an inheritance, and comfortable surroundings, and run away in misery and poverty.

This is a wonderful example that shows us how God works. He requires us to trust his words and promises even when the opposite of the promise is happening to us. Jacob had the promised blessing, but he had to hold on to it by faith and not doubt what he couldn't see. Jacob had nothing but a stick in his hand and a piece of bread in his bag. He was poor, lonely, and outcast, but he believed God's promises. Jacob's example teaches us to live by faith. We should believe God when he promises to love and protect us, take care of us, and listen to us, even though we might not see it happening.

This story is written as an example for us. We must learn to depend on the visible Word of our invisible and incredible God. Because God doesn't lie or deceive us, we wait for him to fulfill his promise with confidence and patience. This is difficult for us because we are used to things we can touch, see, or feel. We have to learn to let go of what we can only experience with our senses and live according to what is invisible.

Keeping Law and Gospel Separate

Does this mean, then, that the laws given to Moses
contradict God's promises? That's unthinkable!

GALATIANS 3:21

❖

HOEVER KNOWS HOW TO TELL the difference between the law and the gospel should thank God and consider himself a true theologian. In times of temptation, I certainly don't know how to do this as I should. You can keep these two separate by placing the gospel in heaven and the law on earth. Call the righteousness of the gospel heavenly and divine, and call the righteousness of the law earthly and human. You should distinguish the righteousness of the gospel from the righteousness of the law as carefully as God has separated heaven from earth, light from darkness, and day from night. You should consider one as light and day, the other as darkness and night. If only you could separate them even further.

So when dealing with matters of faith and conscience, you should exclude the law and let it remain on earth. But when dealing with how we are to live in this world, you should light the lamp of the law. So the immeasurable light of the gospel will illuminate the day, and the lamp of the law will illuminate the night. If you have a conscience terrified by a sense of sin, you should think to yourself, "While I am on earth, I must work. Just as a donkey should work, serve, and carry the burdens given to it, so my body should obey the law. But when I ascend to heaven, I leave the donkey with its burden on earth. My conscience doesn't have anything to do with the law, works, or earthly righteousness." So the donkey remains in the valley, while the conscience climbs with Isaac up the mountain. It knows absolutely nothing of the law and its works. Instead, the conscience only keeps its eye on the forgiveness of sins and Christ's righteousness.

JOHN POINTS US TO CHRIST

John came to declare the truth about the light so that everyone would become believers through his message.

JOHN 1:7

❖

OHN, THE WRITER OF THIS BOOK, doesn't put much emphasis on John the Baptizer. All the writer says about him is that John the Baptizer spoke the truth, preaching to the people about Christ, the light and life of all humanity. The writer doesn't say that John the Baptizer taught the people all about his strict ascetic lifestyle—drinking only water, wearing clothing made of camel's hair, and living on wild honey and locusts. John the Baptizer didn't teach about these as a way to start a new sect. He didn't want people to follow his example as a way to be saved. If he had done that, John the Baptizer would have attracted a large group of followers and would have become the founder of a new sect with a new set of doctrines.

John the Baptizer didn't do anything like that! He came to speak the truth. He had the God-given responsibility of pointing people to Christ and telling them that Christ is the Lamb of God. His mission was to direct everyone, including his own disciples, away from himself and to the Lord Christ. He was saying, "I am not Christ. I am not the light. I can't enlighten you. I can't give you life. However, as his representative, I want you to believe in Christ and let him guide you. I must only preach about Christ. I don't want to talk about my camel-skin clothes or any other aspect of my ascetic lifestyle. My repulsive appearance is meant to force you to pay closer attention to my message than to me. Christ is the life and the light of humanity. He is eternal, and he created heaven and earth. But at this point in time, he has taken our human nature on himself. He is right here with you."

WAITING FOR MARRIAGE

*Isaac was 40 years old when he married Rebekah,
daughter of Bethuel the Aramean from Paddan
Aram and sister of Laban the Aramean.*

GENESIS 25:20

❖

SAAC WAS FORTY YEARS OLD before he got married. In those forty years, he undoubtedly experienced periods of frustration and fiery passion because of his physical desires. A person's physical desires are at war with his spiritual nature. Yet Isaac was obedient to his father Abraham, who taught him how to meditate on God's commands and promises in the battle against his corrupt nature. Later on, God gave Rebekah to Isaac as his wife, and they lived together in harmony.

There is a lesson buried in this passage: Isaac is a great example to young people of a person who abstains from sex before marriage. This is an important subject because all young people have to face this battle. Isaac's purity and moral integrity are clear indications of the way he was raised. His father taught him to avoid bad friends. Isaac meditated on God's promises, prayed, and did useful work. Though not specifically stated in the text, it's safe to assume that he diligently dedicated himself to meditation and prayer during the first forty years of his life when he wasn't yet married.

But some might say, "Waiting for marriage is unbearable and aggravating!" They're right. It's very similar to other difficulties requiring patience that believers must face, such as fasting, imprisonment, cold, sickness, and persecution. Lust is a serious burden. You must resist it and fight against it. But after you have overcome it through prayer, lust will have caused you to pray more and grow in faith.

BEWARE OF JUDGING OTHERS

Stop judging so that you will not be judged.
Otherwise, you will be judged by the same
standard you use to judge others.

MATTHEW 7:1–2

❖

ORGIVENESS OF SINS and tolerance for others are indispensable to the Christian life. We should bear with each other and forgive one another, as Paul taught: "Those of us who have a strong ⌊faith⌋ must be patient with the weaknesses of those whose ⌊faith⌋ is not so strong. We must not think only of ourselves" (Romans 15:1). This is what Christ meant when he said, "Stop judging." Some Christians have greater and better gifts than others. This is necessary, especially for preachers. No one should act superior to others or think of himself better than those who don't have such gifts. Among believers, no one should try to dominate anyone else. On the surface, there is a difference between people. A prince has a higher position than a farmer. A preacher has more education than an ordinary worker. But in their hearts, Christians should be of one mind despite their different positions in society. They should disregard external differences.

As a Christian, you should accept others by making allowances for your neighbor, even if your neighbor occupies a lower position in society and has fewer gifts than you do. You should respect the work of a servant tending horses as much as you respect your own work, whether it is governing or preaching. Your work may appear to have a greater impact than your neighbor's, but you must not judge by outward appearances. You should always remember that your Christian neighbor has the same faith and the same Christ as you do. Your neighbor receives as much of God's kindness as you do. There is one God who creates everyone and gives each person his own gifts. God is pleased by the least as well as the greatest.

Love Covers Many Sins

Above all, love each other warmly,
because love covers many sins.

1 PETER 4:8

❖

ERE, PETER BUILDS UPON a passage from the book of Proverbs: "Hate starts quarrels, but love covers every wrong" (Proverbs 10:12). And this is what Peter means: If you don't restrain your sinful nature and desires, you will easily become angry with others. You will be unable to forgive others easily. So make sure you curb your evil desires. Then you will be able to love and forgive others, for love covers sin.

Some interpret this verse as if it goes against faith. They may say, "You claim that faith alone makes a person godly and that no one can get rid of sin through his works. Then why do Solomon and Peter say that love covers sin?" You can answer them this way: "Solomon is saying whoever hates another person doesn't stop quarreling and bickering. But wherever love is, it covers sin by gladly forgiving it. Where there is anger, you will find a defiant person who won't reconcile and remains full of hatred. On the other hand, a person full of love doesn't become angry no matter how much someone tries to offend him. He covers all these sins and pretends not to see them. Though he can overlook his neighbor's sin, he cannot make God overlook it. No one can cover his own sin before God. Only faith can do that. But with our love, we can cover our neighbor's sin. And just as God covers our sins with his love if we believe, so we should also cover our neighbor's sin. Peter says that we should love one another so that one person can cover the sin of another. Love doesn't cover just one, two, or three sins, but a whole multitude of sins."

GIVING THANKS TO GOD

Praise the LORD, Jerusalem! Praise your God, Zion!

PSALM 147:12

❖

E SHOULD BE ASHAMED that we're so lazy we need to be prodded into praising God or awakened to do so, as if we were sleeping. We're showered with blessings every day, and we're always using what God gives us. Why do we need to be continually reminded of the wonderful things God does for us? We should be able to remember to thank him without reminders from the psalms. God's gifts alone should inspire us to praise God. But this doesn't happen. We have to be yelled at before we start praising the Lord. The words have to be written down for us and spoon-fed into our mouths, as this psalm does.

More shocking still is that the one who is giving us all these blessings has to be pointed out to us. Jerusalem must be admonished, "Do praise the Lord," and Zion told, "Go ahead and praise your God." We all use God's blessings every day, but we never think about where they come from—God. He is the one who gives us everything. Instead, we accept his gifts as if they simply appeared out of nowhere or as if we had earned them through our own efforts, diligence, or wisdom. We think that God somehow owes us these things, and therefore we don't need to thank him. Even animals don't live that shamefully. Pigs recognize the person who gives them their food. They'll run after her and cry to her. But the world doesn't even recognize God, let alone thank and praise him for these blessings. If God's people must be encouraged to praise him, how can the world be expected to do any better? It's astounding how unwilling people are to acknowledge what God has done for them and to praise him for it.

JUDGING BY APPEARANCES

Stop judging by outward appearance!
Instead, judge correctly.

JOHN 7:24

❖

ESUS WARNED THE PHARISEES that they shouldn't judge others by their foolish thinking or according to their own opinions. Looking through colored glass distorts the color of everything. In the same way, the distorted thinking of the spiritually blind doesn't allow them to perceive the truth accurately, even though they have the truth right before their eyes. Their hearts are bitter and they burn with hatred. Like colored glass, their hearts color the way they look at others. They see people as enemies, whom they resent and find repulsive.

In the world, no one sees anyone else through clear glass except for Christians because their eyes are bright and pure. A Christian sees his enemy with the eyes of mercy and compassion. He doesn't wish evil on that person. If his enemy is bitter and mean towards him, a believer thinks, "This big shot is miserable. He is already eternally condemned. Why would I want to wish more evil on him? If he keeps going this way, he will certainly belong to the devil." A Christian has compassion on his enemy and hopes for his salvation. Meanwhile, others only view their neighbors with hatred, envy, and pride. So it follows that they also view us as scoundrels. To the Pharisees, Jesus said, "Stop judging by outward appearance! Instead, judge correctly." In other words, he's saying, "Look at what I do and who I am through clear glass."

Our enemies will always criticize us. They will always look at us through colored glass. We must let it be. No matter what we do, they will still view us through colored glass.

LEAVING THE OUTCOME TO GOD

*Jacob saw Esau coming with 400 men.
So he divided the children among Leah,
Rachel, and the two slaves.*

GENESIS 33:1

❖

HIS STORY IS A GOOD EXAMPLE of doing what you can and leaving the outcome to God. Jacob doesn't hesitate to do what he is able to do in this situation. He divides the people who are with him into two groups, sends presents to his brother, and travels ahead to take care of every possible thing. Someone in despair would have said, "I'm not going to do anything. If I'm meant to be killed, I can't prevent it anyway."

People will draw the same conclusion regarding their salvation and say, "If I'm meant to be saved, I won't be lost no matter what I do." Beware of those wicked words! Certainly, it's true that what is meant to happen will happen. But you have to remember that you don't know what will happen. You don't even know if you will be dead or alive tomorrow. God doesn't want you to know. That's why it's foolish to search for something that God in his wisdom has intentionally hidden from you.

Similarly, it's foolish to blame everything on what God has predestined. God's plan includes his secret wisdom. We can't understand it. God doesn't want you to know the future. So stick with your calling, remain within the limits of God's Word, and use whatever resources and wisdom God has given you. For instance, I can't foresee what my preaching will produce—who will be converted and who won't. What if I were to say, "Those who are meant to be converted will be converted even without my efforts, and what's the use of trying to convert those who aren't meant to be saved?" Saying that would be foolish and irreverent. Who are we to ask such questions? Take care of your responsibilities and leave the outcome to God.

IMPOSSIBLE TO BELIEVE

*No one has gone to heaven except the Son of Man,
who came from heaven.*

JOHN 3:13

❖

 NLY CHRIST WOULD BE ABLE to testify to a truth this remarkable. How can human reason make sense of this strange teaching, or how can it understand how it all fits together? How can Jesus come down from heaven and at the same time live above? How can Jesus ascend back to heaven and yet continuously be in heaven? No one could have conceived of such a thought, whether in his heart or in his mind. Human reason says it's impossible for someone to *descend from* heaven and *be in* heaven at the same time. That is why Christians are considered foolish. We believe something directly contrary to reason.

Whoever has a difficult time believing that Christ can come from heaven and yet be in heaven shouldn't worry about it. It doesn't matter if we can't grasp this truth right away. If we are considered fools because of believing this, our foolishness won't hurt us. For Christians are certainly not foolish. We know perfectly well what we believe. We know where we can find counsel and help in all situations. We know we will live eternally after we have been delivered from this world.

But if some people refuse to believe this truth, then they should leave it alone. Instead, they want to figure it out. These people want to resolve the paradox in their own crazy head—first this way, then that way. All of them think they will find God by figuring it out, but they won't.

However, you must hold tightly to the testimony that was brought down from heaven by Jesus, God's Son. You must believe it, for all Christians dare to believe what Jesus says.

CHRIST IS OUR RANSOM

I no longer live, but Christ lives in me.
The life I now live I live by believing in God's Son,
who loved me and took the punishment for my sins.

GALATIANS 2:20

❖

THE PHRASES, "GOD'S SON," "loved me," and "took the punishment for my sins," are lightning and thunder from heaven against the idea that we are saved by good works. Our will and understanding contained such great wickedness, error, darkness, and ignorance that we could only be freed by an exceedingly high-priced ransom. Why do we think that our human reason is naturally inclined to the best and can correctly lead us? Why do we think each person should do as much as he can? Why do we bring our terrible sins, which are mere straw, to an angry God, who Moses calls "a raging fire"? Why do we want to haggle with God, trying to exchange our stubble for grace and eternal life? Listen to this passage. It says there's so much evil in our nature that the world and all creation can't reconcile us to God. God's Son had to be offered for our sins.

But consider the price of this ransom carefully. Look at Christ, who was captured and offered for you. He is infinitely greater than and superior to anything else in creation. How will you respond when you hear that such a priceless ransom was offered for you? Do you still want to bring God your own good works? What is that compared to Christ's work? He shed his most precious blood for your sins.

THE WORD IS GOD'S SON

The Word became human and lived among us.
We saw his glory. It was the glory that the Father shares
with his only Son, a glory full of kindness and truth.

JOHN 1:14

❖

HIS IS THE FIRST TIME that John called the Word the only Son of the Father. You might have wondered who the Word was when John said, "In the beginning the Word already existed" (John 1:1), "Everything came into existence through him" (John 1:3), and "He was the source of life, and that life was the light of humanity" (John 1:4). In this passage you can see that the Word, who existed with the Father from eternity and is the light for humanity, is God's only Son. The Word alone is the Son, and no one else. Now we know what John meant when he used the term *Word* earlier. From this point on, John will speak plainly about Christ's kingdom. Up to this point, he spoke with strange and unusual words. They weren't clear in any language. But now he says, "The Word is God's only Son."

God also has many other children. However, he has only one Son through whom he created everything. The other children are not the Word, through whom everything was created. Rather, these children were created through this only Son, who is coequal Creator of heaven and earth with the Father. All the others became children through the Son. The Word alone is, as Paul states, the only "Son of God" (Romans 1:4). Through him, God makes and rules all things.

We must hold this passage from the book of John in the highest honor. We should comfort ourselves with it in times of sorrow and temptation. We should hold on to it in faith because it reminds us that we are children of God.

YOUR WILL BE DONE

Father, if it is your will, take this cup ⌊of suffering⌋ away
from me. However, your will must be done, not mine.

LUKE 22:42

❖

 OME PEOPLE HAVE an evil will. It's easy to spot
because it doesn't tolerate any opposition.
Other people have another type of will that
appears to be good but is actually evil. It can be recognized by its fruit—impatience. A truly good will, if it's
hindered, says, "O God, I thought what I wanted would
be good. If it's not to be, I'm satisfied. Let your will be
done." Wherever there's conflict and impatience, there's
nothing good—no matter how good it may seem.

Besides these two types of evil wills, there's also a
good will that God doesn't want us to do. This was the
kind of will that David had when he wanted to build a
temple for God. God praised him for it, and yet God
didn't let it happen (2 Samuel 7:2–29). This was the
kind of will that Christ had in the garden of
Gethsemane. Even though it was good, his will had to be
set aside (Luke 22:42). So if you would like to save the
whole world, raise the dead, lead yourself and everyone
else to heaven, and perform miracles, you should first
seek God's will and submit your own will to his will. You
must pray, "Dear God, this or that seems good to me. If
it pleases you, let it be done. If it doesn't please you, let
it remain undone."

God often breaks a good will in order that a false,
evil will won't sneak in by appearing good. He does this
so we learn that as good as our will might be, it's still
immeasurably inferior to his will. So our inferior good
will must yield to the infinitely good will of God.

WILLING TO LET GO

The LORD has given, and the LORD has taken away!
May the name of the Lord be praised.

JOB 1:21

❖

SN'T IT TRUE THAT YOUR MONEY, property, body, spouse, children, and friends are good things created and given to you by God himself? Ultimately, they all belong to God and not to you. What if he were to test your loyalty by taking them away from you? What if he wanted to learn whether you were willing to let go of them for his sake? What if he wanted to see whether you would hold tighter to him or to his gifts? What if you became separated from your loved ones? Do you think you would have the right to rant and rave, forcibly attempt to get them back, or sulk until they were returned to you? But if you argue that these are God's good gifts to you and that you want to get them back no matter what the cost, then you would be making a big mistake.

If you want to do the right thing, don't rush ahead without thinking. You must fear God and say, "Dear Lord, the people and things you have given me are good, as you have said in Scripture. Yet, I don't know whether you will let me keep them. If I knew that you didn't want me have them, I wouldn't even try to get them back. However, if I knew that you wanted me to have them, I would do what you want by taking them back. But I don't know what you want me to do. All I can see now is that you have allowed them to be taken away from me. So I'll turn the whole matter over to you. I'll wait until I know what to do. I'm ready to live either with them or without them."

Loving the World

Don't love the world and what it offers.
Those who love the world don't have
the Father's love in them.

1 JOHN 2:15

❖

 EING IN THE WORLD, seeing the world, and experiencing the world are all different from loving the world, just as having sin and feeling sin are both different from loving sin. Abraham certainly had property, but he didn't love it. He recognized that God made him a steward over these possessions, and he managed them accordingly. David was a mighty king but didn't demand his own way. Rather, he governed according to God's will. For he said of himself, "I am a foreign resident with you, a stranger like all my ancestors" (Psalm 39:12). In other words, he considered himself to be a traveler, merely a guest on this earth. David didn't rule his kingdom according to his own will, but according to God's will and for God's honor. So he didn't love the world. But when someone oppresses and troubles the poor and uses other people's possessions as his own, then you see someone loving the world. This is unjust. Christ doesn't take us out of the world. Rather, he leaves us in the world after baptism so that others will be strengthened and encouraged by our example. So anyone who flees the world lives in a godless way.

Christ says that the Holy Spirit "will come to convict the world of sin" (John 16:8). The world is filled with people who have turned away from God and know nothing about God. They have turned instead to what God has created and have used his creation for their own honor.

KEEP YOUR EYES OPEN

A wise person uses the eyes in his head,
but a fool walks in the dark.

ECCLESIASTES 2:14

❖

'VE NOTICED THAT the same kinds of things happen to both wise and foolish people. Both end up making mistakes. Nevertheless, wisdom is better than foolishness. You may be familiar with the expression: "If you want to play chess, don't hide your eyes in your pocket." That means that not only do you have to know the game well, but you also have to be an observant and careful player. The author of Ecclesiastes says here, "A wise person uses the eyes in his head." In other words, wise people aren't merely clever managers, but they're also alert, conscientious, and watchful. They see how things ought to be done although they can never assure the outcome. Foolish people, on the other hand, don't use the eyes in their heads because they let themselves be swept up by boldness and audacity. In the end, the affairs of both appear to be determined by coincidence and luck. In reality, God directs everything. Neither wisdom nor boldness determines how things will turn out.

Both wise and foolish plans sometimes fail and sometimes succeed. But God doesn't want us to base our rules for living on whether or not something is successful. That's because what God has created is in his hands, not ours. He allows us to use these things, but he accomplishes what he wants through us. It's pointless to add anything to what God wants or to try to determine how God should do things. In this way, God teaches us not to rely on our own wisdom and insight, but to deal with matters as they come along. If they don't turn out well, then we should simply commit them to God.

GENUINE FORGIVENESS

When they persisted in asking him questions,
he straightened up and said, "The person who is sinless
should be the first to throw a stone at her."

JOHN 8:7

❖

HE POOR WOMAN CAUGHT in adultery was in dire need. Her predicament was no joke to her. She had been brought before the judge and sentenced according to what the law stated: "Stone her to death." This was not music to her ears. Her heart froze in fear. Her only hope was in the man who was writing on the ground. But she was surprised when he said, "The person who is sinless should be the first to throw a stone at her."

Sinners, like this woman, are the ones who belong in Christ's kingdom. Christ doesn't want sinners who refuse to admit that they're sinners. They think that because they haven't sinned notoriously, they don't need the help of God. I used to act like this when I was a monk. I would say, "Today I did nothing evil. I was obedient to my superior. I fasted and prayed. Therefore, may God be merciful to me." I thought that God should forgive me for the sins that I didn't really consider sinful. In fact, these sins weren't real sins at all. Yes, I was inventing them.

Sins that we invent ourselves are stupid sins. God's compassion isn't concerned with made-up sins. They must be real sins—such as not fearing, trusting, or believing God, not loving your neighbor, not praying, not listening to sermons, not doing what the law of Moses commands. In other words, real sins break God's law, which no one can ignore. These are the sins that require genuine forgiveness, not meaningless forgiveness. Let's go back to the woman caught in adultery. She was not caught merely in imaginary sins, but in adultery. So we must guard against real sins. But it's also to real sinners that the gospel reaches out.

THE BENEFITS OF SUFFERING

Joseph prepared his chariot and went to meet his father Israel. As soon as he saw his father, he threw his arms around him and cried on his shoulder a long time.

GENESIS 46:29

❖

ISRAEL, OR JACOB, didn't despair even though he faced many troubles. He appeared to be rejected, but God didn't abandon him. He remained God's child, and God remained in him in a hidden and wonderful way. Much later, when the events had played themselves out, Jacob saw that his son Joseph was still alive and had become an important leader in Egypt. Then Jacob was happy to have gone through so much suffering. He thought, "I wouldn't have experienced this much happiness if my family had been taken care of the way that I had planned. Joseph would've been just a shepherd like the rest of my sons. But now he has been elevated to a position of royalty, and he will save many people."

So when we are being disciplined and feel sad, we shouldn't fight against our troubles, but rather remind ourselves, "I will not die, but I will live" (Psalm 118:17). Even when the opposite seems to be true, we should be able to say, "Whenever I feel helpless, I can put my trust in God, who is able to make everything out of nothing. When I am totally devastated, no one can lift me up again the way he can."

The more severe the suffering, the greater the wonderful benefits to God's holy people. Being tested through suffering is a sure sign of God's kindness and mercy to his faithful people. When they faithfully cling to God's promises, unbelievable blessings result. James says, "Blessed are those who endure when they are tested. When they pass the test, they will receive the crown of life that God has promised to those who love him" (James 1:12).

THE FRUIT OF FAITH

Laws have nothing to do with faith,
but, "Whoever obeys laws will live
because of the laws he obeys."

GALATIANS 3:12

OU CAN'T SHOW ME one person in the whole world, outside the promise of the gospel, that you could rightfully call "a doer of the law." Therefore, the expression "doer of the law" is an imaginary term that no one understands unless he is a true believer—one who is above the law and in the blessing and faith of Abraham. A true doer of the law is a person who has received the Holy Spirit through faith in Christ and begins to love God and do good to his neighbor. The good that this person does includes faith at the same time. In other words, faith brings about a tree, and then the fruit, which is good works, grows. First, the tree must be there, then the fruit will follow. The fruit doesn't produce the tree, but the tree produces the fruit.

Similarly, faith first transforms the person into someone who then can do good works. So if someone wants to fulfill the law without faith, it's like producing fruit without a tree or making fruit out of wood and clay. The result isn't real fruit but simply an illusion. After the tree is planted—after faith in Christ creates a new person—then the works will follow. The doer must come before the work, not the work before the doer.

KNOWING GOD

*What can be known about God is clear to them
because he has made it clear to them.*

ROMANS 1:19

❖

E ARE SO HORRIBLY CORRUPTED by sin that, on our own, we are no longer aware of God. We have strayed from the righteousness of the law and have fallen into a pit of lies. We think we can reconcile ourselves to God through the works we invent. Using our human reason, we can recognize God in the laws of Moses, as Romans 1:19 teaches. But the gospel message shows that we can't truly know God through our human reason. The gospel is a new revelation that came from heaven. It not only teaches us about the Ten Commandments, but also tells us that all of us were conceived in sin and are hopelessly lost. No one fully obeys the laws of Moses. We will only be saved by the kindness and truth of Jesus Christ. This is the depth of his nature and the will of God.

Whether they're tempted to cling to the laws of Moses or to their own righteousness, all people must acknowledge that no one can be saved or even know God apart from Christ. No one finds God's approval unless that person is first covered by the kindness and truth of the Son. This truth is hidden from our human reason; therefore, many people don't know anything about it.

We must find protection in Christ by crawling to him in humility, attaining everything through his kindness and truth. This is what God intends and wants. This is what it means to know God in the right way. So we can't see God through the laws of Moses or through our human reason. No one can imagine what he is like. No one can climb to his heights. He is too exalted for us. Only those born of God will see God.

THE PURPOSE OF WORSHIP

Then God blessed the seventh day and set it apart as holy,
because on that day he stopped all his work of creation.

GENESIS 2:3

❖

UMAN BEINGS WERE CREATED primarily to know
God and to worship him. The day of worship was not established for sheep and cows,
but for people so that they might learn to know God.
Even after the human race lost its knowledge of God
because of sin, God intended that the command to set
apart the day of worship as holy would stay in effect.
Furthermore, God wanted people to use the seventh
day for study of his Word and for participating in the
kind of worship he had established. He did this so that
first and foremost, we would realize our fundamental
calling and purpose in life is acknowledging and
praising God.

In addition, this day was established to assure us of
eternal life in the future. Everything that God commands us to observe on the day of worship gives us
clear indications of another life to follow. Why would
God bother to talk to us through his Word if we were
not going to receive eternal life in the future? If there
were no hope of any future life, why wouldn't we live
our lives as if God had nothing to say to us? Wouldn't
we rather pretend that we didn't know him? Because
the Lord of all speaks only to humans, and they are the
only ones who can know him and know about him, it
follows that there must be a life beyond this one. In
order to reach the next life, we need to know God and
his Word in this life.

PATIENCE IN SUFFERING

*I am happy to suffer for you now. In my body I am
completing whatever remains of Christ's sufferings.
I am doing this on behalf of his body, the church.*

COLOSSIANS 1:24

❖

LL CHRISTIANS SHOULD know they won't be
spared from suffering. But it should be the
kind of suffering and cross that is worthy of
its name. It should really hurt and weigh us down, such
as a serious threat to our possessions, body, or life. We
should really feel it, for it wouldn't be suffering if it
didn't hurt. Moreover, we shouldn't choose our own
suffering, as some people do. It should be the kind of
suffering the devil or the world sends our way. We
would want to be spared of it if at all possible. Then we
need to hold on tight and reconcile ourselves to this
suffering. As I have said before, we have to suffer so that
we will become more and more like Christ. It cannot
and may not be any different. Everyone will face his
cross and suffering.

If you know this, then the suffering is easier and more
bearable for you. You can comfort yourself by saying,
"Well now, if I want to be a Christian, I must wear the
colors of the team. Our dear Christ doesn't give out any
other clothing for his side. I must endure this suffering."

People who insist on choosing their own cross cannot do this. They become upset and fight against it.
What commendable behavior that is! Yet they criticize
the way we teach about suffering as if they were the
only ones who could teach how to handle it.
Nevertheless, we still teach that no one should choose
his own suffering and take up his own cross. But when
the cross comes, patiently endure it and carry it.

FINDING THE MIDDLE WAY

*It's good to hold on to the one and not let go
of the other, because the one who fears God
will be able to avoid both extremes.*

ECCLESIASTES 7:18

❖

EADING ECCLESIASTES TENDS to have the same
effect on foolish people that preaching the
gospel has on unbelieving people. When
unbelievers hear about freedom in Christ and about
God's approval coming from faith instead of what they
do, they conclude that they don't need to perform any
good works. They think they can go on sinning because
faith is enough. On the other hand, when we preach
that good works are the fruit of faith, they think this is
how they are saved. Then, they try to earn their salvation by doing these works. So hearing God's Word often
leads to either arrogance or despair. It's very difficult to
avoid either extreme and find the middle way.

The same thing happens when foolish people hear
the teaching of Ecclesiastes on having a calm and quiet
heart and leaving everything in God's hands. They infer
from all of this that they don't have to do any work if
everything is in God's hands. Others, who are just as
foolish, do the opposite. They are much too worried
and always try to control everything in every way.

However, we must find the middle way. We should
work diligently, doing whatever we can that doesn't go
against God's Word. But we shouldn't evaluate our work
on the basis of our own efforts. Rather, we should commit all of our accomplishments, solutions, and successes
to God. The author speaks both to those who are lazy in
their work and to those who are too worried about it. He
tells them to submit themselves fully to God's Word, as
well as to work diligently. So the author of Ecclesiastes
provides a good warning to those who aren't sticking to
the middle way.

TRUE DISCIPLES

So Jesus said to those Jews who believed in him,
"If you live by what I say, you are truly my disciples."

JOHN 8:31

❖

HRIST PREACHES ABOUT true and false followers
of God's Word. He is saying, "Many hear the
gospel and stick with it because it's useful to
them. They gain money, possessions, and honor from
it. Yes, dear friends, who wouldn't want that? This is
why I teach that if you live by what I say, you are truly
my disciples. For I have two kinds of disciples. The first
kind believes in me. They praise and listen to the gospel
and say, 'This is the real truth.' I consider these people
excellent disciples. They continue to believe. Then,
there are others who hear the gospel. But when the battle heats up, they say, 'Oh my, I don't know whether I
should give up this or that thing for the sake of the
gospel.' There are only a few who hold tightly to the
gospel when there's a cross to carry. Where can I find
those who will stand firm? Therefore, I say, 'If you live
by what I say, you are truly my disciples.' "

People would gladly believe in Christ if it meant
becoming rich and acquiring a kingdom. But if it
involves suffering, then their faith is finished. So Christ
knows many of them won't keep on following his
teaching. Remaining true to his teaching is rare, especially when evil winds begin to blow. Many become
Christians and hold to the gospel in the beginning.
Afterwards, they fall away just as the believers in this
passage did. It's similar to the parable about the seed
that fell on the rock. When the heat of the sun beat
down on it, it wilted and dried up (Luke 8:6). But those
who stick with the gospel are true disciples of Christ.

How the World Rewards Service

When Potiphar heard his wife's story . . . he became very angry. So Joseph's master arrested him and put him in the same prison where the king's prisoners were kept.

GENESIS 39:19-20

❖

LOSING HIS GOOD REPUTATION and being thrown in prison was certainly Joseph's worst hardship. What disgraceful wages he received for his years of faithful service! All of his impeccable character and hard work were rewarded with punishment and a ruined reputation. We serve, teach, counsel, comfort, and do what God tells us to do. For the most part, we do this for undeserving people from whom we get nothing in return except hatred, envy, and suffering. It seems that our lives are wasted on being kind to people who don't appreciate it.

Don't ever expect the world to acknowledge or reward your faithfulness and hard work. The opposite often happens, as Joseph's life shows. Therefore, make sure that you direct your service and life elsewhere. Don't look for favor and kindness from the world. Its favor can quickly turn into furious anger.

If you are called as a pastor or teacher, or if you are in some other position, set this goal for yourself: I will do my job faithfully without expecting any reward from the people I serve. I won't assume that they will be grateful to me. Rather, I will bless others the same way my heavenly Father hands out his blessings. He gives money, talents, peace, and health to even the most ungrateful and evil people. I will remember Christ's command, "You must be perfect as your Father in heaven is perfect" (Matthew 5:48). This means that we must serve people who are wicked, undeserving, and ungrateful. A few will acknowledge our service and thank us. But the others might even threaten our lives. Joseph's example shows us what reward we can expect from the world for even the greatest of kindness—being tied up and thrown in prison.

WE ARE GOD'S CHILDREN

You are all God's children
by believing in Christ Jesus.

GALATIANS 3:26

❖

AUL, AS AN EXTREMELY GOOD teacher of the
faith, always has these words on his lips: "by
faith," "in faith," "by believing in Christ
Jesus." He doesn't say here, "You are God's children
because you are circumcised, have listened to the law,
and obeyed it." This is what the Jews imagined and the
false apostles taught. Instead he says, "by believing in
Christ Jesus."

The law, much less human laws, doesn't make us
children of God. It can't create a new creature or produce a new birth. But it places before our eyes the old
birth by which we are born into the kingdom of the
devil. By doing so, the law prepares us for the new
birth, which takes place through faith in Jesus Christ,
not through the law. Paul testifies to this in the clearest
way, "You are all God's children by believing." It's as if
he were saying, "Although you are tormented, humiliated, and killed by the law, it still has not made you
righteous. But faith has made you righteous. Which
faith? Faith in Christ." It's faith in Christ, not the law,
that creates children of God. The book of John testifies
to this, "However, he gave the right to become God's
children to everyone who believed in him" (John 1:12).

True and False Christians

Jesus saw Nathanael coming toward him and remarked,
"Here is a true Israelite who is sincere."

JOHN 1:47

❖

HE LORD CHRIST DOES NOT want us to brag about being a Christian or, as in the case of Nathanael, being an Israelite. It's not enough to say, "I am baptized" or even to say, "I am a bishop," "I am a cardinal," or "I am a preacher." You must believe in Christ and live like a Christian. You must be righteous both on the inside and on the outside. You must not be embarrassed of the Lord Christ and the Christian faith. If you are, then you are a false Christian. If you don't believe in your heart, your entire life is a lie and you remain in darkness. You aren't righteous, and you only appear to be Christian. Your actions don't reflect your Christian faith.

If we could separate Christians from one another and divide them into true and false Christians, how many true Christians would we find? The world is crazy, foolish, and wild. It's filled with all kinds of evil—adultery, drunkenness, vindictiveness, and other sins. It's no longer considered a sin for people to cheat each other. Yet these same people want to be considered good Christians.

Believe me, you're not fooling anyone but yourself. God isn't fooled or mocked. He will know what you are really like in an instant, just as he knew that Nathanael was a true Israelite who believed in the prophets. He will look at you and say, "Yes, here is a true Christian!"

THE PATTERN OF TEMPTATION

The woman saw that the tree had fruit that was good to eat,
nice to look at, and desirable for making someone wise.
So she took some of the fruit and ate it.

GENESIS 3:6

❖

LL OF SATAN'S TEMPTATIONS follow the same pattern. First, Satan tests the faith of people and lures them away from God's Word. This leads them to commit sins against others. We can see from our own experience that Satan always works this way.

When an idea first strikes us, we don't think that we're about to do something wrong. If we did, we might have second thoughts and consider the potential results. We would think about the harm and misery we would cause. We might even change the way we were thinking and acting. But such thoughts are usually kept hidden. So we go right ahead with our sinful action and abandon our faith.

Eve picked the fruit from the tree. She was convinced that she would not die, even though God said that she would. She believed what Satan had told her. She thought that her eyes would be opened and that she would gain wisdom. After the devil's poisonous words entered her ears, she reached out with her hand, took hold of the forbidden fruit, and tasted it with her mouth. Therefore, she sinned with every part of her body and soul. Still, she was not yet aware of the terrible sin she had committed. She cheerfully ate the fruit and brought some to her husband who also ate it.

Lust, anger, and greed all work the same way. While sin is working, we don't feel it. Sin doesn't scare us. It doesn't sting. Instead, it seems friendly, kind, and cheerful. We often don't feel guilt as we're sinning. But later, when God's law exposes sin, the consequences crush us.

The Word Was with God

In the beginning the Word already existed.
The Word was with God, and the Word was God.
He was already with God in the beginning.

JOHN 1:1–2

❖

OTICE THAT JOHN STRONGLY emphasizes the word *with*. He repeats the word again so that he may clearly express the difference between the separate persons of God. He does this to counteract natural reason and future heretics. Natural reason clearly understands that there is only one God. Many verses in Scripture support this, and of course it's true. But reason struggles against the idea that three persons can be the same God.

This is why the heretic Sabellius claimed that the Father, Son, and Holy Spirit are all one person. Then another heretic Arius admitted that the Word was with God but didn't confess that the Word was true God. Sabellius teaches too great a simplicity in God. Arius teaches too great a multiplicity. Sabellius mixes the persons together, while Arius divides the nature of God into three parts.

But the truth of the Christian faith stays in the middle, teaching and confessing the individuality of the persons and the indivisibility of God's nature. The Father is a different person from the Son, but he is not a different god. Whether or not our natural reason comprehends it, it's still correct. Faith alone must grasp it. Natural reason leads to heresy and error. Faith teaches and holds to the truth. Faith simply clings to the Scripture, which never deceives us or lies to us.

Hardships before Honor

*Joseph named his firstborn son Manasseh . . . because
God helped him forget all his troubles. . . . He named the
second son Ephraim . . . because God gave him children.*

GENESIS 41:51–52

❖

OSEPH BECAME AN IMPORTANT ruler in Egypt,
and Jacob eventually saw his descendants
become a large nation. But both men had to
go through hardships first. Joseph learned this lesson
firsthand. When naming his sons, he thought, "I was
the firstborn son and an heir of a noble mother. But I
lost everything, and I had no hope of inheriting anything. One must totally forget any material gain he
might find in this world." So Joseph named his son
Manasseh in God's honor because God brought him to
his knees and to the point where he forgot all about his
father's family. Joseph named his other son Ephraim
because God had lifted him up again and had given
him children. Later, Ephraim received a wonderful
blessing from his grandfather, Jacob. Ephraim's descendants would become the powerful tribe we read about
in Joshua, Judges, 1 Kings, and 2 Kings.

We learn from this passage that we are brought
down before we are raised up. We must become like
Joseph. We must be reduced to nothing. Our human
natures find this idea very painful and hard to take. All
of creation hates destruction and decay. You can't cut
down a tree or a bush without hearing a loud crash.
Even Christ himself was brought low. He cried out from
the cross, "My God, my God, why have you abandoned
me?" (Matthew 27:46). That's why we should have the
same modest attitude as Joseph. Even after receiving
honor, he didn't become proud, but remained humble.

SERVING EACH OTHER

You were indeed called to be free, brothers and sisters. Don't turn this freedom into an excuse for your corrupt nature to express itself. Rather, serve each other through love.

GALATIANS 5:13

❖

IF GRACE OR FAITH IS NOT PREACHED, then no one will be saved, for faith alone justifies and saves. On the other hand, if faith is preached as it should be preached, then the majority of people understand this teaching about faith in a worldly way. They turn the freedom of the Spirit into the freedom of the corrupt nature. One can see this today in all classes, whether higher or lower. All boast that they are evangelical and praise Christian freedom. Meanwhile, they follow their own desires, turning to greed, lust, pride, envy, and so on. No one faithfully carries out his duty. No one serves others in love. This shameful behavior makes me so impatient that I often wish that such pigs who trample the pearls with their feet were still under the tyranny of Rome. It's practically impossible for these people of Gomorrah to be ruled by the gospel of peace.

We know that the devil hounds those of us who have God's Word. For he holds everyone else captive and is eager to take away this freedom of the Spirit or at least to turn it into unrestrained living. Christ acquired this freedom of the Spirit for us through his death. Therefore, we follow Paul's example, by teaching and encouraging people that this freedom of the Spirit gives them an opportunity to serve, not an opportunity to act on their evil desires. As Peter says, "Don't hide behind your freedom when you do evil. Instead, use your freedom to serve God" (1 Peter 2:16).

WHEN WE DON'T UNDERSTAND

*Nicodemus asked him, "How can anyone be born
when he's an old man? He can't go back inside
his mother a second time to be born, can he?"*

JOHN 3:4

❖

HRIST ISN'T TALKING ABOUT physical birth in this
passage, but rather about spiritual birth,
which is accomplished through water and the
Spirit. If Nicodemus didn't understand what Christ was
saying up to this point, how much less will he understand this spiritual rebirth? Our opponents think it's
ridiculous to teach that a person must be born anew by
water and the Spirit—nothing else. They don't understand or believe this teaching. That is why they shout,
"You must do good works!" In this way, they discredit
what's most important: If a person isn't reborn by water
and the Spirit, then all is lost. Don't think that anyone
will enter the kingdom of God unless he first is born
anew by water and the Spirit. These are plain but powerful words: "You must be born from above" (John 3:7).
We have to pass from the birth of sin to the birth of righteousness. Otherwise, we will never go to heaven. After
this new birth, good works will naturally follow.

Christ tells Nicodemus much about this new birth.
But Nicodemus can't understand it. You won't be able
to understand it either, unless you have been born
anew and have experienced spiritual rebirth. Let these
words stay as they are. Don't try to reinterpret them,
even though they might seem foolish and strange to
human reason. Understand the simple meaning of
these words, the way they are usually read.

You shouldn't dare to reinterpret the Word of God
your own way. It's better to think, "I don't understand
these words. But before I change them, take something
away from them, or add to them, I would rather leave
them alone. I'll give them to God." The Scriptures
should always be handled with reverence and respect.

ETERNAL LIFE IS CERTAIN

Enoch walked with God;
then he was gone because God took him.

GENESIS 5:24

❖

THE FIRST PEOPLE OF THE EARTH eagerly anticipated eternal life because they knew that
Abel and Enoch were living with God. We
have an even greater anticipation because we know that
Christ has already come and has gone back to the
Father to prepare a place for us. Our human nature
spends all of its energy pursuing the fleeting things of
this world but doesn't look forward to the joys of eternal life. Nothing could be more certain than eternal life.
We have so much evidence! We know that Abel, Enoch,
and Elijah are living with God—even with Christ himself. Christ is the first of those who have died to come
back to life (1 Corinthians 15:20, 23).

People who are devoted to seeking worldly pleasures
are worthy of contempt. Similarly, our own human
nature, which makes us look for pleasure, is worthy of
contempt. Because we are so wrapped up in the concerns
of this world, we care little for the riches of eternal life.

We should pay attention to this passage and keep it
in our hearts. Enoch was not taken from this world by
one of his devout ancestors or an angel. He was taken
by God himself. This is the comfort that relieved the
pain of death for the Old Testament believers. They had
so little fear of death that they didn't even call it *death*.
Instead, they referred to it as mere sleep from which
they would awaken into eternal life. For believers, death
is not death but simply sleep. When death no longer
brings dread and fear—when it no longer has sting and
power—it can no longer be called *death*. Consequently,
when faith becomes stronger, death becomes proportionately weaker. Lack of faith, on the other hand,
increases the bitterness of death.

GOD'S HOLY NAME

This is how you should pray:
Our Father in heaven, let your name be kept holy.

MATTHEW 6:9

❖

LTHOUGH IT'S SHORT, the Lord's Prayer is delightful and profound when prayed from the heart. Among the seven parts of the Lord's Prayer, the greatest part is "Let your name be kept holy." Notice, however, that God's name is holy in and of itself. It's not made holy by us. God is the one who makes all things holy and makes us holy as well. So "let your name be kept holy" means that God's name should be made holy in us. When this happens, God becomes everything, and we become nothing. The other six parts of the Lord's Prayer point to the same end—keeping God's name holy. When we keep God's name holy, we do everything well.

To learn how to keep God's name holy in us, we should first look at how it's dishonored and made unholy in us. Clearly, it's dishonored in us in two ways. First, we dishonor God's name when we misuse it to sin. Second, we dishonor his name when we steal it from him. To illustrate, consider a holy object at church. We can desecrate it in two ways: when we use it for human purposes instead of for God's purposes, and when we steal it from the church.

God's name is made unholy through misuse. Instead of using it for improving our souls and making us more faithful, we might actually use God's name to sin and damage our souls. This happens in various ways— through witchcraft, magic, lies, oaths, curses, and deceptions—which are all covered in the commandment: "Never use the name of the LORD your God carelessly" (Deuteronomy 5:11). In summary, we dishonor God's name when we fail to live as God's children.

RESPONDING TO GOD'S PROMISES

Tear your hearts, not your clothes. Return to the LORD your God. He is merciful and compassionate, patient, and always ready to forgive and to change his plans about disaster.

JOEL 2:13

❖

PROMISES LIKE THIS ONE are very beautiful, rich, and far-reaching. The Holy Spirit holds them before us so that people who are deeply discouraged in their soul may find refuge and comfort in these promises when they sense the Lord's anger. It's wonderful to see the way the Holy Spirit works. He highlights and emphasizes the threat in order to show us the goodness and mercy of God. This is what all the prophets do: They frighten us with the strongest and most severe threats. Then they immediately add the greatest promises of the mercy and kindness of God.

But the effect of these threats and promises is different for God-fearing people than for ungodly people. The ungodly don't apply the promises or the threats correctly. When they hear the threats, they don't think these threats pertain to them. They continue in their hypocrisy and godless ways and even consider their ways to be very spiritual. Therefore, these rich promises have no effect on them. Because the threats don't result in troubled hearts for the godless, the promises are equally ineffective for them.

On the other hand, God-fearing people apply these promises to themselves in the right way. They are disheartened and crushed by the anger of God and the threats of punishment. They know they deserve divine judgment. They recognize the seriousness of their sin and its condemnation. So, when they hear these promises, they turn to God's mercy, and their consciences are lifted up again and calmed. So, this is the way our God works: he leads his faithful people to hell before he brings them back. After terrifying them with threats, he comforts them with his promises.

COME TO THE FATHER

*Jesus answered him, "I am the way, the truth, and the life.
No one goes to the Father except through me."*

JOHN 14:6

❖

HAT DOES IT MEAN to come to the Father? It means nothing else but to come from death to life, from sin and condemnation to innocence and godliness, from distress and sorrow to eternal joy and blessedness. Christ is saying, "No one should try to come to the Father through a different way than through me. I alone am the way, the truth, and the life." Christ clearly rules out and powerfully disproves all teaching that salvation can be obtained by works. He completely denies that we can get to heaven by any other way. For Jesus says, "No one comes to the Father except through me." There is no other way.

Salvation can only be obtained by a faith that clings to Christ. No work of ours—or of any other person or saint—can have this same honor. On the other hand, we shouldn't think that we don't have to do good works. Rather, we must first come to Christ in order to receive God's mercy and eternal life. After that, we should do good works and show love. We should make this distinction clear. We should never consider the way we live or the works we do as powerful enough to take us up to the Father.

Though everyone else may abandon me and leave me lying in ruins, I will still have an eternal treasure that can never fail me. This treasure isn't the result of my own works or efforts. The treasure is Christ—the way, the truth, and the life. Only through Christ do I come to the Father. I will hold to this, live by this, and die by it.

WAITING FOR GOD

The Lord isn't slow to do what he promised. . . . Rather, he
is patient for your sake. He doesn't want to destroy anyone
but wants all people to have an opportunity to turn to him.

2 PETER 3:9

❖

OD SOMETIMES POSTPONES answering prayers.
He doesn't do this in order to destroy or
abandon his people. Instead, he does it to
fulfill his promises even more generously. Paul tells us
that God "can do infinitely more than we can ask or
imagine" (Ephesians 3:20). Therefore, God wants us to
wait patiently during the delay, trusting with certainty
that he will give us even more than he has promised.

Human nature makes us so overconfident and
wicked that we distrust God's promises and ignore his
threats. Because punishment doesn't come right away,
we don't take God's warnings seriously. Foolish people
hear that sin will bring judgment and punishment, but
they just brush it off and say, "That won't happen for a
long time. I wish I had lots of money to count in the
meantime." But God wants us to fear his warnings and
wait for his promises to be fulfilled. Of course, that can
only be done if we have faith.

People of the world couldn't care less about God's
warnings. They take his warnings about as seriously as
a goose hissing at them. But God is patient. He postpones both fulfilling his promises and carrying out his
threats. That doesn't mean he's lying. God will eventually punish the wicked and shower even greater and
richer blessings on the faithful because of the delay. But
in the end, he will certainly come.

Unbelievers don't fear God, don't believe in him,
don't hope in him, and don't even care about God.
Believers, on the other hand, pay attention to God's
warnings and trust his promises.

THE INTERNAL BATTLE

What your spiritual nature wants is contrary to what your
corrupt nature wants. They are opposed to each other.

GALATIANS 5:17

❖

OU SHOULDN'T DESPAIR when you feel that the
corrupt nature continuously struggles against
the Spirit. You shouldn't despair if you can't
immediately force the corrupt nature to be subject to
the Spirit.

Don't be surprised or frightened when you become
aware of this conflict between the corrupt nature and
the Spirit in your body. But you should take courage
when Paul says the desires of the corrupt nature are
against the Spirit. "They are opposed to each other. As
a result, you don't always do what you intend to do."
With these words, he comforts those who are being
tested. It's as if Paul wanted to say, "It's impossible to
follow the Spirit as your leader in all situations without
the corrupt nature interfering. The corrupt nature will
get in the way so that you can't do what you really want
to do. At that point, it's enough to resist the corrupt
nature so that you won't gratify its desires. Follow the
Spirit, not the corrupt nature, which quickly becomes
powerless because it's so impatient. It seeks revenge,
bites, doubts, complains, hates God, fights against him,
and despairs."

If you are aware of this battle with the corrupt
nature, don't lose heart, but resist in the Spirit and say,
"I am a sinner and feel sinful because I am still in this
body. As long as I live, sin will cling to this body. I will
obey the Spirit, not the corrupt nature. I will grasp
Christ by faith, trust in him, and find comfort in his
word." You won't gratify your evil desires when you are
strengthened this way.

Jesus Is Both God and Man

The Father loves his Son
and has put everything in his power.

JOHN 3:35

❖

OW DO WE BRING TOGETHER the two truths that Jesus is Lord over all and at the same time is a human being? If Jesus is God, how could God put everything in Jesus' power? If Jesus is God, he already has everything. So how can anything else be given to him?

You already know that there are two natures in Jesus Christ, but there is only one person. These two natures keep their characteristics, but also transfer them to each other. This has caused some confusion. For example, Mary gave birth to Jesus 1,539 years ago. So some ask, "If he's only 1,539 years old, then how can he be eternal?" Jesus suffered on the cross when Pontius Pilate was governor in Judea. So some wonder, "If he suffered under Pilate, then how can he have everything in his power?" How do we reconcile all of this?

The two natures of Christ, the human and divine, are inseparable, and they are united in one person. The characteristics of one nature are attributed to the other nature. For instance, dying is a part of being human. When human nature is united with the divine in one person, death also becomes a divine attribute. Therefore we can say, "God became a man. God suffered. God died." If you separate the human from the divine, that statement would be a lie, for God cannot die. But if we say that two natures reside in one person, then we have spoken correctly.

REAL BLESSINGS

May God give you dew from the sky, fertile fields on the earth, and plenty of fresh grain and new wine. May nations serve you. May people bow down to you.

GENESIS 27:28–29

❖

ISHING YOU GOOD THINGS or nice, obedient children could hardly be considered giving you a blessing because of the uncertainty of the outcome. But the blessing Isaac gave Jacob was neither empty words nor good wishes from one person to another. Isaac's blessing was definite and would certainly come to pass. It wasn't just a wish. Isaac actually gave Jacob something, telling him in effect, "Take the gifts that I am promising with my word."

Saying, "I wish you a strong and healthy body and mind," doesn't mean much. But if I were to hand you a thousand dollars and say, "I would like you to have this money," now that would be different. Similarly, Jesus told the paralyzed man, "Get up, pick up your stretcher, and go home" (Matthew 9:6). If he were merely wishing the best, he would have said, "Poor man, I wish you were healthy and strong." But that wouldn't have cured or strengthened the sick man. Those good wishes would have accomplished little.

The Bible isn't filled with good wishes. It contains real blessings that actually come to pass. We have these kinds of blessings in the New Testament through Christ. We receive a blessing when the pastor says, "Receive forgiveness for your sins." If he were to say, "I *wish* that God would show you favor and mercy, give you eternal life, and forgive your sins," it would be merely an expression of love. Instead, he says, "I forgive you all your sins in the name of the Father, the Son, and the Holy Spirit." These words have the power to actually forgive you, if you believe.

Believe in God

Don't be troubled.
Believe in God, and believe in me.

JOHN 14:1

❖

HRIST IS SAYING HERE, "You have heard that you should trust in God. But I want to show you how to really find him so you won't start worshiping something you made up in your head. If you want to believe in the true God, then believe in me. If you want to invest your faith and trust in the right place, where it will never fail, then invest in me. For all of God lives in me." Later he tells them, "I am the way, the truth, and the life" (John 14:6). In other words, "Whoever sees me, sees the Father. Whoever hears me, hears the Father. Therefore, if you want to meet God, then take hold of him in me and through me. If you have me, you also have the Father. The Father himself testifies about me." In the Gospels, Jesus repeatedly declares that he is from the Father. He doesn't speak and act on his own. Instead, the Father commands that the whole world should believe that Christ is God. No one should believe in any other person or accept any other way to know God than through Christ.

So it's certain that whoever tries to go around Christ won't meet the true God. God is completely in Christ and places himself in Christ for us. No one will be able to succeed in dealing with God apart from Christ. No one will find God on the basis of human thoughts and devotion.

Whoever wants to take the right path with his faith and not lose his way should begin where God has placed the path and where God wants to be found. Otherwise, everything he does and believes is useless.

In Need of Comfort

I will never again curse the ground because of humans, even though from birth their hearts are set on nothing but evil. I will never again kill every living creature as I have just done.

GENESIS 8:21

❖

GOD IS SPEAKING HERE as if he were sorry that he had punished the earth because of humans. It almost sounds as if he is criticizing himself for dealing so harshly with the world. We shouldn't take this as meaning that God changed his mind about his creation. Instead, we should take comfort from this passage. God, in effect, blames himself in order to encourage and lift the spirits of his little flock. He tells his people that he wants to be merciful from this point on.

Noah and his family needed comfort. They were terrified by God's anger, which had just destroyed the world. Because their faith was shaken, God wanted to show himself in a way that would make them expect nothing else but his good will and mercy. So he was present at their sacrifice, talked to them, and told them he was pleased with them. He told them that he was displeased about destroying the human race and promised never to do it again. God wasn't being inconsistent or changing. No, he wanted these people, who were witnesses of the effects of his anger, to change their attitudes and perceptions of him.

People who are going through spiritual trials know how important it is to hear words of comfort. They need to be told to hope in God's good will and dismiss discouraging thoughts of impending doom. A whole day, even an entire month, may not be enough time to comfort them. Recovery from sickness often takes a long time. In the same way, wounded hearts can't be quickly healed with one little word. Because God is aware of this, he uses a variety of ways to show people his good will and mercy—even blaming himself.

WHY WE SAY AMEN

Certainly, Christ made God's many promises come true.
For that reason, because of our message,
people also honor God by saying, "Amen!"

2 CORINTHIANS 1:20

❖

HE LITTLE WORD *AMEN* indicates strong affirmation and means "let it be so." It expresses the faith we should have when we pray. Christ said, "Have faith that you will receive whatever you ask for in prayer" (Matthew 21:22). He also said, "That's why I tell you to have faith that you have already received whatever you pray for, and it will be yours" (Mark 11:24). The Samaritan woman received what she asked for because she didn't stop asking and firmly believed. In response, the Lord said to her, "Woman, you have strong faith! What you wanted will be done for you" (Matthew 15:28). James also said, "When you ask for something, don't have any doubts. A person who has doubts is like a wave that is blown by the wind and tossed by the sea" (James 1:6).

So as the author of Ecclesiastes said, "The end of something is better than its beginning" (Ecclesiastes 7:8). For at the end of your prayers, you say *Amen* with heartfelt confidence and faith. When you say *Amen*, the prayer is sealed, and it will be certainly heard. Without this ending, neither the beginning nor the middle of the prayer will be of any benefit.

GROWING UP IN CHRIST

This is to continue . . . until we become mature,
until we measure up to Christ, who is the standard.
Then we will no longer be little children.

EPHESIANS 4:13–14

❖

UMAN REASON ENJOYS finding fault with the messengers of God's Word. It can quickly detect if these teachers' lives and habits aren't consistent with the absolutely pure teachings that they proclaim. Somehow, reason can judge their lives on the basis of their doctrine while, at the same time, rejecting their doctrine. In this way, our enemies complain that they're always hearing the gospel from us but not seeing behavior that matches it. They say we preach one thing and do another.

But our critics should remember that human beings are merely creatures with the ability to reason. Yet, God has given these human beings the authority to rule over all of creation (Genesis 1:28). Now, look at a baby. Where is this mighty authority God has given to him? An infant is the most pitiful of all living beings. He can't help himself in the least. He depends solely on outside help; otherwise, he would die. Despite his helplessness, the baby still possesses authority over all creation. Although we can't easily see this authority, the hope and promise of it remain. So the parents cherish, nourish, and take care of the child so that when he grows up and becomes strong, he can take on this authority.

Just as all people begin life as a weak baby does and mature over time, the same is true for all believers in spiritual matters. Day by day, we grow in our faith and by our faith. We keep growing until we eventually meet our Lord as mature people, just as Paul wrote in Ephesians 4:13. Meanwhile, God, our merciful Father, watches over us in our weakness and continually forgives us.

Living on the Vine

*I am the vine. You are the branches. Those who live
in me while I live in them will produce a lot of fruit.
But you can't produce anything without me.*

JOHN 15:5

❖

Y SAYING THAT BELIEVERS live in him and he lives
in them, Jesus is making it clear that
Christianity is not something we put on exter-
nally. We don't put it on like clothes. We don't adopt it as
a new lifestyle that focuses on our own efforts, as do
those who practice a holy lifestyle they have invented
themselves. Rather, Christian faith is a new birth brought
about by God's Word and Spirit. A Christian must be a
new person from the depths of his heart. Once the heart
is born anew in Christ, these fruits will follow: confession
of the gospel, love, obedience, patience, purity, and so on.

In this passage, Christ warns his disciples that they
must remain in his Word. Remaining in the Word leads
to genuine, newborn Christians. These true Christians
produce much fruit. They guard themselves from the
teaching that perverts God's Word and that tries to
make grapes from thistles and thorns. This will never
happen, however, because each kind produces its own
kind. Even if you teach about, strive for, and pile up
good works, your nature won't change. You must first
possess a new nature. You won't accomplish anything
by striving and exhausting yourself.

The two types of works remain vastly different. The
one type of work is produced by human effort, while
the other grows naturally. The works we make up
always require us to strive harder, but they never do as
well as natural growth. In contrast, natural growth
stands, moves, lives, and does what it should naturally.
So Christ says, "All other human teaching cannot succeed because it instructs people to make up works. But
if you live in me, as natural branches live on the vine,
you will certainly produce good fruit."

God Will Take Care of You

*So he made you suffer from hunger and then fed you with
manna. . . . He did this to teach you that a person cannot
live on bread alone but on every word that the LORD speaks.*

DEUTERONOMY 8:3

❖

OW DOES PROVIDING MANNA show that a person should live on every word that the Lord speaks? Is this manna God's Word? No, but God uses this example to explain what he said about hunger: "he made you suffer from hunger and then fed you with manna." He did this to show you that even if you don't have manna, God's Word can keep you alive. God's Word promises that he will never leave you, and he will always take care of you. For even in times of hunger, faith in what God says nourishes, not only the soul, but also the body—the whole person. God will never abandon you. In his own time, he will provide food for your body the same way he used ravens and the widow of Zarephath to feed Elijah, and manna to feed the Israelites.

When Moses says that a person can't live on bread alone, he isn't only talking about manna. These words apply both to times when you're hungry and to times when you have plenty of food. The point is that God wants to show you his goodness through all your experiences. When you're hungry, you should learn to trust God's Word. God promises to take care of you and not let you die of hunger. When you trust in him, he will provide nourishment to your body because of your faith. He does all this to prevent you from worshiping your appetites and to teach you that life doesn't depend on a full stomach. God sustains both the body and the soul. You would've never learned this truth if your stomach had always been full. This is how you learn to trust in God.

BE AWARE OF SINFUL TENDENCIES

Those who belong to Christ Jesus have crucified their
corrupt nature along with its passions and desires.

GALATIANS 5:24

 T'S VERY ADVANTAGEOUS for believers to be aware of the sinful tendencies of their corrupt nature. This awareness keeps them from becoming filled with pride through the useless, godless delusion of trying to become righteous by works, as if this would make them acceptable to God. Puffed up by this delusion, the monks believed they were so holy because of their self-chosen works that they sold their righteousness and holiness to others. In their own hearts, however, they were convinced that they were impure. Trusting in our own righteousness and imagining ourselves to be pure is very damaging.

But if we are aware of the sinfulness in our own hearts, we cannot trust in our own righteousness. This awareness humbles us so that we let go of our pride and stop trusting in our own works. It compels us to run to Christ, our Reconciler. He doesn't have a corrupt, impure nature, but a completely clean and holy one, which he gave for the life of the world. In him we find a trustworthy and complete righteousness. So we remain humble—not with false humility but with true humility—because of the sinful tendencies and shortcomings of our corrupt nature. Therefore, we would be guilty of eternal death if God were to strictly judge us. But we are not proud in the sight of God. We humbly acknowledge our sins and desire forgiveness with a broken heart. Trusting in the work of Christ as Mediator, we enter God's presence and plead for forgiveness of sins. Consequently, God spreads his immeasurable heaven of kindness over us, and for the sake of Christ, he does not credit our sins to us.

Not to Condemn the World

God sent his Son into the world,
not to condemn the world, but to save the world.

JOHN 3:17

❖

A FATHER AND MOTHER don't scold, spank, or punish their children because they want to see their children die. They discipline their children so that they won't fall into the hands of the executioner later. In the same way, God doesn't want us to run wild. He directs and disciplines us in order to restrain us and keep us from being punished. Instead, God wants to protect us and make us heirs in the kingdom of heaven.

God disciplines his chosen ones and even sends them many trials and troubles. When you find yourself thinking, "Oh, God is so angry with me," then, say to yourself, "I believe in you and in your Word. You won't deceive me. Even if you send me many troubles, it's not because you are condemning me. You will never throw me out. As Psalm 143:2 says, 'Do not take me to court,' for you haven't been sent to judge the world." Even if God were to send plagues, don't think that he wants to destroy everything. When the Corinthians behaved foolishly at the Lord's Supper, and God allowed many to become ill and die, Paul declared, "If we were judging ourselves correctly, we would not be judged. But when the Lord judges us, he disciplines us so that we won't be condemned along with the rest of the world" (1 Corinthians 11:31–32).

We should understand that God disciplines us so that we will be saved, not condemned. By disciplining us, he hopes to pull us back from the condemnation and judgment reserved for the world. He doesn't want us to be judged along with the world. Christ didn't come to judge. We shouldn't look on him as an executioner. He isn't angry. He doesn't want to condemn us. Instead, Christ wants to help us.

Using Possessions Wisely

*Abram was very rich because
he had livestock, silver, and gold.*

GENESIS 13:2

❖

EOPLE HAVE MANY WRONG ideas about wealth
and material possessions. The Bible gives us
numerous examples, such as this passage,
for countering these errors. The Scriptures teach us that
riches are not wrong in and of themselves because they
are gifts from God. Rather, the problem begins with the
people who own and use them.

No good philosopher or theologian would find fault
with what God has created and given to his people.
Instead, he would condemn the misuse of God's gifts.
David says, "When riches increase, do not depend on
them" (Psalm 62:10). It's as if he meant to say, "Riches are
good, but be careful that you don't use them in the wrong
way." Similarly, it isn't necessarily wrong to admire a
woman. After all, she is one of God's beautiful creatures.
But desiring someone you're not supposed to is sinful. In
order to remain pure, monks shut themselves up in
monasteries to avoid seeing any women. But even when
they were alone, they would burn with desire for women
because they had sinful hearts. Refusing to look at women
can't stop these improper thoughts, just as abstaining
from certain things doesn't put an end to sinful longings.
Rather, we learn how to control ourselves by interacting
with people and actually using our possessions.

Your primary goal in life should be devotion to God.
After that, strive to make use of what you own with a
pure heart. Keep in mind that material possessions
aren't evil in and of themselves. Those who use their
possessions wrongly are like a fool who slouches when
he stands in the sunlight and then becomes upset
because his shadow is crooked. These people don't realize that the problem is inside of them.

PERSECUTED AND BLESSED

In every way we're troubled, but we aren't crushed by our troubles. We're frustrated, but we don't give up. We're persecuted, but we're not abandoned. We're captured, but we're not killed.

2 CORINTHIANS 4:8-9

❖

F THE WORLD CANNOT enthrall us with its delights and draw us into its sins, then it tries to drive us out with suffering and torment. The whole time we are on earth the world tries to deceive us by showing us examples of sin or by cruelly torturing us. It's like a mythical monster with the head of a beautiful maiden, the body of a lion, and the tail of a poisonous serpent. The final destiny of the world, with its pleasures and cruelty, is poison and eternal death.

Therefore, God has ordained matters so that the sins of the world end up bringing us blessing. So also the persecutions of the world aren't useless, but God intended for them to increase our blessings. So when the world tries to harm us, it ends up serving us and making us better people.

So we see that the entire Bible and all the early church fathers agree that those who try to harm us end up being very useful to us if we patiently endure the suffering. That is why Peter says, "Who will harm you if you are devoted to doing what is good?" (1 Peter 3:13). And we read in the Psalms, "No enemy will take him by surprise. No wicked person will mistreat him" (Psalm 89:22). But how can our enemies not harm us when they try so hard to kill us and sometimes even succeed? It's precisely when they harm us that they do us the most good. If we are wise, we understand we're living in the middle of blessing and evil at the same time. It's amazing how God in his goodness moderates it all!

CRYING OUT TO GOD

*Jonah prayed: "I called to the LORD in my distress,
and he answered me. From the depths of my ⌊watery⌋
grave I cried for help, and you heard my cry."*

JONAH 2:2

❖

E SHOULD CRY OUT TO GOD in such a way that
we're convinced in our heart that he will
answer. It should be a cry that allows us to
boast, as Jonah did, that God answers when we cry out
in our need. This is simply crying out with the heart's
true voice of faith. Unless we first lift up our hearts to
God, we are unable to lift up our heads or hold up our
hands.

With the help and support of the Spirit, we run to an
angry God, looking for his undeserved kindness in the
middle of his anger. When we lift our heart in this way,
we willingly endure punishment from God and we continue to look for his mercy. Notice what strong character such a heart must have. Though surrounded by
God's anger and punishment, it doesn't seem to be
aware of them. Instead it sees and feels only God's
kindness and mercy. Though the heart is clearly aware
of God's anger and punishment, it simply doesn't *want*
to see or feel them. Rather, it's determined to look for
God's kindness and mercy—no matter how hidden
they might be.

Turning to God is difficult. Breaking through his
anger, punishment, and displeasure is like running
through a row of thorns or even through a line of spears
and swords. It's only with a sincere cry of faith that we
can break through. When we cry out in this way, we
know in our heart that God hears us.

THE PRAYERS OF BELIEVERS

If you live in me and what I say lives in you,
then ask for anything you want, and it will be yours.

JOHN 15:7

❖

HIS IS A MISERABLE WORLD for unbelievers. They work so hard, yet accomplish nothing. They may even pray a lot, search all over, and knock at the door. Yet nothing is gained, found, or achieved, for they're knocking on the wrong door. They do all these things and even pray as if they were doing any other work. In other words, they do all this without any faith. That's why they can't really pray.

Prayer is the work of faith alone. No one, except a believer, can truly pray. Believers don't pray on their own merits, but in the name of the Son of God, in whom they were baptized. They're certain that their prayers please God because he commanded them to pray in the name of Christ and promised he would listen to them. But the others don't know this. Instead, they pray in their own name and believe they can prepare themselves. They think they can read enough to make themselves worthy and smart enough to make prayer into an acceptable work. And when we ask them whether their prayers have been heard, they reply, "I prayed, but if my prayers were heard only God knows." If you don't know what you are doing or whether God is listening, what kind of a prayer is that?

But Christians don't approach prayer this way. We pray in response to God's command and promise. We offer our prayers to God in the name of Christ, and we know that what we ask for will be given to us. We experience God's help in all kinds of needy situations. And if relief doesn't come soon, we still know that our prayers are pleasing to God. We know that God has answered us because he gives us the strength to endure.

Pray for God's Rich Blessings

*Certainly, goodness and mercy will stay close to me
all the days of my life, and I will remain
in the LORD's house for days without end.*

PSALM 23:6

❖

HE DEVIL NEVER STOPS tormenting believers. On the inside, he afflicts them with fears. On the outside, he torments them with the tricks of false teachers and the power of tyrants. So at the conclusion of this psalm, David earnestly prayed that God, who had given him rich blessings, would continue to take care of him until the end. He was asking God to grant him favor so that "goodness and mercy will stay close" to him all the days of his life. Then, David explained how God would show his goodness and mercy: "I will remain in the LORD's house for days without end." He was saying, "Lord, you are the one who started all this. You gave me your holy Word and made me one of your people who know, honor, and praise you. Continue to show me your favor so that I may stay close to your Word and never be separated from your holy kingdom."

David asked for the same in Psalm 27. He said, "I have asked one thing from the LORD. This I will seek: to remain in the LORD's house all the days of my life in order to gaze at the LORD's beauty and to search for an answer in his temple" (Psalm 27:4).

By his example, David teaches all believers that they should not become overconfident, proud, or presumptuous. Instead, they should be afraid and pray that they don't lose God's rich blessings. David's example should wake us up so that we will pray diligently.

BELIEVERS ARE STILL SINNERS

If we, the same people who are searching for God's
approval in Christ, are still sinners, does that mean that
Christ encourages us to sin? That's unthinkable!

GALATIANS 2:17

❖

OW CAN THOSE WHO have God's approval in Christ not be sinners and yet be sinners at the same time? For the Scripture asserts both about the person who has God's approval. John writes in 1 John 1:8, "If we say, 'We aren't sinful' we are deceiving ourselves, and the truth is not in us." He also writes in 1 John 5:18, "We know that those who have been born from God don't go on sinning." He says the same in 1 John 3:9, "Those who have been born from God don't live sinful lives. What God has said lives in them, and they can't live sinful lives." In other words, John is saying that believers don't sin. But if they were to claim they had no sin, they would be lying.

We can see a similar difficulty in the book of Job. God, who cannot lie, says Job is a man of integrity in Job 1:8. Yet, Job confesses later in Job 9:20 and other passages that he is a sinner. In Job 7:21, he says, "Why don't you forgive my disobedience and take away my sin?" Job must be telling the truth because if he were lying to God, God wouldn't call him a righteous person. So, Job is at the same time righteous and sinful.

If we look at faith, God's laws are fulfilled, sin is destroyed, and no law is left. But if we look at our corrupt nature, there is nothing good. Therefore, we must always remember that all of us who are righteous through faith are still sinners.

ETERNAL FOOD

Don't work for food that spoils.
Instead, work for the food that lasts into eternal life.
This is the food the Son of Man will give you.

JOHN 6:27

❖

N THIS PASSAGE, Christ compares what perishes with what lasts forever. If we were truly concerned about this difference, we would keep holding on to what is eternal and stop clinging to what is temporary. Christ is saying here, "If I were to give you right now the type of things you already have, such as the bread you get from the baker, and if I were to give you enough of it to satisfy the entire world, how much would it really help you? If I had more wheat, barley, oats, money, and property than the richest person in the world to give you, what would be gained? I would have food to give you, but it would be perishable food that wouldn't last forever."

There isn't a farmer so foolish that he would give one hundred bushels of grain for a crumbled piece of paper. There isn't a merchant who would exchange a hundred bottles of beer for a glass of water. Both would rather sell their possessions at a premium price.

Christ, however, is saying that everything we own is perishable and that we should willingly give it all away in order to get eternal food. But in this world, we tend to be more concerned about what will pass away than what will last forever. We grab for a handful of food and end up letting go of the gospel.

PRESERVING HARMONY

Abram answered Sarai, "Here, she's your slave.
Do what you like with her." Then Sarai mistreated
Hagar so much that she ran away.

GENESIS 16:6

❖

N THE DISPUTE BETWEEN Hagar and Sarai, Abram sided with his childless, elderly wife instead of her pregnant servant. Abram doesn't want to make his godly wife sad. So he allowed Sarai to deal with her servant as she pleased, despite the fact that Hagar was pregnant with Abram's child. This little incident describes the hazards, struggles, and conflicts that are a part of marriage. Sarai was being tested, yet God comforted her through Abram. The fact that God always watches over marriages and families shows us that he is pleased with these institutions.

Family life often leads to quarreling and conflict between husbands and wives. Furthermore, frequent disagreements and disputes occur in government. Splinter groups form in the church. Anyone who has watched all these conflicts would assume that nothing good could come from all of this.

This passage is warning us to be prepared for troubles and to patiently tolerate them. Don't think that you will escape marital conflicts or political disputes. Only foolish people, who are naive about life, think this way. Problems are common in church administration as well. Splinter groups and other troublemakers in the church cause all kinds of disruptions. Here on earth we live among unappreciative, stubborn people who will never stop spreading confusion and bitterness. In light of this, we must remember this story and believe and trust in God, just as faithful Abram did. We must try to get along in peace and preserve harmony as best we can.

CONCENTRATING ON PRAYER

The end of everything is near. Therefore, practice self-control,
and keep your minds clear so that you can pray.

1 PETER 4:7

❖

F IT WERE POSSIBLE to see into a person's heart,
nothing would be more ridiculous than seeing the thoughts of a cold, undevoted heart
in prayer. When someone forgets what he just said, he
isn't praying a good prayer. Praise God that I now
understand this clearly. In true prayer, one remembers
all the words and thoughts from the beginning to the
end of the prayer.

To illustrate, a good barber must keep his thoughts,
mind, and eyes on the razor and on the hair he's cutting. He can't forget where he is. If he starts chatting
away, thinking about something else, or looking somewhere else, he might cut his customer's mouth, nose, or
throat. So doing anything well requires total concentration of the whole person. As the saying goes, "Whoever
thinks about many things, thinks about nothing and
doesn't do anything right." Praying a good prayer
requires even more concentration than this. It demands
the whole heart.

This is how I pray the Lord's Prayer. For even today,
I keep on eating and drinking from the Lord's Prayer, as
if I were a hungry baby or a famished adult who can
never get enough. It's the best prayer of all.

IN A SINGLE DAY

"Look at the stone I have set in front of Joshua. . . . I am engraving an inscription on it," declares the LORD of Armies. "I will remove this land's sin in a single day."

ZECHARIAH 3:9

❖

THE STONE WAS GOING to be engraved, and God promised he would take away all sin in one day. We know very well, of course, that sin isn't taken away by anything except Christ's suffering. His suffering will result in the forgiveness of sins, as Isaiah 53 states. Peter and Paul also teach the same in many places. So, the engraving of the stone symbolizes the suffering of Christ, not his conception or birth.

God's promise to remove the sin of the land shows that the sacrifices of the old priesthood were incapable of providing forgiveness of sins. Only Christ's suffering can take away sin, nothing else. All good works are worthless and are even sinful before God. Only the engraved foundation stone can achieve forgiveness of sins for us, nothing else.

God shows us just how strong and powerful this forgiveness is when he said he wanted to accomplish it all "in a single day." This phrase means he wanted to accomplish this in one day—once and only once. The forgiveness and reconciliation achieved on that day would be enough for the sins of the entire world—from its very beginning into eternity. God didn't want to continually arrange for forgiveness of new sins on a daily or yearly basis, as was true under the old priesthood. The people of Israel had to regularly seek forgiveness through sacrifices and worship. But God wanted to provide complete forgiveness in one day. Christ's suffering would be enough, satisfying everything. The author of Hebrews sums this up beautifully: "With one sacrifice he accomplished the work of setting them apart for God forever" (Hebrews 10:14).

JOY AND SORROW

You will cry because you are sad, but the world will be happy.
You will feel pain, but your pain will turn to happiness.

JOHN 16:20

❖

E MUST SEE THE SADNESS, crying, and wailing described in this passage from a Christian perspective, not a worldly one. This sadness accompanies all of the positions in life that are ordained by God.

God designed the world in such a way that he places people in positions in life before they understand everything that goes with it. For example, young people are hurried into marriage with music and dancing. They joyfully approach marriage and imagine it will be as sweet as pure sugar. In the same way, God gives great honor and glory to princes and lords. He hangs gold chains around their necks, sets them on velvet cushions, and allows people to bow before them and call them "your honor." He gives them large castles and great fame. Those who haven't experienced this lifestyle would think these people's lives are filled with nothing but joy and pleasure. Then, having caught them, it's as if God tosses a rope over their horns. When they are caught in their positions, they discover their life is far different than they thought it would be. The thrill fades. Misfortune and sorrow spoil the joy and pleasure.

This is nothing compared to the lofty truths Christ is talking about in this passage. This is how life goes. It alternates back and forth between bad and good, joy and sorrow, summer and winter, sun and rain, good years and bad years, times of sadness and times of laughter and then times of trouble again. This is the way it is for everyone in his position in life. It's very difficult and unpleasant, but we must all patiently endure part of the punishment placed on Adam.

WHITER THAN SNOW

Purify me from sin with hyssop, and I will be clean.
Wash me, and I will be whiter than snow.

PSALM 51:7

❖

OW CAN WE BECOME whiter than snow when sin remains in us and sticks to us? Because of our sins, we are never as clean and holy as we should be. But we have received baptism, which is pure. We have received God's Word, which is also pure. And through baptism and God's Word, we have received Christ's blood, which is absolutely pure. Because of the purity we receive in faith through Christ, we can certainly say that we are whiter than snow. We are purer than the sun and stars, even though sin still sticks to us. Our sin is covered by the purity and innocence of Christ, which we receive when we hear and believe God's Word. We should keep in mind, though, that this purity comes from completely outside of ourselves. In other words, Christ clothes us with his own perfection.

If we look at a Christian apart from Christ and see him as he really is, we would notice how much he is contaminated by sin. Even if he were a fine person, we would not only see that he's thoroughly contaminated, but also that he's covered over with a thick, dark film of sin. If someone tried to separate us from Christ and take away our baptism and God's promises, we would no longer have Christ's purity. We would be left with nothing but sin.

So when someone asks you, "If sin always sticks to people, how can they be washed so clean that they are whiter than snow?" You can answer, "We should view people, not as they are on their own, but as they are in Christ."

Carry Each Other's Burdens

Help carry each other's burdens.
In this way you will follow Christ's teachings.

GALATIANS 6:2

❖

VERYWHERE LOVE TURNS it finds burdens to carry and ways to help. Love is the teaching of Christ. To love means to wish another person good from the heart. It means to seek what is best for the other person.

What if there were no one who made a mistake? What if no one fell? What if no one needed someone to help him? To whom would you show love? To whom could you show favor? Whose best could you seek? Love would not be able to exist if there were no people who made mistakes and sinned. The philosophers say that each of these people is the appropriate and adequate "object" of love or the "material" with which love has to work.

The corrupt nature—or the kind of love that is really lust—wants others to wish it well and to give it what it desires. In other words, it seeks its own interests. The "material" it works with is a righteous, holy, godly, and good person. People who follow this corrupt nature completely reverse God's teaching. They want others to bear their burdens, serve them, and carry them. These are the kind of people who despise having uneducated, useless, angry, foolish, troublesome, and gloomy people as their life companions. Instead, they look for friendly, charming, good-natured, quiet, and holy people. They don't want to live on earth but in paradise, not among sinners but among angels, not in the world but in heaven. We should feel sorry for these people because they are receiving their reward here on earth and possessing their heaven in this life.

LIFE AFTER DEATH

My Father wants all those who see
the Son and believe in him to have eternal life.
He wants me to bring them back to life on the last day.

JOHN 6:40

❖

 HIS PASSAGE IS A GLORIOUS promise to us. It's repeated twice because we tend to think: "That doesn't quite make sense. These words are difficult to believe." No one could foresee that faith would be so important until Christ actually said, "Everyone who believes in me will have eternal life." Now Jerome, Ambrose, and Cyprian all believed in Christ, yet they were executed. How do we fit this together with the promise of eternal life? When we see how people who believe in Christ are cursed, condemned, exiled, even beheaded and burned, it's like having the rug pulled out from under us. Christians aren't allowed to live in peace. This promise about eternal life seems like a lie to us. If this is what eternal life means—that one is pursued and killed—then let the devil have that type of life.

But faith must close its eyes and refuse to pass judgment on what it sees or feels in the world. Believers won't become aware of eternal life until Christ raises them from the dead. Meanwhile, their eternal life is hidden in death. It's covered up and out of sight. But remember that as long as you live, and even when you're dying, you have forgiveness. If you feel the weight of sin crushing you, you can still say, "My sins are forgiven." When your sins hunt you down, bite at you, and terrify you, you can look to Christ, put your feeble faith in him, and hold on tightly.

LOT'S PRAYER

Though you've been very kind to me by saving my life, I can't run as far as the hills. . . . Look, there's a city near enough to flee to, and it's small. Why don't you let me run there?

GENESIS 19:19–20

❖

AKE A LOOK at the different parts of Lot's prayer. The first part of a good prayer is giving thanks to God. Giving thanks includes acknowledging God's wonderful acts of kindness and praising God. When we pray the Lord's Prayer, we certainly do ask for daily bread. But we first address God as our Father right at the beginning of the prayer. With these very words, we are acknowledging that he has already provided food and protection for us, as a father would, up to that very day. Praising and thanking God are good ways to acknowledge his kindness.

The second part of a prayer is to pour out our deepest concerns to God about personal problems and needs. In Lot's case, he was saying, "I'll be in danger if I do what you say and run for the hills. In the past, I have gotten into trouble for being too slow. I could be in bigger trouble now if I'm too slow. Please give me what I'm asking, for I know you are merciful."

In the third part of Lot's prayer, he proposed his own solution to the problem and asked God's permission to carry it out. He wanted to run to a nearby city where he thought he would be safe. He pointed out it was a small town, which would provide a safe place to stay.

This was Lot's prayer. Think carefully about this incident and what happened as a result. Lot prayed, and then God changed his plan. At this point, we shouldn't debate about whether or not God changes his mind. Rather, we should learn what Psalm 145:19 teaches, "He fills the needs of those who fear him. He hears their cries for help and saves them."

What It Means to See God

Blessed are those whose thoughts are pure.
They will see God.

MATTHEW 5:8

❖

IT'S VERY IMPORTANT for believers to have a pure heart that follows God. They need to do this on the basis of God's pure and holy Word. What reward will they have? What has God promised to those who have pure thoughts? We are told, "They will see God." Surely this is wonderful—an excellent treasure! But what does it mean to "see God?"

Some people have their own ideas about how to see God. They crouch in a corner, lift their thoughts toward heaven, and engage in a life of idle speculation. Is this any way to try to see God? They use their own ideas to try to stroll into God's presence. They try to climb up to heaven under their own power. They insist on using their own intellect to figure out everything about God and his Word.

However, if you believe that Christ is your Savior, you'll soon realize that you have a gracious God. Faith leads you to heaven and lets you see inside of God's heart. There, you will get a glimpse of his infinite kindness and love. This is what it really means to "see God." You can't physically see him with your eyes because no one can see God in this life. Instead, you see God by faith.

GOD'S POWER

We have been born into a new life which has an
inheritance that . . . is kept in heaven for you,
since you are guarded by God's power through faith.

1 PETER 1:4–5

ETER SAYS, "You are guarded by God's power
through faith." He says this because when
certain people hear the gospel—how faith
alone without works makes us godly—they jump in
and say, "Yes, I believe too." They confuse their own
thoughts, which they make up, with faith. We have previously taught from Scripture that none of us can do
even the smallest works without God's Spirit. How then
out of our own strength could we do the greatest
work—to believe? Such thoughts are nothing but a
dream. If we are to believe, then God's power must be
working in us. Paul says, "I pray that the glorious
Father, the God of our Lord Jesus Christ, would give
you a spirit of wisdom. . . . You will also know the
unlimited greatness of his power as it works with might
and strength for us, the believers" (Ephesians 1:17–19).
Not only is it God's will, but he also has the power to
spend a great deal on us. For when God creates faith in
us, it is a great work. It's as if he were creating heaven
and earth again.

People are being foolish when they say, "How can
faith alone save us? There are some people who believe,
yet they don't do any good works." For they think that
their own thoughts are faith and that faith can exist
without good works. In contrast, we agree with Peter
who says faith is a power that comes from God. When
God gives faith, the individual is born again and
becomes a new creature. As a result, good works naturally flow from faith.

Between Arrogance and Despair

God opposes arrogant people,
but he is kind to humble people.

JAMES 4:6

❖

E SHOULDN'T BECOME proud in times of prosperity nor despair in times of trouble. On the one hand, we must keep our arrogance in check by fearing God. On the other hand, we should cling to his mercy in those times when we think he is angry with us. By doing so, we won't crash into heaven with our big heads or fall flat on our faces on the earth.

But the person who is humble and has a broken heart is neither proud nor full of despair. Yet, it's difficult for us to avoid both arrogance and despair. In our weakness, we sometimes swerve to the right and sometimes to the left. Whenever we feel overconfident or full of despair, we must make an effort to resist such tendencies. We cannot give in to either one. When an archer misses the bull's eye, he is still awarded points for hitting the target. Similarly, God is pleased when we at least fight against arrogance and despair. Even if we may not show enough joy in times of trouble or enough reverence for God in times of prosperity, he won't hold it against his faithful people. We have Christ as our mediator. Through him, we are considered true saints even though we have barely started to act like holy people.

In summary, those with many troubles should lift their spirits by acknowledging God's mercy and remembering what Christ has done for them. Those with few troubles should drive out arrogance by living in the fear of God.

LETTING GO OF OUR POSSESSIONS

You are already totally defeated because you have lawsuits against each other. Why don't you accept the fact that you have been wronged?

1 CORINTHIANS 6:7

❖

UNFORTUNATELY IN THIS WORLD, we have lawsuits. It would be better if there were none. But God allows them to exist in order to avoid greater evil. He permits lawsuits because people are imperfect. When someone takes something from them, they don't want to let go of it and give it back to God.

Nevertheless, we should strive toward the goal of keeping God's name holy. We should learn from day to day how to give God's honor and goods back to him. This includes giving back to God anything that is taken away from us. In this way, we are made completely holy. The Lord's Prayer was given to us to help us remember that we should always want to keep God's name holy.

It shouldn't surprise Christians if they have everything taken away from them—all of their property, honor, friends, health, wisdom, and so on. For ultimately all their possessions will be destroyed, and they will be separated from all things before they can be made holy and keep God's name holy. For if something exists, its name also exists. So everything must be taken away so that only God, the things of God, and the names of God remain.

ABSOLUTE FAITH

*No one receives God's approval by obeying the law's
standards since, "The person who has God's
approval will live by faith."*

GALATIANS 3:11

❖

E ARE USED TO SPEAKING about faith in two
ways. We sometimes speak about faith apart
from works, and at other times we speak
about faith accompanied by works. Just as a craftsman
speaks about his material in various ways and a gardener speaks of a tree sometimes being barren and sometimes bearing fruit, so the Holy Spirit speaks in Scripture
in various ways about faith. Sometimes Scripture refers
to an abstract or absolute faith. Other times it refers to
faith as it appears outwardly, as it relates to other things,
or as we live it out. Faith is absolute and not connected
to other things when the Scripture speaks absolutely
about receiving God's approval or those who receive it,
as we can see in Romans and Galatians.

But when Scripture speaks of rewards and works, it's
speaking of faith as it relates to other things—how it
appears or how we live it out. The Bible gives several
examples of this faith. "What matters is a faith that
expresses itself through love" (Galatians 5:6). "Do this,
and life will be yours" (Luke 10:28). "If you want to
enter into life, obey the commandments" (Matthew
19:17). "Whoever obeys laws will live because of the
laws he obeys" (Galatians 3:12). "Turn away from evil,
and do good" (Psalm 34:14). There are countless verses like this in Scripture. In these and similar verses
where "doing" is mentioned, Scriptures always speak of
"doing in faith." If you have faith, then you are able to
do good works.

THE BEST PRAYER OF ALL

This is how you should pray:
Our Father in heaven, let your name be kept holy.

MATTHEW 6:9

❖

FTER HAVING DENOUNCED showy and meaning-less prayers, Christ introduced a splendid short prayer of his own. With it, he instruct-ed us on how to pray and what we should pray for. He gave us a prayer that touches upon a variety of needs. By themselves, these needs should compel us to approach God daily with these few easily remembered words. No one can excuse himself by saying he doesn't know how to pray or what to pray for.

Praying the Lord's Prayer every day is certainly a worth-while habit, especially for ordinary people and children. We can pray it in the morning, in the evening, and at the dinner table—at any time for that matter. As we pray this prayer together, we bring our needs before God.

As has been said many times before, the Lord's Prayer is the finest prayer that anyone could have ever thought up or that was ever sent from heaven. Because God the Father gave his Son the words for the prayer and sent him to introduce it, we know beyond a doubt that this prayer pleases the Father immensely.

Right at the beginning of the prayer, with the words, "Our Father," Jesus reminds us of what God demands and promises. God insists that we give him the respect, honor, and reverence he deserves, just as earthly fathers expect this from their children. Also, God the Father wants us to trust that he will meet our needs. We are overjoyed to be his children through Christ. And so, because we trust that he will give us what he promised, we can pray to him with confidence, in the name of Christ, our Lord.

Angels Hear the Harmony

As Jacob went on his way, God's angels met him.

GENESIS 32:1

❖

NGELS ARE SPIRITS who serve all of creation. Their job on earth is to fight for the good of the world and the welfare of God's people. Their job in heaven is to sing, "Glory to God in the highest. . . ." and "Lord God, we praise you. . . ." Christ says that the "angels in heaven always see the face of my Father" (Matthew 18:10).

The angels have a good understanding of how the world works. They know that there's a correlation between the fortunate circumstances of wicked people and the adverse conditions of faithful believers. While we, Christians, are still on earth, we cannot fully understand this or see how it can be true. At the end of the world, after this life, we will understand how all of this fits together.

People who are unfamiliar with the principles of musical harmony have trouble appreciating how the various sounds produced by an organ or harp can result in such beautiful music. In this life, we hear the sounds, not the symphony. It appears to us that God is asleep and the devil is wide awake and ruling everything. Human reason concludes that neither God nor people are in control of the world, but that everything on earth happens by chance. Human wisdom can't comprehend the infinite, heavenly truth that God is in charge and allows many more things in this world to succeed than fail. God's kindness is more widespread than the devil's cruelty. But human reason makes us uncertain because we experience so much disorder and injustice. We feel uncertain because we don't see by the same light as the angels do. We can't understand how right and wrong, life and death, light and darkness all harmonize.

HOLD ON TO CHRIST

God loved the world this way: He gave his only Son
so that everyone who believes in him will not die
but will have eternal life.

JOHN 3:16

❖

N THIS PASSAGE, Jesus tells us how he destroyed death and how we will survive it. Jesus is the antidote for death. Nevertheless, death and the law condemned Jesus so that he had to die and be buried. Yet Jesus rose again from the dead.

But how do we approach our Redeemer and Savior? Do we approach him with personal sacrifice and religious rules? No! Just hold on to the Son in faith. He has overcome death and stabbed the devil's stomach. Although he was crucified under Annas and Caiaphas, Jesus will rule and reign. So we must remain in him. Then, you will be able to tear right through death and the devil, for the passage says: "Everyone who believes in him will not die but will have eternal life." Accept it as true. Accept this wonderful truth that God loved the world and say, "I believe in the Son of God, who was also the son of Mary, who was nailed to the cross and lifted up." Then, you will experience the new birth. Death and sin will no longer condemn you. They will no longer bring you harm, sorrow, or pain. Whoever believes in the Son will have eternal life.

Cling to Christ's neck, or hold on to his clothes. This means believing that Jesus became a man and suffered for you. Make the sign of the cross and say, "I am a Christian, and I will prevail." Death won't prevail. Death couldn't hold on to Christ. It "had no power to hold him" (Acts 2:24) because deity and humanity were united in one person, Jesus Christ. In the same way, we won't remain dead. We will destroy death if we remain in the faith and cling to the destroyer of death, Jesus Christ.

OPPOSING EVIL

But I tell you not to oppose an evil person. . . .
If someone wants to sue you in order to take
your shirt, let him have your coat too.

MATTHEW 5:39–40

❖

 ETTING INVOLVED IN SECULAR matters isn't a sin for Christians. Believers are simply carrying out the responsibilities that all citizens have—whether Christian or non-Christian. Yet, believers have to consciously avoid sin and do what Christ expects of them. In contrast, the people of the world don't do what Christ requires.

That's why when a Christian fights in a war, files a lawsuit, or imposes a punishment, he's functioning in his role as a soldier, lawyer, or judge. But within these roles, a Christian will want to keep his conscience clear and his motives pure. He doesn't want to hurt anyone. So he lives life simultaneously as a Christian and as a secular person. He lives as a Christian in all situations, enduring hardships in this world. He lives as a secular person obeying all national laws, community regulations, and domestic rules.

In summary, Christians don't live for visible things in this life. These things fall under the authority of secular government, which Christ doesn't intend to abolish. Outwardly and physically, Christ doesn't want us to evade governmental authority or expect us to abandon our civic duties. Instead, he wants us to submit to and make use of the organizational and regulatory powers of the government, which keep society intact. But inwardly and spiritually, we live under Christ's authority. His kingdom isn't concerned with governmental authority and doesn't interfere with it, but is willing to accept it. So as a Christian and as an individual, you shouldn't resist an evil person. On the other hand, as a citizen with responsibilities in society, you should oppose evil to the full extent of your authority.

OPEN TO CORRECTION

People who do what is wrong
hate the light and don't come to the light.
They don't want their actions to be exposed.

JOHN 3:20

❖

HE WORLD DOESN'T WANT to be punished. It wants to remain in darkness. It doesn't want to be told that what it believes is false. If you also don't want to be corrected, then you might as well leave the church and spend your time at the bar and brothel. But if you want to be saved—and remember that there's another life after this one—you must accept correction.

If you don't want to be saved, what's the use of me being concerned about it? If you aren't sure you believe in hell, the devil, death, eternal condemnation, and the wrath of God, then just ask your neighbor about it. Anyone can tell you that all of us will die.

In short, if the church and secular government are to exist, they must shed light on evil. The civil authorities must punish the obvious darkness of public vices and the offensive ways of people, while we preachers in the church must bring to light the subtle darkness of false teachers and false belief. We must confront those who teach and think that they have God's approval because of what they do.

If the church and government stopped admonishing people, the whole world would collapse in a heap. If you want to be saved and be a Christian, then stay open to correction. A preacher has to rebuke, or he should leave his position. The Christian who won't accept correction is only pretending to be a Christian.

THE GOOD OLD DAYS

Don't ask, "Why were things better in the old days than they are now?" It isn't wisdom that leads you to ask this!

ECCLESIASTES 7:10

❖

HEN PEOPLE ARE UNGRATEFUL to us, we often start complaining, "Things are worse now than they ever were." But we shouldn't talk like this. Elderly people tend to say, "When I was a child, everything was better." They are the "people who praise the days gone by," as one poet calls them. But the author of Ecclesiastes says that this isn't true. Things never really went that well. We only realize how bad things are now because as we grow older, the number of things that annoy us also increases.

A child doesn't pay much attention to news about someone deceiving or murdering someone else. He keeps on playing, running, and riding. He thinks it's the worst thing in the world when someone steals another's marbles. Only then does he become angry. But when he becomes an adult, he becomes sensitive to the troubles and disloyalty of people around him. He gets angry when a horse breaks a leg, or when the cattle don't fatten properly, and so on.

The world has always been filled with troubles, but we haven't always been aware of them all. When we were children, nothing bothered us. Our lives remained relatively calm. But the world has always been wicked. Therefore, make sure that you have a quiet and peaceful heart. Don't become upset when you see these evils. Though you can't change the world, make sure you are changed into a new person.

THE LIMITS OF GOVERNMENT

Honor everyone. Love your brothers and sisters in the faith.
Fear God. Honor the emperor.

1 PETER 2:17

❖

HE SECULAR GOVERNMENT doesn't extend any further than external and physical matters. God can tolerate secular government because it doesn't concern itself with sins, good works, or spiritual matters. Instead, it handles other matters, such as guarding cities, building bridges, collecting tolls and taxes, providing protection, defending the land and the people, and punishing criminals. So Christians should obey government officials as long as these officials don't command them to do something against their conscience. Christians obey without having to be forced because they're free in all matters.

If an emperor or prince were to ask me about my faith, I surely would tell him, not because of his governmental authority, but because I should confess my faith publicly. If, however, he ordered me to believe this or that, I would say, "Sir, take care of the secular government. You have no authority intruding on God's kingdom. I will not obey you. You cannot tolerate anyone intruding on your domain. If someone oversteps their boundary without your permission, you shoot him. Do you think that God should tolerate your desire to push him off his throne and seat yourself in his place?"

Peter calls the secular government merely a human institution. It has no power to interfere with the way God has arranged the world. It has no power to give orders about faith.

ETERNAL LIFE BEGINS NOW

I can guarantee this truth:
Every believer has eternal life.

JOHN 6:47

❖

NE COULD PREACH a hundred thousand years about these words and emphasize them again and again. Yes, one can't speak enough about it. Here, Christ explicitly promises eternal life to the believer. He doesn't say that if you believe in him you *will have* eternal life. Rather he says that as soon as you believe in him you *already have* eternal life. He doesn't speak of future gifts but of present ones. He is saying, "If you believe in me, you are saved. You already have eternal life."

This passage is the cornerstone of our justification. With it, we can settle the disputes we're having about how we receive God's approval. Good works don't lead us to heaven or help us in the sight of God. Only faith can do this. Of course, you should do good works and live a holy life in obedience to God. But these efforts won't help you earn salvation. You already have eternal life. If you don't receive it while here on earth, you'll never receive it after you leave. Eternal life must be attained and received in this body.

Yet how does a person acquire eternal life? God becomes your teacher, for he tells you about eternal life through those who preach his Word. He convinces you that you should accept his Word and believe in him. That is how it begins. Those same words that you hear and believe will lead you to none other than the person of Christ, born of the virgin Mary. God will take you nowhere else. If you believe in Christ and cling to him, you are redeemed from both physical and spiritual death. You already have eternal life.

Bought with a Price

You were bought for a price.
Don't become anyone's slaves.
1 CORINTHIANS 7:23

❖

 ERE PAUL FORBIDS US to become slaves. No doubt he says this as a general guideline against people who try to destroy the freedom and equality of belief and clamp down too tightly on consciences. For example, if someone teaches that a Christian man absolutely cannot marry a non-Christian woman and stay married to her, as some churches teach, then that person hinders the freedom taught here by Paul. That person actually steers people to be more obedient to him than to God's Word. Paul says that this is serving people. The people following this teacher think they are God's slaves and serving him when in fact they are serving human teaching and becoming slaves of others. This is also true of those who preached that Christians must be circumcised and nullified Christian freedom as a result.

So in every way, Paul is concerned about Christian freedom and guards it against the chains and prison of human rules. Paul verifies this when he says, "You were bought for a price." Paul means that Christ bought us with his own blood and set us free from all sins and laws, as it says in Galatians 5:1.

The freedom Christ purchased, however, isn't what the world means by freedom. It doesn't affect the roles people have with one another, such as a servant with a master or a wife with a husband. God doesn't want these roles to be changed. Instead, he wants them to be honored. He changes us inwardly and spiritually. Before God, no law binds us or holds us captive. We are truly free in all things. Before, we were caught in our sins, but now all of our sins are gone. So whatever outward roles or relationships still exist, they have nothing to do with sin or merit before God.

LISTEN TO CHRIST

*Blessed are your eyes because they see
and your ears because they hear.*

MATTHEW 13:16

❖

OME PEOPLE LISTEN to what Jesus says but don't believe that the Father is speaking. They don't believe that his words are the words of the Father. That's why God must draw them further along. When they hear the Word, God impresses it on their hearts. Then they're able to believe that they're hearing the Father's Word when they hear Christ speaking.

I plead with you to learn what it means for the Father to draw you. This means you must listen to the words from Christ's mouth. You must learn from him. You must not stray from his words.

So it's not reason that brings you to faith. Christ overthrows your own self-deceit and reason. He condemns people who reject his spoken Word and want to wait for something special to happen. They hope the Father will speak personally to them from heaven and give them the Spirit directly. They want to hear an audible voice from heaven, but it won't happen.

The only way to hear the Father speak is through the Son. You will hear the words of Christ, but these aren't enough to draw you. Your reason says that Christ is only a man, and his words are only the words of a man. But if you delight in reflecting on the Word—reading it, listening to it being preached, and loving it—soon you will come to the point where you say, "Truly, this is God's Word!" In this way, faith comes alongside reason.

GOD CAN FIX MISTAKES

The fear of the LORD is the beginning of wisdom. Good sense is shown by everyone who follows ₍God's guiding principles₎. His praise continues forever.

PSALM 111:10

❖

OU SHOULD BEWARE of two extremes. One is becoming arrogant about your wisdom and plans. The other is becoming depressed when things go wrong. God forgives and even blesses the mistakes of faithful people. In my ignorance, I often made the biggest mistakes and did the most foolish things when I was sincerely trying to help people and give them good advice. When I made these mistakes, I prayed fervently to God, asking him to forgive me and correct what I had done. Important and faithful leaders often cause great harm through their advice and actions. If God didn't have mercy on them and didn't straighten everything out, the world would be in a terrible mess.

All of us make mistakes. We consider ourselves wise and knowledgeable. Yet, in our sincere desire to help, we can end up causing a lot of damage. If God in his wisdom and compassion didn't correct our mistakes, we would make a mess out of our lives. We are like the farmer whose horses had trouble moving a heavy load. Thinking the wheels on the wagon were too wide, he sharpened them. This only made the load sink so deep into the mud that the wagon couldn't be moved at all.

Does that mean that people should do nothing and just run away from all their responsibilities? Not at all. You should faithfully do the job that God has given you to do. Don't rely on your own wisdom and strength, and don't pretend to be so smart and important that everything has to be done your way. Don't be ashamed to get on your knees and pray, "Dear God, you gave me this job. Please teach and guide me. Give me the knowledge, wisdom, and strength to perform my duties tirelessly and well."

Worrying about Daily Necessities

So I tell you to stop worrying about what you will eat,
drink, or wear. Isn't life more than food
and the body more than clothes?

MATTHEW 6:25

❖

N THIS PASSAGE, Jesus delivers a scathing sermon against worry. Worry shows lack of
trust, and therefore it's opposed to the
gospel of Christ. Worry is a problem for the world at
large as well as for Christians.

The devil hates anyone who wants to live a Christian
life and declares that Christ is Lord. The devil, the ruler of
this world, keeps opposing and antagonizing believers.
He can't attack them through God's Word and faith, so he
attacks them with what is under his authority and control. Believers are trapped in their bodies, which are still
in Satan's kingdom. So, he harasses and imprisons them,
deprives them of food and drink, and constantly threat-
ens to take away all their wealth and possessions. As this
is happening, believers naturally try to find ways to
escape these calamities and avoid losing their property.

The people of this world, however, praise those who
strive for wealth and possessions. Instead of seeing striving for wealth as a failure to trust God, they consider it a
commendable virtue and a praiseworthy character trait.

Take note of what it means to serve wealth. It's undue
concern about the needs and necessities of life, such as
worrying about what you will eat and what you will
wear. In short, it means thinking only about this life and
accumulating a large fortune under the mistaken notion
that this life will go on forever. We don't have to
consider daily necessities, such as eating, drinking, and
buying clothes, as serving and worshiping wealth.
Purchasing and storing food is essential for life. The sin,
however, is being concerned about them and setting our
heart on them as a source of comfort and security.

EVIL DESIRES WITHIN US

Dear friends, since you are foreigners and temporary residents ⌊in the world⌋ , I'm encouraging you to keep away from the desires of your corrupt nature. These desires constantly attack you.

1 PETER 2:11

❖

ETER POINTS OUT HERE that no believer is completely perfect and pure. Some think this passage only refers to sinners, as if believers don't have any evil desires. But study Scripture carefully and take note: On one hand, the prophets sometimes speak of believers as if they were pure in every respect. On the other hand, they also speak of them as still having evil desires and struggling against sin. Some people cannot get comfortable with both truths. So look at Christians as having two parts—the inner being, which is faith, and the outer being, which is the corrupt nature. If you look at a Christian only according to faith, he appears pure and totally clean, for the Word of God finds nothing impure in him. When faith enters a person's heart and his heart accepts it, the Word makes it completely clean. Therefore, all things are perfect in faith, and we are kings, priests, and God's people. But because faith lives in us and we still live on earth, we at times feel evil inclinations, such as impatience, fear of death, and so on. These are still shortcomings of the old man, for faith doesn't yet have full power over our corrupt nature.

In Luke 10:30–37, a man was traveling from Jerusalem to Jericho and fell among robbers who beat him and left him lying half dead. Later, a Samaritan bound his wounds, took him, and had him cared for. Because this man was being taken care of, he was no longer deathly ill and was sure to live. He had life, but he didn't have complete health. In the same way, we have Christ and we are certain of eternal life, but we don't yet enjoy total health. Some of our evil desires still remain with us.

GOD IS GOOD

Give thanks to the LORD because he is good,
because his mercy endures forever.

PSALM 118:1

❖

OU SHOULDN'T READ the words *good* and *mercy* in a dispassionate way. Don't skim over these words. Don't say them too quickly or irreverently in church. Instead, remember that these are vibrant, relevant, and meaningful words that emphasize the goodness of God.

God is good—much better than humans. God, from the very bottom of his heart, is inclined to help people and continually do what is good. He doesn't like to get angry or punish people. He only does so when it's necessary—when he's forced into it by a person's wickedness and stubborn refusal to change. People could never be as patient as God is. They would punish a hundred thousand times sooner and more severely than God does.

God proves beyond a shadow of a doubt that he is good and merciful. His daily and continual goodness shows this in rich and powerful ways. This psalm says, "his mercy endures forever." In other words, God continually does what is best for us. He provides for our bodies and souls and protects us day and night. He continues to preserve our lives. He lets the sun and moon shine for us and allows the sky, fire, air, and water to serve us. The Lord causes the earth to give us everything we need—grain, food, cattle feed, wood, and the resources for making wine and clothes. He gives us gold and silver, homes and families, wives and children, animals, birds, and fish. Who can count all the Lord's blessings?

STRENGTH IN WEAKNESS

When the festival was half over,
Jesus went to the temple courtyard
and began to teach.

JOHN 7:14

❖

ESUS TRAVELED TO THE FESTIVAL secretly. This made his opponents proud. But Jesus was obedient to God and wasn't afraid of their defiance. He didn't merely go to Jerusalem, he went to the middle of the temple. This was the place where his worst enemies, the priests and Pharisees, had great power and ruled. Setting aside all fear, Christ took them on at their own game. He didn't ask if it was okay with them if he could preach. He ignored their religious authority and civil status and didn't ask for permission. Instead, he entered the temple with enthusiasm and spiritual power and began to teach. Christ didn't ask, "Mr. Annas, Mr. Caiaphas, do you mind if I preach?" Instead, he took over the priestly ministry for himself. He was very brave to walk up right before their eyes. Earlier, they had challenged him and called him afraid and timid. Now they had to stand there and listen to him preach.

John describes this event for our comfort. No one should become worried when God allows himself to appear as weak, while the world boasts and struts around. The same is true for all Christians, especially preachers. They are often weak and timid, while their powerful adversaries stomp their feet and threaten. This is nothing new. We have to get used to it. It doesn't only happen to us. It happened to all the prophets and apostles. They appeared weak compared to their oppressors. Yet it was in their weakness that they were the strongest.

PRETENDING TO BE SORRY

God came to Laban the Aramean in a dream at night and said to him, "Be careful not to say anything at all to Jacob."

GENESIS 31:24

❖

ABAN WAS WARNED in his dream not to treat Jacob harshly. But he continued to chase Jacob anyway. He was told not to harm Jacob, but he was so angry that he still threatened to hurt him. Laban didn't want to be called a failure. He didn't want people to think that his plans went wrong and that he had to return without doing what he intended to do. He felt he would be disgraced if he didn't carry out all the furious threats he had made in front of everyone.

Laban is a good example of a hypocrite pretending to repent. Unbelievers often pretend to be truly sorry and say they're going to change the way they think and act, but inside they know it's a lie. When David admitted that he had sinned (2 Samuel 12:13), it was entirely different from the time when Saul admitted that he had sinned (1 Samuel 15:24). They used the same words, the same tone of voice, and showed the same feeling of remorse, but the motivation was quite different.

When unbelievers say they're sorry for their sins, their sorrow is really expressing disappointment that they will no longer be able to do what they want. They don't really want to change their behavior. When thieves express sorrow, they mean they're sorry they can't steal anymore. Laban is portrayed in this same way. Deep down, he didn't really repent. His sorrow was only an outward show. Someone who is truly repentant isn't afraid of anything except God's anger and displeasure. He isn't concerned about being humiliated and disgraced in front of other people as long as he knows that God is on his side.

FAITH BRINGS FREEDOM

Yet, we know that people don't receive God's approval
because of their own efforts to live according to a set of
standards, but only by believing in Jesus Christ.

GALATIANS 2:16

❖

ON'T MAKE THE MISTAKE of thinking that Christians are people who never sin or feel sinful. Rather, because of their faith in Christ, God simply doesn't attribute their sin to them. This teaching is comforting to those who have terrified consciences. For good reason, we often try to impress on people that sins are forgiven and that righteousness is attributed to believers for the sake of Christ. In the same way, Christians shouldn't have anything to do with the law and sin, especially in times of temptation.

To the extent we are Christians, we stand above the law and sin. Christ is the Lord of the law. He is present and locked in our hearts, just as a precious stone is firmly mounted in a ring. When the law accuses us and sin terrifies us, all we need to do is look to Christ. When we have taken hold of him in faith, we have the victor over the law, sin, death, and the devil with us. Because Christ rules over all of these, we won't be harmed.

That's why a Christian, correctly defined, is free from all laws and subject to no one, either inwardly or outwardly. But notice that I said, "to the extent we are Christians," not just to the extent we are human and have a conscience. We are free to the extent we have a conscience that is transformed and made rich through faith. This faith is a great and immeasurable treasure, as Paul says, a "gift that words cannot describe" (2 Corinthians 9:15), a gift that cannot be raised high enough or praised enough. It makes us children and heirs of God.

Jesus Is the Light

John came to declare the truth about the light so that every-
one would become believers through his message. John was
not the light, but he came to declare the truth about the light.

JOHN 1:7–8

❖

Y OPPONENTS ACCUSE ME of teaching that God
alone should be respected and revered. They
claim that I treat the saints as though they
had never done anything good or useful in their lives.
They ask, "Wouldn't you at least say that John the
Baptizer was worth something?"

I haven't snubbed John. I honor and respect him.
However, John is a servant of the Lord and is not the
Lord himself. John points to the true light and leads people to it, but he is not the light. He certainly had a more
important role than the prophets did. John didn't
prophesy, as others did, that the Lord would come one
of these days. Instead, he pointed with his finger at the
Lord who was standing right there and said, "Look, there
he is!" That's why I greatly respect John. I am thankful
that God gave us such a faithful prophet, whose mouth
spoke about the true light and whose finger pointed out
the Lamb of God. Yet, I won't depend on John to save
me. I can't rely on his holiness, ascetic life, and good
works. John admitted that he wasn't the Messiah when
he said, "I am not the Messiah" (John 3:28). But regarding Christ, he said, "He must increase in importance,
while I must decrease in importance" (John 3:30).

Christ said that John was the greatest of all people
ever born (Matthew 11:11) and that he was far more than
a prophet (Matthew 11:9). Yet, John was not the light.
So, if John's holiness, ascetic life, strange clothes and
food, and refusal to drink wine can't help you obtain
eternal life and salvation, then any saint who is less sig-
nificant than John will be able to do even less for you.

Praying in Times of Trouble

*Hezekiah took the letter from the messengers,
read it, and went to the Lord's temple. He spread it
out in front of the Lord and prayed to the Lord.*

ISAIAH 37:14–15

❖

 HIS CHAPTER OF ISAIAH contains an interesting story about King Hezekiah. The Assyrians were attacking Jerusalem with a large army and beginning to overpower it. The situation looked hopeless. King Sennacherib ridiculed Hezekiah mercilessly. Sennacherib made fun of Hezekiah's misfortune by writing him a letter filled with insults about God in order to make the devout king lose all hope. Instead of losing hope, Hezekiah went into the temple, spread out the letter in front of God, bowed down with his face touching the ground, and prayed a heartfelt prayer.

Learning to pray when there's an emergency or when something is frightening us requires a lot of discipline. Instead of praying, we tend to torture ourselves with anxiety and worry. All we can think about is trying to get rid of the problem. The devil often tricks us when temptation or suffering first begins, whether dealing with spiritual or physical matters. He immediately barges in and makes us so upset about the problem that we become consumed by it. In this way, he tears us away from praying. He makes us so confused that we don't even think about praying. When we finally begin to pray, we have already tortured ourselves half to death. The devil knows what prayer can accomplish. That's why he creates so many obstacles and makes it so inconvenient for us that we never get around to prayer.

On the basis on this story in Isaiah, you should get into the habit of falling on your knees and spreading out your needs in front of God the moment you have an emergency or become frightened. Prayer is the very best medicine there is. It always works and never fails—if you would just use it!

WHATEVER WE ASK

I will do anything you ask ⌊the Father⌋ in my name so
that the Father will be given glory because of the Son.

JOHN 14:13

❖

 HAT DOES IT MEAN when Christ says, "I will do
anything you ask the Father in my name"? I
would think he should say, "What you ask
the Father in my name, he will do." But Christ is pointing to himself in this passage. These are peculiar words
coming from a human being. How can a mere man
make such lofty claims? With these simple words,
Christ clearly states that he is the true and almighty
God, equal with the Father. For whoever says, "What
you ask, I will do," is saying, "I am God, who can and
will give you everything." Why else should Christians
pray in Jesus' name?

Why do people call on saints as helpers in times of
need—Saint George for protection in war, Saint
Sebastian for protection from pestilence, and on others
for other circumstances—unless they believe that these
saints will answer their prayers? But Christ claims this
role for himself. In other words, he is saying, "I won't
command others to do whatever you ask for. I will do
it myself." So he is the one who can help in every situation with what we need. He is mightier than the devil,
sin, death, the world, and all creation.

No being—whether human or angelic—has ever had
or ever will have such power. Christ possesses all of
God's power and strength. Here, Christ sums up what
we can ask him for in prayer. He doesn't limit his
promise by adding, "that is, only if you ask for gold and
silver or for something that other people can give you."
Rather, he says that he will do "anything you ask."

God's Calling and Choosing

Therefore, brothers and sisters, use more effort to make God's calling and choosing of you secure. If you keep doing this, you will never fall away.

2 PETER 1:10

❖

ALTHOUGH THE CALLING and the choosing Peter talks about here is strong enough by itself, it doesn't feel strong and firm enough to you. This is because you're not yet certain that it's meant for you. So Peter wants to make this calling and choosing feel more firm with good works.

Peter considers the fruits of faith to be very important. These fruits are directed towards our neighbors for service to them. But the fruit doesn't remain outside of us. Faith is strengthened by the fruit so that we do more and more good works. So this power is very different from physical strength. We get tired and injure ourselves if we overuse our physical strength. But with spiritual power, the more we use it, the stronger it becomes. And if we don't exercise it, it diminishes.

We shouldn't let faith rest and lie quietly. It becomes more powerful with cultivation and practice until we become certain of our calling and choosing. We become certain that we cannot fail. In addition, this passage gives us a guideline for dealing with election. There are many frivolous spirits who don't know what strong faith feels like. They jump in, start at the top, and want to find out through their human reason whether God has chosen them. They do this so that they can feel certain of their position. Quickly back away from this approach because it's not the correct way. If you want to become certain, you must approach it the way Peter suggests here. If you choose a different way, you have already failed. You will see if you try it. But if you cultivate and practice your faith over time, you will become certain so that you will never fall away.

SHOWING CONTEMPT FOR THE WORLD

"Absolutely pointless!" says the spokesman.
"Absolutely pointless! Everything is pointless."

ECCLESIASTES 1:2

❖

HE BOOK OF ECCLESIASTES doesn't condemn what God has created, but rather people's evil tendencies and desires. We aren't satisfied with what God created and gave us to use. So we concern ourselves with accumulating more possessions and achieving more fame as if we were going to live on this earth forever. We become bored with what we currently have, then we strive for more things, and then strive for even more. Depriving ourselves of what we presently have because we're desperately concerned about acquiring more for the future is shameful and pointless.

It's these twisted tendencies and human striving that the author is condemning in this book, not the things themselves. Later, in Ecclesiastes 5:18, the author says that nothing is better for a person than being happy and making his life pleasant by eating, drinking, and finding joy in his work. The author would be contradicting himself if he condemned these same things in this passage. Instead, he's only condemning the misuse of these things, which comes from having a wrong attitude.

Some foolish people haven't understood this very well and have taught nonsensical ideas about hating the world and avoiding anything to do with it. But living alone and isolating yourself from others doesn't show the proper contempt for the world. Neither does throwing money away or refusing to touch it show the proper contempt for money. Those who live surrounded by what the world has to offer and yet don't become attached to these things are the ones who display the proper attitude.

A HIGHER AUTHORITY

*The chief priests and Pharisees asked them, "Why didn't
you bring Jesus?" The temple guards answered,
"No human has ever spoken like this man."*

JOHN 7:45-46

❖

HE WORDS OF THE TEMPLE guards were humble
yet powerful. The guards didn't arrogantly
say, "You scoundrels, you want to kill the
man who is from God." Instead, the guards remained
humble and deferred to the authority of the chief
priests and Pharisees. They didn't grab their swords or
resort to force. They remained servants who knew their
place. Their dispute was not about earthy matters. They
didn't raise themselves higher than they were. Their dispute concerned the spiritual realm. The heart of the
matter was that the faith and beliefs of the temple
guards were different than those of the Pharisees. They
refused to go along with the Pharisees.

We must distinguish between civil and spiritual
authority. A servant shouldn't run away from his master,
even though one believes differently from the other. God
doesn't want them separated. The servant shouldn't
resist or murmur against his master, but recognize his
authority. Even though the servant humbly serves his
master, he still has another Master—Christ, who is Lord
over the conscience and soul. Christ should also be
served, for the earthly master has no authority over the
servant's conscience. The servant can say to his master, "I
have put myself in your service with body, hand, and
foot, but not with my conscience. I don't get paid for
learning God's Word and believing in it. In spiritual
matters, I am free. There, I answer to someone else."

So if two people disagree about what to believe, they
should remain unified in external matters of the world,
even though they may be divided in matters of faith
and conscience.

PEOPLE WHO HAVE IT ALL

Esau took his wives, his sons, his daughters, all the members of his household, his possessions, all his cattle, and everything he had accumulated in Canaan and went to another land.

GENESIS 36:6

❖

HE ACCOUNT OF ESAU'S FAMILY is appropriately included in the history of Isaac and Jacob. In this passage, we see that unbelievers have honor and fame on earth. They are wealthy and successful, and they rule the world. They either look down on believers or oppress them, as Esau's descendants did. Because of their arrogance, they despised and oppressed Jacob and his descendants in later years.

On the other hand, Jacob had God's blessing. He was an important leader in the world and among God's people. Yet he had to endure many tragedies in his life. He had so many problems and so much misery that it seemed as if all spiritual blessings and even God's favor had been taken away from him. Yet, in the end, God worked out everything the way Mary described in her song, "He pulled strong rulers from their thrones. He honored humble people" (Luke 1:52). Christ described the end for the godless when he said, "But how horrible it will be for those who are rich. They have had their comfort. How horrible it will be for those who are well-fed. They will be hungry" (Luke 6:24–25). And Christ described the end for believers when he said: "Blessed are those who mourn. They will be comforted" (Matthew 5:4).

Unbelievers will be fortunate for awhile. But in the end, they will be destroyed. Believers, on the other hand, will have to suffer for awhile. But they will find protection, help, and comfort in God. He sustains sad people and relieves their misery. In the end, God will take his little flock away from their suffering and reward his people with eternal life and happiness.

NO LONGER CONDEMNED

*So those who are believers in Christ Jesus
can no longer be condemned.*

ROMANS 8:1

❖

CHRISTIAN IS TRULY HUMBLE when he genuinely feels his sin and recognizes that he is worthy of the wrath and judgment of God and eternal death. So in this life, a Christian will be humbled. At the same time, however, he possesses a pure and holy pride, which makes him turn to Christ. By turning to Christ, he can pull himself out from under this feeling of God's wrath and judgment. A Christian believes that any remaining sin is not counted against him. He also believes that he is loved by the Father. A Christian is loved not for his own sake but for the sake of Christ—the one whom God loves.

From this it becomes clear how faith justifies us without works. It becomes clear why we still need Christ's righteousness credited to us. The sin, which God thoroughly hates, remains in us. Because this sin still remains in us, Christ's righteousness must be credited to us. God gives us that righteousness for the sake of Christ—the one given to us, the one we grasp by faith.

Meanwhile on this earth, we still have sin and godless people. Even believers continue to sin. That's why Paul, in Romans 7:23, complains about how believers still have sin within them. Yet Romans 8:1 says: "Believers in Christ Jesus can no longer be condemned." Who can reconcile these diametrically opposed statements: that the sin in us is not sinful, that those worthy of condemnation will not be condemned, that the wicked will not be rejected, that those worthy of wrath and eternal death will not be punished? The only one who can reconcile these is the one Mediator between God and humans—Jesus Christ (1 Timothy 2:5). As Paul says, "Those who are believers in Christ Jesus can no longer be condemned."

THE KINDNESS AND TRUTH OF CHRIST

The Teachings were given through Moses, but kindness and truth came into existence through Jesus Christ.

JOHN 1:17

❖

E NEED TO LEARN HOW to clearly distinguish the laws in Moses' Teachings from the undeserved kindness in Christ. We must always keep the role of Christ separate from the role of Moses and make a clear distinction between the two. We need to know precisely what purpose each one fulfills so that we don't become confused. I was confused about this distinction myself for over thirty years. I just couldn't believe that Christ wanted to show his kindness to me.

The First Commandment teaches us that God wants us to sincerely trust him. Yet, we must also fear him above everything else. In other words, a Christian is like a child who has been punished but who still loves his father and is confident that his father still loves him. The good works required by the First Commandment are far better than wearing special clothes, fasting, praying, and all the other good works religious people have invented. So, the good works required by the First Commandment are holy and must be obeyed. But who can live up to them? Certainly, no one can completely obey the First Commandment. Everyone is a sinner, except for Christ.

Christ, however, comes to you and says, "I have shed my blood for you. My blood cries out on your behalf." Out of his undeserved kindness, he brings you the forgiveness of your sins at no cost to you whatsoever.

GOD'S PERFECT TIMING

Everything has its own time, and there is a
specific time for every activity under heaven.

ECCLESIASTES 3:1

❖

 O ONE CAN CHANGE THE FUTURE, no matter how hard he might try. How could someone who doesn't know what's coming change something that hasn't happened yet? God wants us to use what he has given to us without telling him when or how he should provide it. All of that is in God's hands. We shouldn't think everything is in our hands to use in whatever way we wish. After all, God must provide everything first.

"Everything has its own time" means that everything happens when God wants it to occur. If someone tries to plan and do everything himself without acknowledging that God is in control, then he will experience nothing but failure. Many people work hard at getting rich but don't succeed. Others acquire wealth without trying at all. That's because God provided the right time for some of them, but not for the others.

So people on earth strive for what they want to have. But all their striving only leads to frustration. They don't accomplish anything because they don't wait for the right time. Knowing this, we should leave everything up to God, use what we presently have, and avoid yearning for things we want in the future. If we don't follow this advice, our lives will be full of trouble and disappointment.

The Father Points to Christ

The Pharisees asked him, "Where is your father?"
Jesus replied, "You don't know me or my Father. If you
knew me, you would also know my Father."

JOHN 8:19

❖

 HEN THE PHARISEES ASKED, "Where is your father?" they were saying, "We don't hear the testimony of the Father. The miracles that you have performed, such as raising the dead, don't amount to anything." The Pharisees wanted Jesus to place the Father right before their eyes, so that they might feel and touch him as they would a wall. Otherwise, they wouldn't believe or accept what he was saying. But Christ didn't point to the Father's testimony so that they might see and touch the Father, but so that they would believe. The Father's testimony should have led them all to his Word. Philip also said to Christ, "Show us the Father" (John 14:8). But Christ doesn't show us the Father the way we might want him to. Rather, the Father shows us Christ, who says, "The Father points you to me, not the other way around. He is the one who shows you Christ. He testifies of me. You must do what he says, and listen to my words and testimony."

This is the main point of the argument: we should always keep Christ before our eyes. The devil continually tempts us to abandon Christ and seek the Father, saying to ourselves, "This or that will please him." Meanwhile, we ignore Christ—the one the Father sent— so that we might listen to him alone. We respond as the Pharisees did and reject Christ. We wonder, "Where is the Father?" That is the question the world asks.

This is the greatest temptation to your faith. You must devote yourself to the Word of Christ and train yourself to hold on to it so that you never lose sight of Jesus.

BECOMING LAZY

Prove that you're working hard so that you will remain confident until the end. Then, instead of being lazy, you will imitate those who are receiving the promises.

HEBREWS 6:11–12

❖

OD'S BLESSINGS DON'T COME to those who are sleepy and lazy. Solomon didn't mean to prohibit work when he said, "The LORD gives ₍food₎ to those he loves while they sleep" (Psalm 127:2). He wanted to say that we should have peaceful, rested consciences. Work shouldn't disturb the restful sleep God gives to those who have faith and confidence in him. We should have peace of mind and clear consciences. Christ says, "So don't ever worry about tomorrow. . . . Each day has enough trouble of its own" (Matthew 6:34). Don't create your own unhappiness. Sleep well, and don't ask, "What are we going to eat? . . . What are we going to drink?" (Matthew 6:31).

I don't mean people should be lazy loafers. They should work. God doesn't give his blessings to those who are lazy and lie around snoring. He wants our corrupt natures to be controlled and killed. As Paul says, "Those who belong to Christ Jesus have crucified their corrupt nature along with its passions and desires" (Galatians 5:24).

Although it's God's blessing that brings us what we need, not our work, God still wants us to do our duty and work diligently at the jobs we are called to do. That way we'll get our exercise so that we don't become lazy. As a non-Christian poet once said, "By nature all people would prefer not to work and would like to do what they want." We can't give in to loafing and laziness. Instead, we should work diligently and faithfully to do what is required of us. Even in times of hardship, exhausting work, and persecution, we should wait cheerfully for the Lord's blessing.

Hammered by the Law

What, then, is the purpose of the laws given to Moses?
They were added to identify what wrongdoing is.

GALATIANS 3:19

❖

LTHOUGH THE LAW DOESN'T justify us, it's still useful and necessary. First, in society, it holds the lawless people in check. Second, it shows each person that he is a sinner guilty of death and worthy of eternal wrath.

Why does the hammer of the law smash us to pieces and crush us? Of what use is this humiliation? It shows us that the way of grace stands open to us. So the law is a servant and prepares us for grace. For God is a God of the humble, the miserable, the troubled, the oppressed, the despairing, and those who have become totally nothing. He lifts the lowly, feeds the hungry, heals the blind, comforts the miserable and troubled, justifies the sinner, raises the dead, and saves the despairing and the condemned. For he is the Almighty Creator who makes everything from nothing. Most of all, he protects us from the most harmful corruption—presuming we're righteous. No one wants to be a sinner who is impure, miserable, and condemned. But everyone wants to be righteous and holy. So God uses this hammer of the law to break, crush, and annihilate this beast with its empty confidence, wisdom, righteousness, and power. As a result, it will learn through its misfortune that it is lost and condemned. When the conscience has been terrified in this way by the law, there's a place for the teaching of the gospel and of grace, which restores and comforts the conscience. This teaching says that Christ came into the world, not to "break off a damaged cattail," not even to "put out a smoking wick" (Isaiah 42:3), but "to deliver good news to humble people . . . to heal those who are brokenhearted, to announce that captives will be set free and prisoners will be released" (Isaiah 61:1).

THE SIN OF THE WORLD

John saw Jesus coming toward him the next day
and said, "Look! This is the Lamb of God
who takes away the sin of the world."

JOHN 1:29

❖

ROM THIS PASSAGE, we learn that all people have been plunged into sin by the devil and that only the Lamb can lead us out. Our unbelief isn't Jesus' fault. The guilt is ours. If we don't believe, then we're stuck in our own sins. In short, the Lamb of God has carried the sins of the world.

You should believe and confess this all of your life. You may wonder, "Yes, I know that Jesus carried the sins of Peter, Paul, and other saints. They were holy people. But who knows if Christ will carry my sins, too? If only I were as good as Peter or Paul." Can't you hear what John is saying? "This is the Lamb of God who takes away the sin of the world." You must admit that you, too, are a part of this world. You were born of a human mother and father—you aren't a cow or pig! It follows, then, that your sins are paid for, just as the sins of Peter and Paul are paid for. You are unable to pay for your own sins. They couldn't pay for their own sins either. There are no exceptions.

Therefore, don't listen to your own thoughts. Listen to God's Word. It promises forgiveness of sins to anyone who believes that this little Lamb carried the sins of the whole world. Did you hear that? The Lamb didn't miss any of it. He carried all the sins of the world from the beginning of time. Therefore, he carried your sin, too, and he offers his undeserved kindness to you.

SATAN SNATCHES THE WORD

Some people are like seeds that were planted along the road. Whenever they hear the word, Satan comes at once and takes away the word that was planted in them.

MARK 4:15

❖

HEN THE GOSPEL IS TAUGHT clearly, believers are confirmed in their faith, and they are able to guard themselves from idolatry. Satan is upset when the truth of the gospel is taught. He uses various methods to distort the Word and keep people from hearing it. In the early church, a number of heresies appeared. One claimed that Christ isn't the Son of God. Another claimed that he isn't Mary's son. In Basil's time, some denied that the Holy Spirit is God.

We have examples of Satan snatching away God's Word in our own day. When I and my followers began to preach the pure message of the gospel, many people arose who were against God's Word and his work in the world. Of course, none of the other temptations lessened. Satan keeps on tempting people to commit sexual sins and other terrible crimes because he doesn't want people to believe in what God says and does. But the church and God's people should regard Satan's attacks on God's Word and work as especially dangerous.

This is how Satan deceived Adam and Eve. They lost their trust in God and no longer believed what he said. Instead, they believed Satan's lies. When Satan deprives people of their trust in God, it's not surprising that they become proud and despise God and other people. Eventually, they will turn to adultery, murder, and so on. Letting go of God's Word is the root of all temptations. It results in the destruction and violation of all God's commandments. Unbelief is the source of every sin. If Satan is able to tamper with God's Word or snatch it out of people's hearts, he will achieve his goal—people will no longer believe in God.

STUCK IN THE MUD

Therefore, God's choice does not depend on a person's desire or effort, but on God's mercy.

ROMANS 9:16

❖

VEN WITH EXTREME EFFORT, learning to depend on God's mercy is difficult—especially for us who have been raised in the doctrine of works and have been told to look to the law and our own efforts. Moreover, our nature leans towards doing works. We are so rooted in our habits, and our hearts are so used to it that we can't stop thinking this way: "If I have lived a holy life and have done great and many works, then God will be merciful to me." So we struggle both against our nature and our ingrained habits. It's extraordinarily difficult to change our thinking and clearly distinguish between faith and love.

Even if we already have faith, the mud still sticks and clings to us. We keep wanting to brag: "I have preached so long, have lived so well, and have done so much. Surely God will take note of that." We want to bargain with God. We want him to look at our lives and change the judgment seat into the mercy seat because of what we have done. But nothing will come of this. You may be able to tell other people, "I have tried to do good to everyone. Where I have fallen short, I will try to make it up." But when you come before God, leave such bragging at home. Remember that you are appealing for grace, not justice. Let anyone try this. He will see how difficult and troublesome it is. A person who has been stuck in his own works his whole life finds it difficult to pull himself out of it and let himself be lifted by faith.

HELPING OTHERS IN NEED

Now, suppose a person has enough to live on and notices another believer in need. How can God's love be in that person if he doesn't bother to help the other believer?

1 JOHN 3:17

❖

F WE SHOULD BE WILLING to die for our fellow believers, shouldn't we be even more willing to give up our property and belongings? If we have possessions and don't share them, if we don't give food, drink, clothing, and so on—in other words, if we are greedy and stingy—then we aren't Christians.

Today, people are loudly complaining that those who have come to know Christ are the ones hoarding money. This is happening to such an extent that they fear God may unleash his wrath soon. Of course, God is merciful, but he isn't idle either. He doesn't let sinners go unpunished. He's merciful to the humble who fear him.

It's foolish to interpret this passage as only referring to people in extreme need. Besides, there are several degrees of love: you shouldn't offend an enemy, you should help out a fellow believer, you should support a member of your household. You know Christ's commandment about loving your enemies. But you owe even more to a believer who loves you in return. You should help out whoever doesn't have enough to live on. But what should you do if that person betrays you? You should help him again. You owe the most, however, to the ones related to you. "If anyone doesn't take care of his own relatives, especially his immediate family, he has denied the Christian faith and is worse than an unbeliever" (1 Timothy 5:8). It's a general rule that if a person who has property and belongings doesn't take the need of his neighbor to heart, then he has no love.

ENJOYING WHAT YOU HAVE

*It is better to look at what is in front of you than to go
looking for what you want. Even this is pointless.
₍It's like₎ trying to catch the wind.*

ECCLESIASTES 6:9

❖

NJOYING WHAT YOU currently have is better
than letting your heart wander. You should
make use of what is in front of you instead
of wandering around full of desires. This is what the
dog in Aesop's writings did when he chased after the
reflection in the water and lost the meat he had in his
mouth. You should use what God has placed before
you and be satisfied with it. You shouldn't try to satisfy
your desires because they will never be satisfied.
Instead, you should use whatever God has placed in
front of you. All of it is very good (Genesis 1:31).

A faithful person is pleased with what he currently
has and considers it all to be a gift from God. The unbeliever, however, acts differently. Everything he sees in
front of him is nothing but a nuisance. He doesn't use
these gifts or enjoy them. Rather, he allows his heart to
roam in discontent. If he has money, he doesn't find
pleasure in it or enjoy it. He always wants something
different. If he has a wife, he wants someone else. If he
acquires a kingdom, he isn't satisfied with just one.
Alexander the Great, for example, wanted another world
to conquer.

We should keep our eyes on what we already have in
front of us. We should delight in all of it. We should
enjoy it and give thanks to God for it. Therefore, God
doesn't want our hearts to wander to thoughts of other
things. This passage points out that we should make
use of what we currently have. Letting our hearts wander around filled with desires is pointless.

FREEDOM FROM SIN

*So if the Son sets you free,
you will be absolutely free.*

JOHN 8:36

❖

RUE FREEDOM IS BEING free from sin. How does this happen? It happens when we hear his Word—Christ was born of Mary, suffered, was crucified, died, was buried, and rose again from the dead on the third day. "Oh," we might say, "I know that message well. It is a very familiar sermon." But let's learn this lesson again from our children, for it tells us how we can be saved and be set free. "Yes," we might even say, "This teaching is too simple. That's why it won't work." But it's a virtue that children can pray these words and understand them so easily. We are old fools. The more educated and intelligent we become, the less we know and understand.

We must preach this message again and again so that all of us may be satisfied and filled with its teaching. My hunger, however, has not yet been satisfied. This teaching is like bread. No one ever grows tired of eating bread. We fill ourselves with all kinds of food, but we never have enough bread, unless we are ill and can't eat. A healthy person will never grow tired of bread. In the same way, Christians will never learn this completely during their lifetimes, whether they are saints or even Mary or John the Baptizer.

So we must sit with the children by the stove and learn the lesson again. There are some who say they have already been taught the message and think they know everything about it. But when troubles come, they desperately need someone to recite these words to them again. They end up needing a four-year-old child to show them how to believe.

MORE THAN WE CAN IMAGINE

*Then Pharaoh said to Joseph, "I now put
you in charge of Egypt." Then Pharaoh took off
his signet ring and put it on Joseph's finger.*

GENESIS 41:41–42

❖

AUL IS ABSOLUTELY CORRECT when he says that
God "can do infinitely more than we can ask
or imagine" (Ephesians 3:20). In contrast,
our prayers tend to be weak and insignificant. Joseph
didn't dare to ask for what he finally received. His heart
was like a damaged cattail and a smoking wick. His
groaning was like smoke that rises straight to heaven.
His heart was a real incense burner! The sweet aroma
that comes from a humble, groaning heart pleases God.
Though Joseph may have felt like he was dying, his
groaning didn't cause any real harm.

Hang on. God will remain faithful. Don't despair.
Cling to the truth the psalmist proclaims: "Wait with
hope for the LORD. Be strong, and let your heart be
courageous" (Psalm 27:14). The Lord won't extinguish
a smoking wick but instead will make it glow brightly.
He won't break the damaged cattail but instead will
strengthen it (Isaiah 42:3).

God wants to give us more than we ask for, not just fulfill our weak prayers. Joseph asked for nothing more than
to be rescued, released from prison, and returned to his
father. God in heaven let him pray that for a long time. In
effect, God was saying, "You don't realize what you're asking (Matthew 20:22). I will give you more than you can
ask or imagine (Ephesians 3:20). That's why you have to
wait a little longer. I want more of the smoke that rises
straight to heaven." But later, Joseph received what he
could never have imagined. He would never have had the
confidence or courage to ask for it. We must recognize that
God's wisdom, kindness, mercy, and power are most certainly with us, as they were with Joseph. However, God
usually doesn't give them to us in the way we ask for them.

A FLICKER OF FAITH

Faith causes us to wait eagerly for the
confidence that comes with God's approval.

GALATIANS 5:5

❖

 ERY FEW PEOPLE KNOW how weak and feeble faith and hope can be when they are suffering and struggling under a cross. At such times, faith and hope appear to be "a smoking wick" that a strong wind could easily blow out (Isaiah 42:3). But during these terrifying struggles, some continue to believe and hope, even when it seems there is nothing left to hope for (Romans 4:18). Trusting in the promises of Christ, they fight against the feelings of sin and God's wrath. Eventually, they will experience this little flicker of faith, at least this is how faith appears to their human reason because they can hardly sense it. They will watch this flicker of faith become a great fire that will fill the entire heavens and devour all terror and sin (2 Peter 3:10–12).

Truly faithful people have nothing more precious in the whole world than this teaching. They hold on to it tightly, and they know what the whole world doesn't. They know that sin, death, misfortune, and physical and spiritual evils work for the good of God's chosen ones. Likewise, they know that God is nearest to them when he seems to be furthest away. He is the most merciful and truly a Savior when he seems to be angry and punishing them. They know that they have eternal righteousness when they are feeling the terrors of sin and death the most. With hope, they look for eternal righteousness as their certain possession laid aside for them in heaven. They are lords over all things when they are the poorest, as Paul says, "We have nothing although we possess everything" (2 Corinthians 6:10). This is what Scripture calls receiving comfort through hope. But we can't learn this skill without going through many great trials.

Born to Do Good Works

*Jesus replied to Nicodemus, "I can guarantee
this truth: No one can see the kingdom of
God without being born from above."*

JOHN 3:3

❖

 CHILD WHO WILL BE BORN two years from now doesn't yet exist. The woman who will carry and give birth to the child is still a virgin, and the child hasn't even been conceived. That child can do nothing, for that child does not yet exist. Everyone can understand that. In the same way, all works, no matter how precious and good they might be, amount to nothing if a person does them before he has been spiritually born. These works lead only to sin and death. This is why Jesus said that Nicodemus and all the Pharisees were nothing if they didn't accept him, for they hadn't been born anew.

But what will become of those who do even less than Nicodemus? What will happen to all those religious people whose works are nothing compared to those of Nicodemus? None of those people will be able to do good works that please God because they haven't been born anew. We aren't condemning good works. People first have to be made ready to do good works by being born anew. Only then will they be capable of doing good works.

If you want to have a carpenter build a house, the carpenter must first exist. For what can be built if the carpenter hasn't been born yet? The same is true for good works. Doing good works doesn't make anyone good. First, ask yourself if you have been born anew. Then after that, ask yourself what works you should do. Many people, however, don't go about it this way. They mistakenly assume that their good works can save them. Just make sure that you are born anew. Because if you are not, your good works are worthless.

GOD'S APPROVAL OF US

The LORD approved of Abel and his offering,
but he didn't approve of Cain and his offering.
So Cain became very angry and was disappointed.

GENESIS 4:4–5

❖

OD'S APPROVAL ISN'T BASED on what a person does. Rather, he accepts what a person does because he already approves of the person. The person hasn't earned God's approval through the good that he does. Because God approved of Abel, he also accepted Abel's offering. God didn't approve of Cain, so he didn't accept his offering. So Abel had God's approval even before he had done anything.

The author of Hebrews writes, "Faith led Abel to offer God a better sacrifice than Cain's sacrifice. Through his faith Abel received God's approval, since God accepted his sacrifices" (Hebrews 11:4). Cain also brought an offering. In fact, he brought his offering before Abel brought his. But he brought his offering with an arrogant and overconfident attitude. He assumed that God would be pleased with his sacrifice for the simple reason that he was the firstborn. Because he lacked faith and didn't acknowledge his sinfulness, he felt no need to pray and didn't place his confidence in the mercy of God.

This is exactly how those who rely on their own efforts to earn God's approval still act today. They concentrate on the good that they do, which they hope will please God. They don't trust in God's mercy and his undeserved kindness. They aren't hoping that God will forgive their sins through Christ. This passage is definite proof that God cannot be influenced by outward appearances or impressed by the good that people do. He only looks at the faith of the individual. Yet God doesn't reject any acts of human kindness, no matter how insignificant or meaningless they seem to be. Indeed, the only thing God hates and condemns is unbelief.

PRAYING WITHOUT WORDS

Dear friends, use your most holy faith to grow.
Pray with the Holy Spirit's help.

JUDE 1:20

❖

LL TEACHERS OF SCRIPTURE conclude that the essence and nature of prayer is simply lifting up the heart to God. But if the essence and nature of prayer is the lifting up of the heart to God, it follows that everything else that doesn't lift the heart to God is not prayer. Therefore singing, talking, and whistling without this lifting up of your heart to God are as much like prayer as scarecrows in the garden are like people. The name and appearance might be there, but the essence is missing.

Jerome confirmed this truth about prayer when he wrote about an early church leader named Agathon. Agathon lived in the desert for thirty years and carried a stone in his mouth so that he would learn to stay quiet. But how did he pray? In his heart, undoubtedly. This is the kind of prayer God likes the best. In fact, this is the only kind of prayer God regards and wants. But hearing the words helps us think about what we're saying and helps us pray correctly. We should consider our spoken words to be like a trumpet, drum, organ, or other kind of sound that moves our heart and lifts it up to God.

You shouldn't attempt to pray without words, relying on your own heart, unless you are well-trained spiritually and skilled in removing stray thoughts from your mind. Otherwise, the devil will lead you astray and quickly destroy the prayer in your heart. So you should cling to the words and let them lift you up—let them lift you until your feathers grow and you're able to soar high without the help of words.

CHRIST WILL REIGN FOREVER

I will be his Father, and he will be my Son. . . .
I will place him in my royal house forever,
and his throne will be established forever.

1 CHRONICLES 17:13–14

❖

UMAN REASON OBJECTS to this passage. Considering itself ten times wiser than God, reason asks, "How can God give his eternal power to someone else? What would he be keeping for himself?" Now, it's true that God has said, "I will not give my glory to anyone else or the praise I deserve to idols" (Isaiah 42:8). It would be especially difficult for God to give his glory to a mere human being, who was born in time and not eternal. But Christians do acknowledge that Jesus was a human being. He was Mary's son and David's descendant. He was born, and he died.

Furthermore, people of other religions deduce that God can't have a son because he doesn't have a wife. Why do these people think they can contain the incomprehensible nature of God in the nutshell of their human reason? Shame on you, Satan, as well as all others who are students of blind, foolish, miserable, human reason. No one can fully understand these lofty matters but God alone. All we know about them is what the Holy Spirit has revealed to us through Scripture.

Christians can answer these objections correctly, clearly, and accurately because they have insight from the New Testament. God's Son has two natures in one inseparable person. He is one Christ, not two Christs. The Father gave Christ, his Son, eternal divinity—not in time, but from all eternity. The Father gave his divinity to Christ completely and fully, just as the Father himself possessed divinity from eternity. When he gave it to Christ, the Father didn't lose any divinity himself. Rather, he gave to the Son the same power, which he still retains in eternity. There are not two deities. Rather, God the Father and Christ are united in one deity.

PATHS IN LIFE

Jesus answered him, "I am the way, the truth, and the life.
No one goes to the Father except through me."

JOHN 14:6

❖

AM THE WAY. You should learn what this eloquent statement of Christ means. Don't
think of a path that you walk on with your
feet. Instead, think of one that you travel on by faith—
a faith that clings only to the Lord Christ.

There are various ways of walking and wandering
through life. First, there are many roads and footpaths
for physically walking from one place to another, as
cows and horses do. The Scripture teaches nothing
about these paths. But there are other kinds of paths in
this life. A second kind of path pertains to everyday life.
On this path, we lead a good and moral life before the
world and seek to preserve government, peace, honor,
and order. Living in this way brings possessions and
respect. Philosophers have given us good principles,
and rulers have issued various laws, for walking on this
path. But these two kinds of paths are still limited to
this life, which is passing away.

Over all of these ways is still another path about
which the Scripture and Christ speak of here. This third
path is the way to get from this life to the next. For this
journey, we need a much different way, a much different path. Here, Christ is saying, "When you have come
to me in faith, you are on the right way. This path is reli-
able and won't mislead you."

GOD'S TRAINING METHODS

Joseph said to his brothers, "I am Joseph!
Is my father still alive?" His brothers could not
answer him because they were afraid of him.

GENESIS 45:3

❖

THE EMOTIONAL CLIMAX to Joseph's story was this sudden revelation to his brothers. They had thought Joseph was a horrible, terrifying tyrant because he had treated them like strangers and scared them to death. Even though he had left them many clues, they couldn't imagine any kindness hidden under his hostile appearance. But then he came straight to the point. Without using an interpreter, he said, "I am Joseph!"

This story is a beautiful example of how God treats his faithful people. He sometimes punishes us and acts as if he weren't our God and Father. Sometimes he even appears to be a tyrant or a strict judge who wants to torture or even destroy us. But at the right time—when he is ready—he will say to us, "I am the Lord your God. Up to now, I treated you as if I wanted to reject you or send you to hell, but it was only an exercise I use to train my people. I would never have trained you this way if I didn't love you from the bottom of my heart."

In this Bible story, God shows us the training methods he uses with his people. This should comfort us. We must get used to the way God tests and instructs us. We should also humble ourselves so that the horrible evil called original sin may be restrained. God doesn't want to condemn or reject us, even when our suffering and punishment nearly destroys and kills us. Rather, he wants to sweep away the sin that clings to us. Only then will we understand what God means when he says, "The LORD kills, and he gives life. He makes ₗpeopleₗ go down to the grave, and he raises them up ₗagainₗ" (1 Samuel 2:6).

COMMANDED TO LOVE

All of Moses' Teachings are summarized in a single statement, "Love your neighbor as you love yourself."

GALATIANS 5:14

❖

EOPLE WHO THINK they have a good understanding of the command to love are badly mistaken. To be sure, they have this command written on their hearts. By nature, they know that they should do for other people what they want done for them (Matthew 7:12). That doesn't mean that they truly understand it, otherwise they would also show it in their actions and prefer love above other works. They wouldn't make such a big deal about their antics and superstitions, which amount to nothing. Some examples of such behavior include: walking around with a sad face and hanging head, being celibate, eating only bread and water, living in the desert, dressing shabbily, and so on. These are strange and superstitious works, which they choose for themselves and which God neither commands nor accepts. They consider these works so glorious and holy that they cast a dark shadow over love, which is the sun that shines over all works. The blindness of human reason is so limitless and incomprehensible that reason cannot come to a correct understanding of faith, much less make correct judgments about life and works.

Therefore, we must strongly resist our own opinions. In matters of salvation, we would by nature rather base our opinions on our hearts than on the Word of God. We should also strongly object to the mask and halo of self-chosen works. Instead, we must learn to value our calling and the responsibilities that go with it. Although these works may appear puny and contemptible, they are commanded by God. In contrast, we should despise the works which reason chooses to do apart from God's command no matter how glorious, meaningful, great, or holy they appear.

CHRIST IS THE CENTER

As Moses lifted up the snake ₍on a pole₎ in the desert,
so the Son of Man must be lifted up.

JOHN 3:14

❖

 HEN MOSES LIFTED UP the snake on a pole, many Israelites disapproved of God's command to look at it because it wasn't pleasant. Only believing Israelites—and no one else—understood and were healed because of their faith in the Word. Who else but our Lord could have used this story to point to Christ? I would have never been so bold to interpret this story the way Christ did. He explains it by pointing to himself and saying, "That is the bronze snake. But I am the Son of Man. The Israelites had to look at the snake with their eyes. But you must look at me with the eyes of faith. They were cured of a physical poison. But through me, you will be redeemed from an eternal poison. Looking at the snake means believing in me. Their bodies were healed. But I will give eternal life to those who believe in me." These are strange statements and an extraordinary teaching.

With these words, the Lord gives us the proper way to interpret the Old Testament. He helps us understand that the writers and prophets of the Old Testament point to Christ with their stories and illustrations. Christ shows us that he is the center point from which the entire circle is drawn. Everyone looks towards him. Whoever follows Christ belongs in that same circle. All the stories in Holy Scripture, if they are interpreted correctly, point towards Christ.

FEELING FORGOTTEN

*God remembered Noah and all the wild
and domestic animals with him in the ship.*

GENESIS 8:1

❖

EING TRAPPED INSIDE that floating container for such a long time was no joke and could hardly be described as fun. Noah and his family saw the torrential downpour and were tossed back and forth on the rising floodwaters. Noah felt that God had forgotten them. Moses makes a point of this when he wrote that God finally remembered Noah and his family. Through faith, Noah and his family were able to overcome their feelings of abandonment. But they had to struggle with their human natures. Because Noah had never experienced anything this serious in the past, he wondered if God would show compassion and remember him and his family. In the end, they conquered their anxieties. But it came with a tremendous struggle. In the same way, a young person who wants to live a pure and virtuous life must make a determined effort to control his sinful desires.

Our human nature is weak. It cannot tolerate the idea that God may have forgotten or abandoned us. We even want to brag and take the credit for ourselves when God remembers us, looks on us with kindness, and gives us success. Is it any wonder that we become hopeless when we feel like God has abandoned us and everything seems to be going wrong?

Don't forget that this story gives us a model of faith, patience, and perseverance. It teaches us that we must believe and trust God. It also makes us aware of our need for patience. Yet patience is unnecessary if we have no personal struggles and doubts. Even Christ calls us to persevere in difficult situations when he says in the New Testament, "But the person who endures to the end will be saved" (Matthew 24:13).

LET YOUR KINGDOM COME

Let your kingdom come.
Let your will be done
on earth as it is done in heaven.

MATTHEW 6:10

❖

E SHOULDN'T PRAY, "Dear Father, let us come into your kingdom," as though it's a place to which we travel. Instead we pray, "Let your kingdom come." For if we're to receive it at all, God's grace and kingdom with all its virtues must come to us. We will never be able to go to him. In the same way, Christ came to us—from heaven down to earth. We didn't go up to him from earth to heaven.

Another mistake of those who pray the Lord's Prayer is that they only think about their eternal happiness. They understand the kingdom of God to mean nothing but joy and pleasure in heaven. Thinking from an earthly, physical perspective and fearing hell, they only seek their own benefit and advantage in heaven. These people don't realize that God's kingdom is nothing but godliness, chastity, purity, gentleness, tenderness, and kindness. His kingdom is full of every virtue and grace. They don't know that God must have his way and that he alone lives and reigns in us. This should be our first and foremost desire. We are saved only when God reigns in us, and we become his kingdom.

We don't have to seek or ask for joy, happiness, or anything else that we may desire. Rather, all of this comes along with God's kingdom. So to help us avoid wanting what is false and selfish, Christ tells us to seek first God's kingdom itself, not the fruits of the kingdom. But those who seek the fruits of God's kingdom seek the back end of God's kingdom. They seek the last part first, and the first part they value only because of its ultimate benefits.

Live Humbly with Your God

You mortals, the LORD has told you what is good. This is what the LORD requires from you: to do what is right, to love mercy, and to live humbly with your God.

MICAH 6:8

❖

VEN THE MOST SPIRITUALLY minded people have a difficult time escaping the temptation to love themselves. As soon as they see that they are better than others in some way, they begin to love themselves and look down on others. The Scripture provides us with a frightening example of this in the story of Saul. He was well-thought-of and had no equal in Israel (1 Samuel 9:2). He was filled with the Spirit of the Lord. But he didn't do what Micah demanded in this passage. Therefore, he fell into terrible disgrace and was rejected by God.

The church fathers spoke about the temptation to love ourselves in the following way: "No matter where you throw the head of a thistle, it will stand straight up." Similar to a thistle, this wicked attitude easily takes root in the hearts of believers. It's difficult for believers to avoid self-love. As Augustine stated, this is the only evil that sticks to good works. That's why God allows his people to slip into sin, just as he allowed Peter and David to fall. Shocked by their fall into sin, believers humble themselves. They're fearful of thinking of themselves too highly, and they want to keep in mind how weak they still are. This is why David cried out, "My sin is always in front of me" (Psalm 51:3).

Believers humble themselves by recognizing and looking at their weaknesses and sin. They try to avoid feeling proud of their works or of the gifts of the Spirit they have received from God. This is what it means, "to live humbly with your God." We should be genuinely modest and humble, wanting to remain in the background. We should never look for honor and praise from the good works we do.

Our Helper

I will ask the Father, and he will give you
another helper who will be with you forever.

JOHN 14:16

❖

T'S CORRECT TO SAY that the Holy Spirit is our
helper because that's what he does and is
supposed to do. Right now, I don't want to
debate about his divine being or substance. Christ indicates here that the Spirit is a distinct person—the Holy
Spirit is neither the Father nor the Son. But in John 15,
we also see that the Spirit is God—the Holy Spirit is
one in essence with the Father and the Son. For now, it's
enough to learn that he is called a helper for us.

The name *helper* shows us how we should think of
the Holy Spirit. A helper is not a lawgiver or someone
like Moses, who frightens us with the devil, death, and
hell. No, a helper fills a troubled heart with joy towards
God. A helper encourages us to be happy that our sins
have been forgiven, death has been conquered, heaven
has been opened, and God is smiling upon us.

Whoever understands what it means for the Spirit to
be our helper will have already won the battle. That person will find nothing but pure comfort and joy in heav-
en and on earth. Because the Father is the one who
sends this helper, and because Christ is the one who
asks him to do so, this is certainly not done out of
anger. Instead, this flows from a fatherly, heartfelt love.
So Christians should remind themselves of this name
and title for the Holy Spirit. He is the helper, and we are
the troubled and timid ones whom he helps.

TRUSTING GOD IN TIMES OF NEED

Never test the LORD your God as you did at Massah.
DEUTERONOMY 6:16

❖

EUTERONOMY 6 TEACHES us to trust that God will take care of us in good and bad times. We shouldn't become overconfident in times of plenty, but we also need to patiently endure times of adversity. God will never leave us. He will be near us in our troubles. Unbelievers don't have this confidence in God because they put their trust in earthly things.

If what we need isn't available to us, we have to rely on God's promises. If we don't rely on God, we are testing him. This is what Moses was writing about when he said, "as you did at Massah." At Massah, Israel complained and asked, "Is the LORD with us or not?" (Exodus 17:7). Here, the people didn't trust God's promises because he didn't fulfill them in the time, place, or manner that they expected. Therefore, they gave up and stopped believing. When we try to dictate to God the time, place, and manner for him to act, we are testing him. At the same time, we're trying to see if he is really there. Doing that is putting limits on God and trying to make him do what we want. It's nothing less than trying to deprive God of his divinity. But we must realize that God is free—not subject to any limitations. He must dictate to us the place, manner, and time.

RESIST THE CORRUPT NATURE

Live your life as your spiritual nature directs you.
Then you will never follow through on
what your corrupt nature wants.

GALATIANS 5:16

❖

OMETIMES BELIEVERS FALL and gratify the desires of the corrupt nature. David fell terribly, committing adultery and causing the murder of many when he wanted Uriah to die in battle. He gave God's enemies opportunity to criticize the people of God, give the credit to idols, and blaspheme the God of Israel. Peter also fell dreadfully when he denied Christ. But as great as these sins were, they were not committed intentionally out of contempt for God, but out of weakness. In addition, when they were confronted, they did not stubbornly persist in their sins but repented. Paul commands that we should accept, instruct, and restore such people (Galatians 6:1). So those who sin and fall because of weakness will not be refused forgiveness if they stand up again and do not persist in their sin. Persisting in sin is disastrous. If they do not repent but stubbornly continue to gratify the desires of the corrupt nature, they show that their spirit is filled with dishonesty.

We will not be without sinful desires as long as we live in these bodies. Consequently, none of us will be free of temptation either. But each person is tempted in a different way according to individual differences. One person will be attacked emotionally, such as with depression, blasphemy, unbelief, or despair. Another will be attacked with coarser sins, such as sexual desire, anger, or hatred. But Paul demands that we live by the Spirit and resist the corrupt nature. Whoever obeys the corrupt nature and continues to gratify its desires should know that he does not belong to Christ. Even though the person may label himself with the name "Christian," he is only deceiving himself.

CHRIST CAME TO SAVE THE WORLD

God sent his Son into the world,
not to condemn the world,
but to save the world.

JOHN 3:17

❖

O ONE SHOULD RUN from Christ or from God the Father. God wants us to stay close to him in the same way that chicks gather under the wings of a hen. Just as children cling to their parents, we also should find refuge in Christ and the Heavenly Father.

The world is already judged because of original sin, the fall, and the laws of Moses, for it was led astray by the devil. The laws of Moses, our conscience, and our heart already judge us. Paul says that our own conscience accuses and condemns us (Romans 2:15). No additional judge is necessary. The world has always been full of judgment and death. It has never been worthy of love. That's why no other judge is needed. But the Son was sent to silence these thoughts.

In the past, no one saw the glory of this passage or took these words to heart: "God sent his Son into the world, not to condemn the world, but to save the world." Christ is not a judge. He is a mediator, helper, comforter, and a throne of mercy. He is our bishop, brother, and intercessor. He is both our gift and our helper in times of need. We have no reason to run away from him. But we still have wounded hearts that have not yet healed. We, by nature, tend to distrust God. Yet all of us should study this passage again, as a young child would. We must learn that Christ didn't come to judge the world.

FAITH CHANGES PEOPLE

*Faith led Abraham to live as a foreigner in the country
that God had promised him. He lived in tents, as did Isaac
and Jacob, who received the same promise from God.*

HEBREWS 11:9

❖

AITH CHANGES PEOPLE. It makes them see everything in a new light. Their ears hear, their
eyes see, and their hearts feel something
completely different from what everyone else perceives.

Faith is living and powerful. It's not a simple-minded
idea. It doesn't float around in the heart like a goose on
the water. Rather, it's like water that's been heated. After
heating, the water is different. It's still water, but it's
warm. The same thing happens when the Holy Spirit
gives us faith. Faith transforms the mind and attitudes.
It creates an entirely new person.

Faith is active, profound, and powerful. If a person
were to describe faith correctly, he would say it's a
process, not a result. In other words, faith changes the
heart and mind.

Reason tends to concentrate on what is present—the
here and now. Faith concerns itself with things that are
intangible and, contrary to reason, regards them as
actually being present. That is why faith isn't as common among people as the five senses are. Considering
the number of people in the world, there are relatively
few believers. Most people concern themselves with
what they can see, touch, and handle rather than listening to God's Word.

THE EVIL WITHIN US

Evil thoughts, sexual sins, stealing, murder, adultery, greed,
wickedness, cheating, shameless lust, envy, cursing,
arrogance, and foolishness come from within a person.

MARK 7:21–22

❖

 HETHER A PERSON BELIEVES it or not, no agony, pain, or burden could be worse than feeling all of the evil that lies within himself. The evil he doesn't feel is even greater and worse than the wickedness he does sense. For if a person were able to feel all of his evil, he would get a taste of what hell is like.

So when the all-powerful God disciplines us in his mercy, he only shows us our lesser evils. He knows that if he shows us all of our wickedness, we would be ruined and would die in an instant. According to the author of Hebrews, God shows us some of the evil within us as a part of fatherly instruction or discipline: "He severely disciplines everyone he accepts as his child" (Hebrews 12:6). By showing us our lesser evils and disciplining us, God wants to drive out the greater evils, so we will never have to see them. As Proverbs says, "Foolishness is firmly attached to a child's heart. Spanking will remove it far from him" (Proverbs 22:15).

Isn't it true that devout and faithful parents experience more suffering, grief, and distress when their children become thieves or are otherwise bad than if their children were wounded? Faithful parents would much rather severely discipline their children than allow them to become bad.

What prevents us from feeling all the evil within us? God has established matters so that people won't die by seeing the evil in their innermost self. So God is the one who hides our wickedness from us. He wants us to see it only through the eyes of faith.

FEAR OF SIN AND PUNISHMENT

Jonah answered them, "I'm a Hebrew. I worship the LORD, the God of heaven. He is the God who made the sea and the land." Then the men were terrified.

JONAH 1:9–10

❖

ROM THE STORY OF JONAH, we learn how to free ourselves from all anxiety and fear. Above all, we should confess our sin. Openly acknowledging sin decreases the immediate danger and lessens our anxiety. The heart must be helped first. Confessing sin makes it lighter and allows it to breathe. After this, it's easier to help the rest of the person. Only after our conscience has been released from its heavy load and is able to breathe freely can we find relief for other areas of distress.

When God's anger is poured out, we immediately become aware of our sin and become afraid. Foolish people cope with this situation in the wrong way. They ignore their sin and only try to get rid of their fear. That doesn't work, so they eventually fall into despair. This is the way human reason always tries to handle the problem in the absence of God's kindness and the Spirit. Wise people, however, try to ignore their fear and focus instead on their sin. They acknowledge their sin and try to get rid of it, even if it means that their fear will remain with them forever. They willingly accept their punishment, as Jonah did in this story.

But godless people do just the opposite. They pay attention to the *punishment* and are afraid of it, but they aren't concerned about their *sin*. If there were no punishment, they would never stop sinning. But this isn't what happens because punishment consistently follows sin. In contrast, godly people pay attention to their *sin* and are afraid of it. They aren't as concerned about the *punishment*. In fact, it's almost as if they would rather endure the punishment without sinning than commit the sin without facing any punishment.

EXTRAORDINARY FRUIT

I am the vine. You are the branches. Those who live in
me while I live in them will produce a lot of fruit.
But you can't produce anything without me.

JOHN 15:5

❖

ALSE CHRISTIANS CANNOT understand what
Jesus is saying in this passage. They wonder,
"What kind of Christians are these people?
They can't do anything more than eat and drink, work
in their homes, take care of their children, and push a
plow. We can do all that and better." False Christians
want to do something different and special—something above the everyday activities of an ordinary person. They want to join a convent, lie on the ground,
wear rough hair shirts, and pray day and night. They
believe these works are Christian fruit and produce a
holy life. Accordingly, they believe that raising children,
doing housework, and other ordinary chores aren't part
of a holy life. For false Christians look on external
appearances and don't consider the source of their
works—whether or not they grow out of the vine.

But in this passage, Christ says that the only works
that are good fruit are those accomplished by people
who live in him. What believers do and how they live
are considered good fruit—even if these works are more
menial than loading a wagon with manure and driving
it away. Those false believers can't understand this. They
see these works as ordinary, everyday tasks. But there is
a big difference between a believer's works and an
unbeliever's works—even if they do the exact same
thing. For an unbeliever's works don't spring from the
vine—Jesus Christ. That's why unbelievers cannot
please God. Their works are not Christian fruit. But
because a believer's works come from faith in Christ,
they are all genuine fruit.

THE SHEPHERD'S ROD AND STAFF

*Even though I walk through the dark valley of death,
because you are with me, I fear no harm.
Your rod and your staff give me courage.*

PSALM 23:4

❖

VEN THOUGH DAVID couldn't see or hear the Lord, David said, "You are with me." The Lord's presence can't be perceived by the five senses. Only faith enables us to know that he's there. Faith convinces us that the Lord is nearer to us than we are to ourselves. In what way is God near? He is near to us through his Word.

When David said, "Your rod and your staff give me courage," it's as if he wanted to say, "Nothing else on earth can help me through my worries and troubles. God's Word alone is my rod and staff. I will hang on to it and use it to pull myself up again. I will be certain that the Lord is with me and that he gives me courage in all anxieties and troubles. He defies the devil and the world and rescues me from my enemies.

With the words, "your rod and your staff," David was referring to the image of a shepherd with his sheep. He wanted to say, "A shepherd guides his sheep with his rod and staff and leads them to graze in the meadow and drink fresh water. He also uses his staff to protect them from all dangers. This is the way the Lord, the True Shepherd, leads and guides me with his staff. In other words, he leads me with his Word. Then, I can walk with him on the right path in firm faith and with a clear conscience. I can also protect myself from false doctrine and false piety. In addition, the Lord protects me from all spiritual and physical dangers and uses his staff to rescue me from all my enemies. God's Word so richly strengthens and comforts me that no spiritual or physical trial is too much to endure and overcome."

WATCH YOURSELF

If a person gets trapped by wrongdoing, those of you who are spiritual should help that person. . . . At the same time watch yourself so that you also are not tempted.

GALATIANS 6:1

❖

HIS PASSAGE GIVES US a very serious warning. It's meant to restrain the severity of those who don't help or console those who have fallen into sin. Augustine says, "There is no sin committed by a person which could not also be committed by someone else." We are always walking on a slippery path. It's very easy to fall off if we become proud or get out of line. "So, people who think they are standing firmly should be careful that they don't fall" (1 Corinthians 10:12).

David was a holy man, full of faith and of the Spirit of God. He received glorious promises from God and did great things for God. But he fell in such a shameful way. After successfully enduring many trials that God used to test him, and even though he was advanced in age, he was carried away by the passion of youth. If this could happen to such a man as David, how can we ever take for granted our own ability to remain steady? Through this example, God shows us our own weakness so that we will not exalt ourselves but stand in fear. God also shows us his judgment. He finds nothing more intolerable than pride, whether against him or against a brother or sister. So Paul does not uselessly say, "Watch yourself so that you also are not tempted."

Those who have faced temptations know how important this is. Some haven't, so they don't understand what Paul is saying, and they lack compassion for those who have fallen.

FOLLOWING FOR WRONG REASONS

Jesus replied to them, "I can guarantee this truth: You're not looking for me because you saw miracles. You are looking for me because you ate as much of those loaves as you wanted."

JOHN 6:26

❖

HRIST TELLS THE PEOPLE that they're not following him because of his teaching but because of their stomachs, which they hold dear. They were thinking to themselves, "Jesus is a great teacher for us! He'll give us freedom. We will all be full and satisfied, getting whatever we want." In this passage, the Lord reveals what type of followers the gospel will attract. Even today, the gospel attracts people who think it will fill their bellies, satisfy their desires, and help them here in this life.

This idea is so common today that I have almost become tired of preaching and teaching it. People, pretending to be sincere disciples, come to hear a sermon. But under this guise, they come only for personal gain. However, the gospel wasn't sent from heaven in order to allow people to fill their own bellies, take whatever they want, and do whatever they please. Christ didn't shed his blood for this purpose!

The gospel proclaims God's glory and teaches us how to praise the Lord. God wants us to praise him. He wants us to do what pleases him. If we make God's honor and kingdom our first priority, then not only will he give us life in this world and everything we need, he will give us eternal life as well.

LIVING WITH INGRATITUDE

[Abram] slept with Hagar, and she became pregnant.
When Hagar realized that she was pregnant, she began
to be disrespectful to Sarai, her owner.

GENESIS 16:4

❖

S A SLAVE, HAGAR OWNED nothing except the food and clothes that Sarai, out of kindness and generosity, had given her. Sarai was even the one who chose her to be the mother of Abram's child. Yet Hagar began to be disrespectful to Sarai, Abram's true wife. The Holy Spirit relates this story about the quarrel between Sarai and Hagar for our comfort. He wants us to understand what God's people had to go through in their lifetimes. The entire family was affected by the fact that Hagar treated Sarai with disrespect.

On the surface, this story seems to be trivial and insignificant. Nevertheless, the Holy Spirit considered it worthwhile to describe it in great detail. This was done so that believers would be comforted and learn the lesson that they should be patient as they wait to be delivered from similar problems.

Hagar owed everything she had, even life itself, to Sarai. Yet she was rude and disrespectful to the person who generously provided for her. So learn to do good to others, but be prepared to put up with ingratitude. Many situations in our lives don't turn out the way we expect. Our hopes for other people aren't always fulfilled. After all, human nature is corrupt, and people are unpredictable. When life suddenly starts going well, it's difficult for anyone to avoid the temptation of becoming rude and disrespectful to others.

Taking Time to Pray

Never stop praying. Whatever happens, give thanks,
because it is God's will in Christ Jesus that you do this.

1 THESSALONIANS 5:17–18

❖

T'S GOOD TO LET PRAYER be the first thing you
do in the morning and the last thing you do
at night. Be on guard against false, deceitful
thoughts that say, "Wait awhile, you can pray in an
hour. First, you must finish this or that." For with such
thoughts, you turn away from prayer towards the business at hand, which surrounds you and holds you back
so that you never get around to praying that day.

Of course, some tasks are as good as or better than
prayer, especially during an emergency. Nevertheless, we
should pray continually. Christ says to keep on asking,
searching, and knocking (Luke 11:9–11). And Paul says
that we should never stop praying (1 Thessalonians
5:17). Likewise, we should continually guard against sin
and wrongdoing, which can't happen if we don't fear
God and keep his commandments in mind at all times.
In Psalm 1 we read, "Blessed is the person who . . .
reflects on his teachings day and night" (Psalm 1:1–2).

We shouldn't neglect the habit of true prayer and get
caught up in necessary work—which usually isn't all
that necessary anyway. We can end up becoming lazy
about prayer, cold towards it, and tired of it, but the
devil doesn't get lazy around us.

RETURN TO GOD

The LORD was very angry with your ancestors. Tell the people,
"This is what the LORD of Armies says: Return to me,
declares the LORD of Armies, and I will return to you."

ZECHARIAH 1:2-3

❖

I N THIS PASSAGE, we see that Zechariah's message was primarily concerned with belief and unbelief. He pointed out that the greatest sin of the Israelites' ancestors was not trusting in God when they were undergoing trials. Rather, they looked to other people for help. In this way, they were rebellious and idolatrous. Zechariah wanted the people of Israel to understand that the words "return to me" should penetrate their hearts deeply.

A person "returns to God" when he trusts in and finds comfort in God at all times, especially in times of need. On the other hand, a person has turned away from God when he doesn't trust in God. When someone doesn't trust God, his good works and sacrifices won't be able to help him. This is what happened to Israel's ancestors.

In Zechariah's time, when the Israelites were trying to rebuild the temple, they needed to turn to the Lord of Armies because of all the trials and troubles they were facing. They had to cling to God and depend on him even if rebuilding the temple angered the emperor of Persia or the neighboring people. God spoke. He wanted to help, could help, and would help them so that Israel's enemies wouldn't overpower them again.

We, too, need to hear these warnings in the book of Zechariah. Let everyone return to Christ, cling to him, and not fall away. Let no one become scared or be led astray. God speaks. And God will do what he says.

SINS THAT LEAD TO DEATH

But if a person has doubts and still eats,
he is condemned because he didn't act in faith.
Anything that is not done in faith is sin.

ROMANS 14:23

❖

FTER COMING TO FAITH, no one should think that sin can be taken lightly. Sin is truly sin, whether it was committed before or after one comes to know Christ. God always hates sin. Every sin is a mortal sin—a sin that leads to death—as far as the act itself is concerned. But it's not a mortal sin for the believer. Christ the Reconciler atoned for sin by his death. For the unbeliever, not only are all his sins mortal ones, but even his good works are sins. As Paul says in Romans, "Anything that is not done in faith is sin" (Romans 14:23).

The philosophers make a fatal error when they classify sins according to the acts themselves rather than according to the person who commits the sin. A believer has the same sin and just as great a sin as an unbeliever. But the sin of the believer is forgiven and not credited to him. The sin of the unbeliever, however, is retained and counted against him. For the believer, the sinful act is a sin that can be easily forgiven. For the unbeliever, it's a mortal sin that leads to death. This is not because of the difference in the sin itself as if the believer's sin is less and the unbeliever's sin is greater. It is because of the difference in the person who committed it.

By faith, believers see that their sins are forgiven for the sake of Christ. Christ offered himself for their sin. So they remain righteous in spite of their sin, although they have sin and continue to sin. But unbelievers remain unrighteous. Although believers aren't free from sin, they know that their sin isn't credited to them because of their faith in Christ. This is the wisdom and the comfort of true believers.

FILTHY IN GOD'S SIGHT

The Messenger said . . . "Remove Joshua's filthy clothes."
Then he said to Joshua, "See, I have taken your sin away
from you, and I will dress you in fine clothing."
ZECHARIAH 3:4

❖

OSHUA, THE CHIEF PRIEST at this time, was
selected by God to lead the people. In these
verses and the ones that follow, God linked
his promises to Joshua's obedience. By doing this, God
guarded against Joshua becoming too proud as a result
of his receiving visions, comfort, and promises earlier.
Rather than assuming that God was bound by his
promises and had to fulfill them, Joshua needed to
remain humble and continue to live in the fear of God.

We who live on this earth are such poor people. We
become easily discouraged and fainthearted when God
punishes us and sends us problems. Then, God has
plenty of work to do to comfort and lift us up again.
After he comforts us and allows us to experience good
times, we become proud and overconfident. Then, he
has to threaten and frighten us. So, we are too weak and
fragile to endure what God allows to happen to us—
whether good or bad. No matter what he does for us,
he ends up having more work to do. We can't hold up
under the bad times, and we can't hold on during the
good times.

After giving Joshua great promises, God needed to
humble him. God couldn't allow Joshua to become
arrogant in the light of such wonderful promises.
Similarly, Saul and many other kings of Israel were
blinded by God's promises. They became too proud
and were destroyed as a result. Though their ancestors
were completely dependent upon God and his promises, they didn't want to obey him. Oh, if only we could
recognize how poor and filthy we are in God's sight!

GOD CHOSE YOU

You didn't choose me, but I chose you. I have appointed you to go, to produce fruit that will last, and to ask the Father in my name to give you whatever you ask for.

JOHN 15:16

❖

A FIERCE BATTLE HAS BEEN RAGING in this world since the very beginning. Cain wanted to choose God on his own terms. He wanted God to value his work and his offering instead of his brother's. The world has followed Cain's example from that day until now. The world always wants to turn this verse in John around and say, "I don't want to be chosen by God, I want to choose him first." But God cannot and will not tolerate this. He turns their words back around and says, "You cannot and should not choose me. I must choose you. It won't happen the way you imagine, but the way I want it to. I want to be your Lord and Master. I don't want to be mastered by you." That's why throughout Scripture God condemns and throws away this type of choosing that goes against what he commands.

Even Paul condemns this vice. He says, "Let no one who delights in ⌊false⌋ humility . . . tell you that you don't deserve a prize" (Colossians 2:18). Likewise, he says, "These things look like wisdom with their self-imposed worship, ⌊false⌋ humility, and harsh treatment of the body. But they have no value" (Colossians 2:23). With these words, he describes those who practice useless, self-chosen worship and justify it by saying, "I mean well and am doing it for God and to honor him. It will please him, and so he will be merciful to me." These people are twice as bad as God's enemies. God called the Israelites out of Egypt and gave them the Ten Commandments, telling them what they should and shouldn't do so that they wouldn't invent ways to serve him. In the same way, God wants to tell us what it means to serve him.

Praying for God's Mercy

Have pity on me, O God, in keeping with your mercy.
In keeping with your unlimited compassion,
wipe out my rebellious acts.

PSALM 51:1

❖

E NATURALLY THINK, "I'm frightened by the sight of God, so I can't look to heaven for help. I know that I'm a sinner and that God hates sin. How can I pray?" With these thoughts, an intense battle begins inside us. Because we know we are sinners, we may think we have to postpone praying until we feel worthy. Or we look for other people to assure us that we have done enough good works to have confidence in our own worthiness. Only then do we pray, "God have mercy on me." But we were born in sin. If we had to wait until we felt pure and free from all sin before we prayed, we would never pray.

We must shake off these kinds of unchristian thoughts. When surrounded by our own sinfulness—even while drowning in our sins—we should cry out to God, just as David did in this psalm. Then, we won't have to postpone our prayer. What purpose do the words, "Have pity on me, O God, in keeping with your mercy," serve if the only people who pray them are pure and don't need any mercy? No matter how sinful we feel, we must encourage ourselves to cry out to God, "Have mercy!"

I have learned from my own experience that praying is often the most difficult thing to do. I don't hold myself up as a master of prayer. In fact, I admit that I have often said these words coldly: "God, have mercy on me." I prayed that way because I was worried about my own unworthiness. Yet, ultimately, the Holy Spirit convinced me, "No matter how you feel, you must pray!" God wants you to pray, and he wants to hear your prayers—not because you are worthy, but because he is merciful.

CONSIDERING OTHERS

You were indeed called to be free, brothers and sisters. Don't turn this freedom into an excuse for your corrupt nature to express itself. Rather, serve each other through love.

GALATIANS 5:13

❖

ECAUSE THERE ARE TWO different types of people, two different offenses occur. On one side the weak are offended, on the other side the strong. Paul is trying to keep them both in the middle and avoid both offenses.

The weak are offended when something is done that they don't understand and can't distinguish from evil. Romans 14 deals with this situation at length. For example, when the weak saw that others were eating foods forbidden by the law as unclean, they did not dare eat these foods because they were inhibited by their consciences. Yet they could not disapprove of what the others did. Here, Paul became a Jew with the Jews, a weak person with the weak to serve them through love so that they would become strong in Christ.

On the other hand, the strong are offended when they become annoyed by the weak and grow impatient with their slowness and clumsiness. Without consideration for others, they overuse their freedom in Christ, resulting in weak people becoming offended. It would be better for them to keep all the laws before offending one person. This is what it means to live by the Spirit. What good does it do to use the Spirit of freedom against the Spirit of love?

But you may insist, "We are free to do this." Certainly. But you must put the weakness of your brother or sister ahead of your own freedom. It doesn't hurt you if you don't exercise your freedom. Yet it hurts them if they are offended by your freedom. Don't forget that the task of love is thinking of what's best for others. Rather than finding out how much freedom you can exercise, find out how much service you can give to your brother or sister.

COME TO CHRIST

Everyone whom the Father gives me will come to me.
I will never turn away anyone who comes to me.

JOHN 6:37

❖

F A SERVANT WERE OBEDIENT and had earned the approval of his master, it would be normal for his master to want him to stay. The master wouldn't be showing any special virtue by doing this. But if a master threw a good servant out of his house, that would be to the disgrace of the master, not the servant. On the other hand, if the servant was disobedient and yet the master kept him in the house, then that would be to the master's credit. So even if you fall and sin, Christ won't push you away. A mother would never want to get rid of a child because he was dirty, sick, or injured. Although a young child often misbehaves, no father would disinherit him or throw him out of the house for his bad behavior. The father would merely scold him, "If you want to be my child, then you better stop doing what's wrong. I will overlook it this time."

The Lord takes the same approach. He's saying, "I see that you don't believe. If anyone is going to have faith, I know that my Father must give it to him. If he gives you faith, then you will certainly be able to believe. Yet you want to be my master. You want me to be your student. That's not going to work. This shows that the Father hasn't called you. But others will come who will accept my message. These people may be weak and clumsy Christians. But if they only believe, I will never turn them away."

GOD'S COMMANDS ARE NECESSARY

The LORD made burning sulfur and fire rain out of heaven on Sodom and Gomorrah. He destroyed those cities, the whole plain, all who lived in the cities.

GENESIS 19:24–25

❖

THE STORY OF SODOM and Gomorrah shows God's fierce anger being poured out on sinful people. Reflecting and meditating on this story is an unsettling experience. That's why I am deeply moved whenever I read or speak about it. Even though I am often furious at wicked people who refuse to change their ways, the terrible suffering and agony that took place at Sodom upsets me. I also feel the mental anguish that Abraham suffered when he interceded with God. Though the wicked people of Sodom refused to change, Abraham sincerely hoped that disaster wouldn't fall on them.

Today, some people want to de-emphasize God's commands. They think that people should only be treated with love and tolerance and shouldn't be frightened by examples of God's anger. Paul says quite the opposite. In the letter to the Corinthians, he tells many stories about God's anger against sinners. Then he states, "These things have become examples for us so that we won't desire what is evil, as they did" (1 Corinthians 10:6).

Arrogant and stubborn people despise the Word of God and laugh at well-intentioned words of caution. They feel so good about themselves that whenever anyone tells them about the extent of God's mercy and undeserved kindness, it only leaves them worse off than they were before. This is what happens when people try to get rid of God's commands. We must guard against this false teaching. It's not enough for these people to bring destruction on themselves. They intend to drag us down with them. Like the people of Sodom, they don't realize that their sins will soon be punished.

HAVING A PURE HEART

Blessed are those whose thoughts are pure.
They will see God.

MATTHEW 5:8

❖

 OME DREAMERS CLAIM that in order to have a
pure heart people have to hide in a corner,
enter a monastery or convent, or seek the
solitude of the desert. They claim people shouldn't
think worldly thoughts or spend any time on secular
matters. Instead, all their thoughts should be about
heaven. These dreamers deceive both themselves and
others with their mistaken notions. They lead people
astray and do a lot of damage. They consider secular
leaders and institutions to be evil. Yet, these are the very
things that ensure a law-abiding and orderly society.
These leaders and institutions keep the world running
and are established by God himself.

Scripture talks about having pure thoughts and a
pure heart in a way that is consistent with being a
spouse, loving and caring for your family, and doing
everything a parent does. In fact, God insists that we
fulfill these responsibilities. Whatever God commands
can't be impure. In fact, it's this very purity that allows
us to see God.

When a judge carries out his responsibilities and
imposes a sentence, he isn't acting on his own. He is
carrying out God's laws and commands. If he's a
Christian, he is performing a good, pure, and holy
function. But a person in this position couldn't do anything if his heart wasn't pure. Even dirty and unpleasant work, such as shoveling manure or washing diapers,
is pure and holy work if it comes from a pure heart.

THE GENUINE GOSPEL

God has given us a new birth because of his great mercy.
We have been born into a new life that has a confidence
which is alive because Jesus Christ has come back to life.

1 PETER 1:3

❖

HE BOOK OF 1 PETER is a wonderful letter and a model for us. Peter begins by explaining who Christ is and what we have received through him. He says that God has given us a new birth to a living hope through Christ's resurrection. Likewise, the Father out of pure mercy has given us everything, apart from our merit. These are genuinely evangelical words that must be preached.

May God help us. How little of this message do we find in other books. Even among the best, such as those written by Jerome and Augustine, we find hardly anything. Therefore, we must preach about Jesus Christ, that he died and rose from the dead and why he died and was resurrected. We must preach so that the people will believe in him and through faith be saved.

This is what it means to preach the true gospel. Any preaching that is different than this is not the gospel, no matter who preaches it.

A Broken and Sorrowful Heart

The sacrifice pleasing to God is a broken spirit. O God,
you do not despise a broken and sorrowful heart.

PSALM 51:17

❖

AVID TALKS ABOUT "a broken and sorrowful heart." In other words, this is a sincerely humble heart that is almost dying out of despair. David is saying that God doesn't hate a broken and sorrowful heart, but rather accepts it with joy. The message we proclaim brings life and God's approval to us because it strengthens us and fights against sin and death. In fact, the gospel demonstrates its power when we are sinful and weak. It's a message of joy that can only be experienced when sorrow and distress are present.

But we want to have the message of life and joy without any sorrow or death. What fine theologians we think we are! We must learn that as Christians we have to live with death all around us, with regret and a trembling conscience—between the teeth of the devil and hell. In spite of all this, we must hang on to the message of God's kindness. Then in all circumstances, we can say, "Lord, you want only the best for me."

In this psalm, we read that God finds no sacrifice more pleasing than a broken heart. The tax collector exemplified this attitude when he said, "God, be merciful to me, a sinner!" (Luke 18:13). The tax collector offered the Lord the most desirable sacrifice, a sorrowful heart that trusts in God's mercy. This is a comforting way to think about God. God's true nature is to love people who are troubled, have mercy on those who are broken-hearted, forgive those who have fallen, and refresh those who are exhausted. This psalm calls us to trust in God's mercy and goodness alone. It encourages us to believe that God is on our side even when we feel abandoned and distressed.

Stay Where You Are

Everyone should live the life that the Lord gave him when God called him. This is the guideline I use in every church.

1 CORINTHIANS 7:17

❖

CHRISTIANS HAVE FREEDOM. Faith and the Christian life aren't restricted to any particular station or position in life. But they are above, in, and throughout all positions in life. Therefore, it's not necessary for you to accept or give up any position in life to receive salvation. Stay in whatever place the gospel finds you. You can remain there and be saved. It's not necessary for you to give up your marriage and run from your non-Christian spouse for the sake of faith or salvation. On the other hand, it's not necessary for you to become married for the sake of faith or salvation. If you are married, whether it be to a Christian or non-Christian, whether with a good or evil person, you are neither saved nor condemned because of that. If you are unmarried, you also are not saved or condemned because of being single. It is all free—free!

As a result, if you are a Christian and remain one, you will be saved, and if you remain a non-Christian, you will be condemned. "This is the guideline I use in every church" means "among all Christians to whom I preach. For I do not teach them to leave their position in life and stir up unrest, but to remain where they are and live in peace." So you see that Paul doesn't call any position in life a blessed one except this one: being a Christian. The others he frees up so that in and of themselves they neither save nor condemn us. But all positions in life—no matter how well kept—can be blessed through faith or cursed through lack of faith.

CLIP THE WINGS OF WISDOM

Jesus responded, "Stop criticizing me! People cannot come to me unless the Father who sent me brings them to me. I will bring these people back to life on the last day."

JOHN 6:43–44

❖

HEN JESUS SAID, "Stop criticizing me," he wanted to curb human wisdom or reason. We should also clip the wings of human reason when it comes to Christian doctrine. God's Word isn't the kind of teaching you can grasp with reason. It doesn't reach the human heart that way. The more educated and the more sharpened a person's reasoning ability, the less he understands. Christian teaching doesn't appeal to reason. That's why our reason complains about it. I don't want to take my salvation out of my own hands and throw away all my good works in order to achieve eternal life. I don't want to place my hands and set my feet on someone outside of myself, someone who was so silly and foolish as to let himself be crucified. How am I supposed to believe that Jesus is my Savior? Reason cannot grasp this. We must take every thought captive so that it's obedient to Christ (2 Corinthians 10:5).

Jesus is saying, "Stop complaining that I claim to be the bread of heaven. You want to understand this on your own. You want to be smarter than I am when you ask, 'Don't we know his mother and father?' But when I tell you how the Father has drawn you to me, it can't be understood by your reason. When you hear about how the Father draws you, reason draws you in a different direction. Whoever wants to understand these words must close his eyes, shut the gates of reason, and let himself become like a blind person." This is what God wants. Whoever refuses to be led by God, but wants instead to be led by reason, will be irritated by the message of Jesus and will continually complain about it.

Prayer Changes Us

Your Father knows what you need before you ask him.

MATTHEW 6:8

❖

 OU MIGHT WONDER, "Why does God insist that we pray to him and tell him our problems? Why doesn't he take care of us without our having to ask? He already knows what we need better than we do." God continually showers his gifts on the whole world every day. He gives people sunshine, rain, good harvests, money, healthy bodies, and so on. But no one asks God for these gifts or thanks him for them. If God already knows that we can't live without light or food for any length of time, then why does he want us to ask for these necessities?

Obviously, he doesn't command us to pray in order to inform him about our needs. God gives us his gifts freely and abundantly. He wants us to recognize that he is willing and able to give us even more. When we pray, we're not telling God anything he doesn't already know. Rather, we are the ones gaining knowledge and insight. Asking God to supply our needs keeps us from becoming like the unbelieving skeptics, who don't acknowledge God and don't thank him for his many gifts.

All of this teaches us to acknowledge God's generosity even more. Because we continue to search for him and keep on knocking at his door, he showers us with more and more blessings. Everything we have is a gift from God. When we pray, we should express our gratitude by saying, "Lord, I know that I can't create a single slice of my daily bread. You are the only one who can supply all of my needs. I have no way to protect myself from disasters. You know what I need ahead of time, so I'm convinced that you will take care of me."

MORE THAN COMMON SENSE

[Abraham] spoke to Ephron so that the people of that region could hear him. He said, ". . . I will pay you the price of the field. Take it from me so that I can bury my wife there."

GENESIS 23:13

❖

PHRON, A LANDOWNER in Hebron, tried to talk Abraham into accepting a piece of land as a gift, free of charge. Ephron was saying, "Something this trivial shouldn't come between us. You are a prince of God, and I am rich. Even if you paid me ten pounds of silver for the land, that money wouldn't matter to me." This was a great show of respect for Abraham, a prophet and teacher. But Abraham used good sense and refused the offer. He preferred to own the land and purchase it at a fair price.

Abraham could have said, "I know that you are generous, devout, and kind. Yet I've known people in other places who taught me a hard lesson about how unpredictable people can be. So I've learned to be cautious. In Egypt and Gerar, the people treated me with respect and dignity at first, but in the end, they threw me out. I helped the people of Sodom, but all they showed me was ingratitude and abuse. If I accept this field as a gift, then your descendants may forget your unselfish gift to me after you're gone. They may decide to take back the land by force, exhume Sarah's body, and take it away. We are foreigners in a strange country. To prevent something like that from happening, I prefer to purchase this piece of land. Then, your descendants will have no right to demand that the property be returned."

Even in purely secular matters, godly people should treat others with respect. As God's people live in the world, they should conduct their business carefully. Like Abraham, they should use common sense, be courteous, and show respect in their dealings with each other and with everyone else.

TRUSTING GOD FOR DAILY NEEDS

*So I tell you to stop worrying about what you will eat,
drink, or wear. Isn't life more than food
and the body more than clothes?*

MATTHEW 6:25

❖

W E CAN'T SEEM TO LET GO of our anxieties and worries as long as we live. Yet, God gives us everything we need hour by hour, without needing any assistance from us. So why do we keep on having foolish fears and anxieties about trivial little needs, as though God can't or won't supply us with food and shelter? We should hang our heads in shame when people point out this foolishness to us. Yet, foolish is the only way to describe those rich, well-fed people who are always worried about having a full pantry. They have plenty of food on hand to serve nourishing meals, but they never share a meal with anyone or invite dinner guests. They have empty beds but never ask anyone to spend the night.

Accordingly, Christ is plainly telling us what foolish people we are. It should be enough to make us want to spit on ourselves in utter disgust. Still, we continue to grope along in our blindness, even though it's obvious that we're incapable of providing for our basic needs without God. This alone should be enough to make us Christians and to keep this thought in mind: "Undoubtedly, I never held in my own hands even one fleeting moment of my life. If I must trust God for my very life and limb, why should I worry about how I'm going to find nourishment from day to day?" Not trusting God for your daily needs is like having a wealthy father who is willing to lavish thousands of dollars on you, yet not being able to trust him for money in an emergency.

SUFFERING FOR DOING GOOD

Who will harm you if you are devoted to doing what is good? But even if you suffer for doing what God approves, you are blessed. Don't be afraid of those who want to harm you.

1 PETER 3:13–14

❖

PETER DOESN'T WANT YOU to say that the person who harmed you was doing right. For there is a much different judgment between me and God and between me and you. For example, I can have anger, hatred, and evil desire in my heart and not hurt you. You remain unharmed and have nothing against me. But before God, I am guilty. If he punishes me, he does what is right, for I have certainly earned it. If he doesn't punish me, then he shows mercy to me. He is right either way. But it doesn't follow from this that the person persecuting me is also doing right. For I have not wronged him in the same way that I have wronged God.

In Ezekiel 29:19–20, God speaks about King Nebuchadnezzar. It's as if God were saying, "Don't you know that he has been my servant and has served me? Now I must give him a reward. I have not yet paid him. I will give him the land of Egypt as his reward." Nebuchadnezzar had no right to the land, but God had the right to punish others through him. In order that these evil scoundrels won't eat their bread free of charge, God has them serve him by persecuting his people. Human reason, then, steps in and thinks that people like this must be doing well. But God is only paying them in return for their work of punishing and persecuting devout Christians. But if you endure the punishment and bless God by saying, "You are right, Lord!" you will do well. Then God will cast those people into hell and punish them for doing wrong. But he will mercifully receive you and give you eternal salvation. So let God do what he will. He will certainly repay in the end.

CALL ON THE LORD

*During times of trouble I called on the LORD. The LORD
answered me ₍and₎ set me ₍free from all of them₎ .*

PSALM 118:5

❖

 OU MUST LEARN TO CALL on the Lord. Don't sit
all alone or lie on the couch, shaking your
head and letting your thoughts torture you.
Don't worry about how to get out of your situation or
brood about your terrible life, how miserable you feel,
and what a bad person you are. Instead, say, "Get a grip
on yourself, you lazy bum! Fall on your knees, and raise
your hands and eyes toward heaven. Read a psalm. Say
the Lord's Prayer, and tearfully tell God what you
need." This passage teaches us to call on him. Similarly,
David said, "I pour out my complaints in his presence
and tell him my troubles" (Psalm 142:2). God wants
you to tell him your troubles. He doesn't want you to
keep them to yourself. He doesn't want you to struggle
with them all alone and torture yourself. Doing this
will only multiply your troubles.

God knows you will be too weak to overcome your
troubles by yourself. He wants you to grow strong in
him. Then, he will be the one who receives the glory.
Out of difficult experiences emerge true Christians.
Without troubles, people talk a lot about faith and the
Spirit but don't really know what these things are or
what they're saying.

You must never doubt that God knows your troubles
and hears your prayers. You must not pray haphazardly
or pray as if you're shouting into the wind. This mocks
prayer and tests God. In this case, it would be better not
to pray at all. You must learn to appreciate the part of the
passage that says, "The LORD answered me ₍and₎ set me
₍free from all of them₎." The psalmist acknowledged that
the Lord heard him and released him from his troubles.

The Gospel from God

Jesus responded to them, "What I teach doesn't come from me but from the one who sent me."

JOHN 7:16

❖

CHRIST ANSWERED HIS adversaries carefully. He showed that he understood them and realized they were accusing and slandering him. They thought that his teaching came from the devil. So Jesus answered them, "What I teach doesn't come from me but from the one who sent me." Does that make sense? If Jesus' words were not his own, why did he preach, promote, and embrace them so strongly? Why did he refuse to accept the honor of his own words? Why didn't he say, "This is *my* teaching"?

Christians often say, "This is my sermon, my baptism, my Christ, my God." Or we might say, "my gospel." Yet none of these are ours, for we didn't create them. They didn't originate in us. They aren't our works. Yet, at the same time, they are ours because God gives them to us. In the same way, we might say, "my child, my husband, or my wife." Yet none of those people are truly ours, for we didn't create them. They are the work of another, and they are presented and given to us. We didn't pour them into a mold or carve them out of wood. They were given to us as gifts. Christ says the same about his teaching.

This is why I insist that this gospel is mine. It's different than the teaching of other preachers. This is my teaching—in other words, Luther's teaching. At the same time, I'm saying, "It's not my teaching. It's not my work, but God's gift." I didn't create it in my head. It didn't grow in my garden. I didn't give birth to it. Rather, it's God's gift. So both are true. The gospel is mine, yet it's not mine, because it's God's.

GOD RESCUES US FROM SATAN

The Messenger of the LORD camps around those
who fear him, and he rescues them.

PSALM 34:7

❖

HIS IS ONE OF THE MOST remarkable passages in the Psalms. We can claim it as our own. But you might say, "I don't see or feel God's angels around me. Actually, I feel like I am under the power of the devil and am being led to hell." My answer would be, "Don't let yourself think that way! If you had been handed over to the devil, he wouldn't let you live one hour without plunging you into a life of crime. As a matter of fact, he probably wouldn't even give you time to do anything wrong, but would kill you right away. You are still alive because of the protection of the holy angels. The time will come when you have to leave this earth and, with God's permission, you may be subjected to Satan's anger. But God, in his mercy and undeserved kindness, will strengthen you through his Word."

When you are handed over to Satan, it will only be for a very short time. This isn't to condemn you but to test you, to bring about salvation and endless blessings. Christ said, "A single grain of wheat doesn't produce anything unless it is planted in the ground and dies. If it dies, it will produce a lot of grain" (John 12:24). In the same way, Christ was handed over to murderers, but only for a short time and to bring about salvation. So when you feel Satan bothering and tempting you, pray and thank God that you won't fail but that you are only going through a trial in order to be purified. Jeremiah comforts us by saying, "I keep this one thing in mind: the LORD's mercy. We were not completely wiped out. His compassion is never limited" (Lamentations 3:21–22).

KEEP YOUR EYES ON CHRIST

I have been crucified with Christ.
I no longer live, but Christ lives in me.
GALATIANS 2:19–20

❖

HE RIGHTEOUSNESS PAUL is speaking about here is external and comes from Christ living in us. It's not internal, and it doesn't come from ourselves. So if we are concerned about Christian righteousness, we must completely set aside the self.

If I focus on myself, then I become concerned about works and become subject to the law—whether I intend to or not. Instead, Christ and my conscience must become one so that I see nothing else except the crucified and risen Christ. If I ignore Christ and only look at myself, then I am ruined. Soon I begin thinking, "Christ is in heaven, I am on earth. How can I come to him? I will try to live a holy life and do what the law requires so that I will find eternal life." If I consider myself—my condition and what I should be doing—then I will always lose sight of Christ. He alone is my righteousness and my life. If I lose him, no one else will be able to help me. Despair and condemnation will certainly follow.

Unfortunately, this happens all the time. When facing temptation or death, it's natural for us to ignore Christ and look at our own lives. If we aren't strengthened through faith during those times, we will perish. So during these struggles of conscience, we must learn to let go of ourselves. We must forget about the law and works. They only drive us to look at ourselves. Instead, we must turn our eyes directly toward the bronze snake, Christ, the one nailed to the cross (John 3:14). We must fix our gaze upon him.

BECOMING GOD'S CHILDREN

*He went to his own people, and his own people didn't
accept him. However, he gave the right to become God's
children to everyone who believed in him.*

JOHN 1:11–12

❖

O EVERYONE WHO BELIEVES in Christ, God offers
the privilege of becoming his children. Yet,
this greatest of all offers is despised,
ridiculed, and laughed at by the blind and condemned
people of this world. In addition, God's offer is abused
and even regarded as blasphemy. Although those who
confess his name and trust his words are children of
God, they're executed as though they were children of
the devil, blasphemers, and revolutionaries. The religious leaders did the same to Christ, God's only Son.
They accused him of stirring up trouble among the people, of keeping the people from paying taxes to the
emperor (Luke 23:2), and of claiming to be the Son of
God (John 19:7).

Sometimes the devil attacks devout Christians so
fiercely with his flaming arrows (Ephesians 6:16) that
they forget about the endless glory they have as God's
children. They begin thinking the opposite and wonder
if God has forgotten about them, abandoned them,
and thrown them so far away that he can't see them
anymore.

Our faith is still very weak and cold. If our faith were
as strong and steady as it should be, we would practically die from sheer joy. But we praise God because we
know that even those who have only a little faith are
also children of God. That's why Christ said, "Don't be
afraid, little flock" (Luke 12:32). So we always need to
pray with the apostles, "Give us more faith" (Luke 17:5),
and pray with the man in the book of Mark who cried
out, "I believe! Help my lack of faith" (Mark 9:24).

THE CROSS OF CHRIST

*It's unthinkable that I could ever brag about anything except
the cross of our Lord Jesus Christ. By his cross my relationship
to the world and its relationship to me have been crucified.*

GALATIANS 6:14

❖

HE CROSS OF CHRIST doesn't refer just to the
wood that Christ carried on his shoulders
and on which he was nailed. It also signifies
all the troubles of the faithful people whose suffering is
Christ's suffering. Paul talks about Christians enduring
these sufferings in 2 Corinthians 1:5–7. In Colossians
1:24, he says, "I am happy to suffer for you now. In my
body I am completing whatever remains of Christ's sufferings. I am doing this on behalf of his body, the
church." Therefore, the cross of Christ generally refers
to all the afflictions that the church suffers for the sake
of Christ.

Christ himself testifies to this in Acts 9:4 when he
says, "Saul! Saul! Why are you persecuting me?" Saul
didn't attack Christ. He persecuted his followers. But
whoever touches them touches the apple of his eye
(Zechariah 2:8). We know by experience that the head
is more sensitive than other parts of the body. For if a
toe or another tiny part of the body is injured, the head
recognizes the feeling, and the face shows it. The nose
wrinkles, the eyes squint, and so on. Similarly Christ,
our head, makes our afflictions his own and suffers
when we, his body, suffer.

It's helpful to remember this so that we don't despair
when our opponents persecute, excommunicate, and
kill us, or when heretics hate us with such deep hostility. We should remember Paul's example and pride ourselves in the cross. We have taken up this cross, not
because of our own sins, but for the sake of Christ.

WHY WE DON'T PRAY

*If your child asks for a fish, would you give him a
snake? . . . So how much more will your Father in heaven
give good things to those who ask him?*

MATTHEW 7:10-11

❖

UR OWN URGENT NEEDS should be enough to
make us pray. But as though that were not
enough, Jesus uses a beautiful illustration
from family life to coax us to pray. Even a problem
child wouldn't receive a snake instead of a fish from his
parents. With this illustration, Jesus is saying, "Your
human nature is corrupt. You aren't nearly as good as
God, but you still give your children good gifts. Because
God, your heavenly Father, is perfect, won't he also give
you good things if you ask him?" If we take this illustration to heart, we will want to pray.

Yet, when you understand what God says in his Word,
begin to live according to it, and teach it to others, then
you'll face many temptations and frequent opposition.
Your corrupt human nature is an enemy of prayer. It
quickly becomes bored, careless, and indifferent to what
God says and the good life he gives us. For this reason,
you will never have as much wisdom, knowledge of
God's Word, faith, love, or patience as you should. Every
day your corrupt nature hangs around your neck and
drags you away from prayer. The world is also an enemy
of prayer. It's so envious that you have faith and God's
precious Word that it refuses to put up with any of it, no
matter how weak you may be. The world condemns you,
tries to take away what you have, and gives you no peace.

These are the two enemies of prayer: our corrupt
nature and the world. On the inside, they try to
decrease our desire to pray, and on the outside, they try
to chase us away from prayer. All we can do is to continue crying out to God. We should pray for strength
and better understanding of his Word.

SHARING IN THE DIVINE NATURE

*Through these promises you will share
in the divine nature because you have escaped the
corruption that sinful desires cause in the world.*

2 PETER 1:4

❖

ETER SAYS THAT THROUGH the power of faith we share in the divine nature and have fellowship with the divine nature. What a verse! We can't find another one like this in either the New or Old Testament. Yet unbelievers consider this a small matter.

But what is the divine nature anyway? It's eternal truth, justice, wisdom, eternal life, peace, joy, happiness, and whatever else can be called good. Whoever shares in the divine nature receives all of this so that he lives eternally and has eternal peace, pleasure, and joy. He is pure and clean, and he has power over the devil, sin, and death. Peter is saying, "Just as one cannot take eternal life and truth from God, no one can take it from you." If someone does something to you, he also does it to God. If someone oppresses a Christian, he also oppresses God. The way Peter uses the little phrase *divine nature* means all of this.

It's truly wonderful when a person believes. However, Peter didn't mean for all these instructions to be a foundation for faith. Instead, he is underscoring what great, rich possessions we receive as a result of faith. This is why Peter adds that you will have all of this if you demonstrate your faith by fleeing sinful desires.

PRAYING THE PSALMS

Be filled with the Spirit by reciting psalms, hymns,
and spiritual songs for your own good. Sing
and make music to the Lord with your hearts.

EPHESIANS 5:18–19

❖

CONSIDER WHAT THE MOST respected church
fathers, especially Athanasius and Augustine,
taught about using psalms. They said we
should adapt and adjust our minds so that we are in
tune with the psalms. We must sing the psalms with the
help of the Holy Spirit. They are like a school for the
attitudes of the heart.

For example, when you read in Psalm 1, "Blessed is
the person who does not follow the advice of wicked
people," you must actually reject the advice that wicked
people give you. When you read, "He delights in the
teachings of the LORD," you shouldn't take it easy and
pat yourself on the back as if you were a person who
already loved the Lord's teachings. For as long as you
live, you will need to think of yourself as a person who
desperately needs to love God's teachings even more.
When you read, "He succeeds in everything he does,"
you should wish this for yourself and feel sorry for
those who find themselves in trouble.

Don't think that you are being asked to do the
impossible. All you need to do is try, and I know you
will be glad you did. First, practice on one psalm or even
one verse of a psalm. You will be successful as soon as
you have learned how to make just one verse come alive
and live in your heart—even if it takes a day or a whole
week. However, after you begin, everything else will follow naturally, and you will find a rich treasure of insight
and love. Just be careful you don't let weariness and dis-
couragement prevent you from getting started.

SPIRITUAL THIRST

*On the last and most important day of the festival, Jesus
was standing ⌊in the temple courtyard⌋ . He said loudly,
"Whoever is thirsty must come to me to drink."*

JOHN 7:37

❖

THIS MESSAGE OF JESUS was eagerly received by
the sad hearts of ordinary people, especially
the ones who were devout. They honored
Christ as the Prophet and Messiah. But the rest of the
people didn't regard Jesus' words very highly. That's
why Jesus chose words that would speak to the heart.
He chose words that would reach those who needed to
hear them. They are comforting, friendly, and precious
words. They refresh, comfort, and strengthen the
thirsty. Christ phrased his message this way because his
Word, unless it's preached to the thirsty, is usually
despised rather than accepted.

Those who are thirsty have a comforting preacher in
Christ himself. He shows them where they can quench
their thirst—in him, the Lord Christ. But first we must
ask, "What kind of thirst is this?" Only then will we
understand what Christ means by drinking and how we
can quench our thirst. This thirst is not a physical thirst,
which can be satisfied by drinking beer and wine. Rather,
it's a spiritual thirst—a thirst of the soul. It's the desire of
a sad, miserable, frightened, and battered conscience. It's
the desire of a despairing and terrified heart that wants to
know how it stands before God. The thirsty are the timid
and faint-hearted people who feel their sinfulness and
the weaknesses of their spirit, soul, and body. They study
God's warnings. They fear the Lord God and take note of
his law, anger, judgment, death, and other punishments.
This fear is true thirst. It happens naturally that those
with fears, temptations, and needs are very thirsty
because of their anxiety. Their tongues become dry. They
become feverish, and their fears dehydrate them. This
fear is what creates spiritual thirst.

LIGHT FOR A DARK WORLD

*Your word is a lamp for my feet
and a light for my path.*

PSALM 119:105

❖

OD CONSIDERS HUMAN reason, wisdom, morality, and even sunlight for that matter, to be
dark and hazy compared to his Word. God's
Word is a flame that shines in the darkness. Through
teaching, preaching, and the sacraments, its glow
spreads. If we use this light, then God will no longer
remain hidden from us.

When we're faced with disasters, when we're overwhelmed by darkness, when things seem so dark that
we doubt that we are part of the church or pleasing to
God, then we should learn to reach for the Bible. We
shouldn't let people who fall away from the faith dis-
tract us. Instead, we should recognize that we live in a
dark world. The only reason we can see at all is that the
light of God's Word shines brightly (2 Peter 1:19).

Jesus said, "Whoever believes and is baptized will be
saved" (Mark 16:16). The light of these words is shining in our hearts. Even if the sun were shining brightly,
it couldn't reveal this truth. Human reason by itself
can't grasp it. Wherever the Bible sheds its light, no real
danger exists. Without the Bible, we wouldn't know or
understand anything.

HONORING GOD

Abraham serves as an example. He believed God, and that faith was regarded by God to be his approval of Abraham.

GALATIANS 3:6

 ITH THESE WORDS, "[Abraham] believed God," Paul shows us that faith in God is the highest worship, the greatest allegiance, the ultimate obedience, and the most pleasing sacrifice. Whoever has a way with words should expand on this topic. That person will discover that faith is all-powerful. Its power is immeasurable and infinite. Faith gives God the greatest honor anyone can give him. Giving God honor is believing him, considering him truthful, wise, righteous, merciful, and all-powerful. In short, it's recognizing that he is the Creator and Giver of every good thing. Reason doesn't do this, only faith does.

Faith makes God real to us and real in us. Without faith, God's honor, glory, wisdom, righteousness, truth, and mercy cannot be in us. Where there is no faith, God has no majesty and divinity. God doesn't require anything more from us than to acknowledge his divinity and give him the glory and honor he deserves. We shouldn't think of him as an idol but as God—the God who accepts us and hears us, who is merciful to us, and who stands by us. When we honor God, his divinity remains complete and intact—he has everything that a believing heart can give him. When we honor God in this way, we are showing the greatest wisdom, the highest justice, and the best worship, while offering the most pleasing sacrifice.

A Pleasure to Obey

The Teachings were given through Moses, but kindness and truth came into existence through Jesus Christ.

JOHN 1:17

❖

OHN WANTED TO MAKE a point about God's laws when he said, "The Teachings were given through Moses, but kindness and truth came into existence through Jesus Christ." It's as if he wanted to say: "The laws given through Moses are laws that lead to life, God's approval, and everything else that is good. But much more was attained through Christ. He came and filled our empty hands. He fulfilled the demands of God's laws. He brought God's kindness and truth."

Christ enabled us to keep the First, Second, and Third Commandments. In this way, we came to trust and have faith in God as our Father. We began to praise him with a cheerful heart and regard his name as holy.

Where did all this kindness come from? We certainly didn't do anything to deserve it. None of our good works performed in obedience to God's laws earned it. Instead, it came from being enlightened by the Holy Spirit, being renewed by the Word of God, and having faith in Christ. Through these, we have received a new spirit that makes God's Word and God's laws a pleasure to obey. Now, we find joy in trusting God above everything else. We feel that we can do it. We have made a new beginning and have already learned the basics. The undeserved kindness that Christ has given us through faith makes the First Commandment a pleasure to obey.

TRUST GOD TO PROVIDE

The eyes of all creatures look to you, and you give them
their food at the proper time. You open your hand,
and you satisfy the desire of every living thing.

PSALM 145:15–16

❖

OOK AT THE WELL-KNOWN religious orders, and you will immediately notice that all their physical needs are completely taken care of. They have a guaranteed income, food, clothing, shelter, and all kinds of extra things acquired by the work and care of others and given to them. Therefore, they don't risk any danger nor would they want to. Rather than having confidence in the things that no one can see (Hebrews 11:1), which is a characteristic of faith, they have confidence in their possessions.

If you find a wife and marry, the first challenge is how to provide for your family. This challenge continues as long as you live. So marriage by its nature teaches and moves you to look to God's hand to provide. It forces you to trust in his kindness and to believe. For where there is no faith in marriage, it's a difficult, miserable existence, full of worry, anxiety, and hard work. In contrast, the less faith these famous religious orders have, the better they seem to have it. For their bellies are fed free of charge, and they don't have to see God's hands supply nor do they have to wait for his goodness.

So tell me, which order could rightly be called the spiritual one? Is it not the one where faith is necessary and has its own work to do? Is it not the one that has reason to trust in God daily, according to Psalm 145:15–16?

The order of marriage has a reason to trust in God. But religious orders don't have this and don't want it, for they were founded and endowed so that they wouldn't have to worry about their needs. By doing so, they have pushed faith out and plugged up all the holes for fear it will come back in.

Victory through Death

Jesus took on flesh and blood to be like them.
He did this so that by dying he would destroy the one
who had power over death (that is, the devil).

HEBREWS 2:14

❖

 E MUST HAVE THE KIND of Savior who can save us from the power of this world's god (2 Corinthians 4:4), and this world's ruler (John 16:11), the devil. We must have a Savior who can save us from the power of sin and death. Christ must be the true, eternal God, through whom all believers receive God's approval and are saved. If Christ weren't greater or better than Moses, Elijah, Isaiah, or John the Baptizer, then he wouldn't have been able to reclaim us. Because he is God's Son, he was able to reclaim us and free us from our sins when he shed his blood. If we believe this, we can rub it in the devil's face whenever he tries to torment or terrify us with our sins. This will quickly defeat the devil. He will be forced to retreat and leave us alone.

Here's an illustration that can help us understand how Christ defeated the devil by dying. The fishing hook, which is Christ's divinity, was concealed by the earthworm, which is Christ's humanity. The devil swallowed both when Christ died and was buried. But Christ's divinity ripped open the devil's stomach so that it couldn't hold Christ anymore. The devil had to throw him up. The devil ate something that proved to be fatal. This truth gives us wonderful comfort. Just as the devil couldn't hold on to Christ in death, so the devil can't hold on to us who believe in Christ.

HE GAVE HIS ONLY SON

*God loved the world this way: He gave
his only Son so that everyone who believes
in him will not die but will have eternal life.*

JOHN 3:16

❖

OMEONE MIGHT ASK: "How is it possible for the Son of man to save us and give us eternal life?" Another might ask: "How could God allow his only Son to be crucified?" Certainly, it's reasonable to say the Son of man died on the cross, but to say that a man can give us eternal life doesn't make sense. It also doesn't seem reasonable that God would let his own Son die for the world. But we must remember that when we speak about Christ, we are not speaking about a mere human being, but one person with two natures—human and divine. All of the characteristics attributed to these two natures can be found in this one person, Jesus Christ. Therefore, we can say that the Son of man created heaven and earth, and we can also say that the Son of God created heaven and earth. We shouldn't divide up Christ into two separate natures, as the heretics do. They claim that it wasn't the Son of God, but only Mary's son, who suffered and died for us.

This passage, however, clearly states that God gave his Son for the world. When Christ was handed over to Pilate to be crucified and was led by Pilate to the judgment hall, Pilate took hold of the hand of not only a human being, but also the hand of God. That's why Paul said that if the people of Jerusalem had known, they wouldn't have crucified the Lord of glory—the one all creation adores (1 Corinthians 2:8). Therefore, it was not only the Son of man, but also God's Son who was conceived by Mary, suffered and died, was buried, descended into hell, and was raised again from the dead.

SEEING OUR LORD

*Then, together with them, we who are still alive will be
taken in the clouds to meet the Lord in the air.
In this way we will always be with the Lord.*

1 THESSALONIANS 4:17

❖

E WILL ALL BE TAKEN UP to the Lord together at
the same time, both those who previously
died and those who live until Christ's coming. In one moment, all will hover together and see
each other again. Although we who are still living will
have our eyes wide open, we will not see the Lord
Christ before those who have died. It would make more
sense that we, who are still living, should be the first to
see the Lord because the dead have long since decayed
and, to our thinking, are no more.

But Christ has determined that the dead will rise
with us at the same moment and will have beautiful
eyes that see as well as we do. God will do for
Christians what he did for Christ. He pulled Christ out
from the closed and sealed grave in an instant, so
quickly that in one moment he was both in and out. So
in the last moment, God will bring together both. He
will bring us, who are still alive and have our five
senses, together with those who are dead, decayed,
pulverized, and scattered all over the world. We will all,
at the same time, be drawn to heaven and soar in the
clouds. We will be lighter than the birds and much
more beautiful than the sun.

WE ARE GOD'S CHILDREN

The Father has given us his love. He loves us so much
that we are actually called God's dear children.
. . . What we will be isn't completely clear yet.

1 JOHN 3:1–2

❖

OHN WANTS TO PROTECT against fainthearted-
ness by giving each of us this reassurance—
God loves you. He repeats this and wants to
deeply impress it on our hearts. He also reassures us
that we are called God's children. It's difficult to recognize that we are God's children because we are still in
these bodies and we experience troubles from the
world and from ourselves. We don't yet feel like God's
children because we are still in these bodies. But we
shouldn't let that lead us astray because "what we will
be isn't completely clear yet."

John tells us about the hidden Son of God. Previously,
Christ revealed himself in the shadows, but he didn't
reveal himself completely. And God could not conceal
himself any more than he does now. Nevertheless, God
doesn't withdraw himself from us. But the world, the
corrupt nature, and the devil obscure our vision so that
we don't see God. The world is one layer, the corrupt
nature the second, and the devil the third. We must break
through all these layers with faith, which comes from the
Word of God. This is how we are God's children—not by
physically seeing God, but by believing in God.

Faith in the Word promises great things to us about
what we will become. Yet as long as we are in the world,
our corrupt nature entices us and the devil seduces us. It
isn't yet clear to us what our future happiness will be, nor
will it become clear. "No eye has seen, no ear has heard,
and no mind has imagined the things that God has prepared for those who love him" (1 Corinthians 2:9).

CONTENTMENT COMES FROM GOD

God gives wisdom, knowledge, and joy to anyone who pleases him. But to the person who continues to sin, he gives the job of gathering and collecting ⌊wealth⌋.

ECCLESIASTES 2:26

❖

HENEVER SOMEONE IS ABLE to feel content with what he has, it's a gift from God. God gives those who please him contentment without having to strive for it. God sees only two kinds of people: those who are faithful, and those who are sinners. Besides the gifts he gives to all people, God gives wisdom and discretion to the faithful. On top of that, he adds joy. The faithful are content with what they have and are not tormented by the same kind of thoughts and desires sinners have. They go about their business with joy and peace.

On the other hand, sinners are always troubled. They are preoccupied with gathering and collecting wealth, but they're never satisfied. Even if they've been given wisdom and skill, so many difficulties are mixed in with these gifts that they feel more like punishment. Sinners don't enjoy their work, whether it's farming or building—even though others enjoy doing these things and find happiness in them. What sinners produce cannot be used in the right way by anyone except those who have God's approval. So, whatever sinners accumulate belongs to those who have God's approval. The faithful know how to use God's gifts with joy and thanksgiving, even when they have very little.

But sinners don't even use what they have, in spite of all the trouble they go through to accumulate their possessions. In the end, faithful people truly own the whole world because they enjoy it with happiness and contentment. Even when they possess a lot, sinners have nothing. That's how pointless their lives are.

CHRIST DIDN'T COME TO JUDGE

You judge the way humans do.
I don't judge anyone.

JOHN 8:15

❖

HRIST DOESN'T WANT TO JUDGE. He wants to help. So don't picture Christ as a judge for whom you must do this or that to be reconciled. No, he is the Light of the world. He judges no one. Whoever follows him will no longer walk in darkness. Christ says, "If you feel your sin and admit it, and if you're terrified by it, then hold tightly to me, follow me, and believe in me. Think of me as the Light. Then you won't have to be afraid of being brought to court and being convicted. I have come to save the world. However, those who reject my help will bring judgment on themselves because they don't want to be saved."

Christ's words are similar to what a physician would say to a patient, "I haven't come to poison you. I want to help you. If you follow my advice, you won't need to worry. If you refuse my advice and call me a scoundrel, if you hate me and reject my medicine, then you are willfully sentencing yourself to death. Then it's your own fault. Certainly, I am not putting you to death. No, I'll have to let you to die because you despise and reject my medicine."

We're in the same situation. Christ will certainly keep his promise to us: "I don't judge anyone. So don't judge yourselves. You aren't condemned in my eyes, for I am the Light that illumines the way to eternal life and salvation."

BAD EXAMPLES GIVE US HOPE

Judah was told, "Your daughter-in-law Tamar has been acting like a prostitute. What's more, because of it she's pregnant." Judah ordered, "Bring her out to be burned."

GENESIS 38:24

❖

OD'S PEOPLE OFTEN FALL into sin. Their examples show us God's endless kindness and mercy. He saves not only those people who were faithful and moral like Abraham, Isaac, and Jacob, but also those who were immoral like Judah, Tamar, Reuben, Simeon, and Levi. Therefore, no one should be self-righteous about his own morality or wisdom. On the other hand, no one should give up because of his sins. Scripture praises the examples of Abraham, Isaac, and Jacob. At the same time, it describes the worst kinds of sinners. We see the virtues of the most godly people and the sins of the most wicked people—yet they all come from the same family.

This teaches us about repentance, faith, and forgiveness for sins. No one should brag about how good he is, but those who have fallen into sin shouldn't give up either. The Bible records the mistakes, weaknesses, and horrible sins of God's people. This is meant to uplift and comfort those who are depressed because of their sins. Sinners need to be told, "Don't give up. God wants you to trust him and believe in his promises. He can forgive you, make you holy, and bless you just like he blessed Judah, Tamar, and other sinners." God doesn't want us to depend on our own efforts or despair because of our sins. He wants us to trust entirely in his mercy and undeserved kindness.

We would have no hope if Peter hadn't denied Christ, if the apostles hadn't taken offense at Christ, and if Moses, Aaron, and David hadn't fallen into sin. God wants to comfort sinners with these examples. It's as if he were saying to each of us, "If you have sinned, turn around. The door of grace is open to you."

CHRIST THE SUN

Christ paid the price to free us from the curse that God's laws bring by becoming cursed instead of us. Scripture says, "Everyone who is hung on a tree is cursed."

GALATIANS 3:13

❖

HE GOSPEL—THE MOST LOVED and comforting doctrine of all—doesn't focus on our works or the works of the law. Rather, it shows us the incomprehensible, inexpressible mercy and love of God towards us, who are unworthy and lost people. The merciful Father saw that we were oppressed by the curse of the law and held under it. On our own and through our own efforts, we could never have freed ourselves. He sent his only Son into the world. He put all the sin of all the people on his Son and said, "You will be Peter, who denied me; Paul, who persecuted, blasphemed, and acted violently; David, who committed adultery; the sinner who ate the apple in paradise; the thief on the cross. In summary, you will be the one who committed all the sins of all the people. Make sure you pay for these sins and make atonement for them."

At this point the law said, "I find Christ to be a sinner—the one who has taken the sins of all the people upon himself. I do not see sin on anyone else except him. Therefore, he must die on the cross." Then the law grabbed him and killed him.

Since this happened, the entire world has been cleansed and atoned of all sin and freed from death and all evil. If everyone in the whole world believed, God would only see purity and righteousness. This is because Christ would have taken away all sin and death. And even if there were any remnants of sin remaining, God wouldn't see them because of the brightness of Christ, the Sun.

THE LAMB OF GOD

*John saw Jesus coming toward him the next day
and said, "Look! This is the Lamb of God
who takes away the sin of the world."*

JOHN 1:29

❖

OD'S LAWS TELL US how we should live. They command us: "Never desire to take your neighbor's wife. Never murder. Never commit adultery. Give to the poor." It's good to follow God's laws in order to guard against outward sins. Before God, however, it won't work to try to get rid of sin by obeying God's laws. What does work is stated in this verse: "Look! This is the Lamb of God who takes away the sin of the world." Isaiah explains that "the LORD has laid all our sins on him" (Isaiah 53:6) and "he was killed because of my people's rebellion" (Isaiah 53:8). Everything points to Christ.

As a Christian, you should hold tightly to these words and not let them be taken away from you. Then, you will know that godless people and religious people who hope to satisfy God with their pilgrimages and good works are blind. Many boast of their good works and console themselves by thinking they will get a second chance to be saved. The Holy Scripture, in contrast, says that the sins of the world aren't laid on the world. John's sins weren't laid on John, and Peter's sins weren't laid on Peter, for no one can bear his own sins. Rather, the sins of the world were laid on Christ. He is the Lamb of God. He stepped forward to become a sinner for us, to even become sin itself, and to act as though he had committed the sins of the entire world from the beginning of its creation (2 Corinthians 5:21). The Lamb's mission, role, and function were to take away the sins of the world. The Lamb carried them all.

THE PROBLEM OF TEMPTATION

The snake was more clever than all the wild animals the
LORD *God had made. He asked the woman, "Did God really*
say, 'You must never eat the fruit of any tree in the garden'?"

GENESIS 3:1

❖

 HIS PASSAGE RAISES a lot of questions. Some
people become curious and ask, "Well, why
did God permit Satan to lure Eve into sin?
Why did Satan appear to Eve in the form of a snake
instead of some other animal?"

No one can explain why God permits things to happen. No one understands what he does or why he does
it. So we should remember the lesson that Job learned:
no one can summon God into court to account for
what he does or allows to happen. We might as well
argue with him about why the grass and trees aren't
green all year long. It's enough for us to know that all
these things are under God's power. He can do as he
pleases. Idle curiosity causes guessing and questioning.
Since we are merely clay in God's hands (Isaiah 64:8),
we should avoid debating these matters. We can't sit in
judgment over the all-knowing God. Instead, we
should allow him to judge us.

The only satisfactory answer to these and similar
questions should be that it pleased God for Adam to be
tempted in order to test his ability to resist. That is how
God still works today. After we have been baptized and
brought into Christ's kingdom, God doesn't want us to
become idle. Instead, he wants us to pay attention to
his Word and make use of his gifts. So even today, he
allows poor, weak people like us to be sifted and
strained by the devil.

THE MERCY SEAT

All of us must appear in front of Christ's judgment seat.
Then all people will receive what they deserve for the good
or evil they have done while living in their bodies.

2 CORINTHIANS 5:10

❖

SCRIPTURE TEACHES US that God has set up two seats. One is the judgment seat for those who are proud and don't acknowledge or want to confess their sins. The other is the mercy seat for the poor, timid consciences who feel their sins and confess them, who despair of his judgment, and who hope to find God's kindness.

In Romans 3:25, Paul says this mercy seat is Christ. God has given this seat to us as a place where we can find refuge because we cannot withstand God's judgment on our own. I want to find my refuge there too, for I have done and am still doing too little. I keep sinning against God's law even after my justification and sanctification. My heart and conscience, no matter how pure they might appear to others, will count for nothing there. But they will be covered with a vaulted ceiling called mercy and forgiveness of sins. It will serve as a strong protection and defense for me. My heart and conscience will crawl under it and be safe.

For God has led his apostles to preach and proclaim that everyone who believes in his name will receive forgiveness of sins (Acts 10:43). Likewise, "Whoever believes and is baptized will be saved" (Mark 16:16). And Jesus says, "God loved the world this way: He gave his only Son so that everyone who believes in him will not die but will have eternal life" (John 3:16). Therefore, God himself has established this mercy seat. He is the one who directs us away from the judgment seat and towards the mercy seat.

ACCEPTING WHAT CAN'T BE CHANGED

What advantage do they gain from working so hard for the wind? They spend their entire lives in darkness, in constant frustration, sickness, and resentment.

ECCLESIASTES 5:16–17

❖

IVING IN DARKNESS is a Hebrew expression for "living in sadness." The phrase is derived from the way people look when they're feeling sad. When a person's heart is sad, his eyes almost look as though they are covered by a cloud. But when a person's heart is happy, his face lights up and shines. Light represents happiness, and darkness represents sadness. For example, we read in the Psalms, "The LORD is my light and my salvation" (Psalm 27:1), and "O LORD my God! Light up my eyes" (Psalm 13:3). To live in darkness, therefore, means to lead a harsh life of sadness.

The only cases that come before judges are bad ones. A judge who is unwise will torture himself and wear himself out with worry because he doesn't think he's making any difference. But someone who is wise will say, "I plan and do everything that I can. But what I can't change, I'll accept. I have to endure it. In the meantime, I'll commit everything to God. He alone knows how to make things better according to his will. He is the only one who can make my efforts succeed."

Therefore, just like a judge, our eyes and ears must get used to seeing and hearing bad things, even if this isn't what we want. We shouldn't think we'll see and hear only good things that please us. That's not what the world offers. So, we should prepare ourselves for bad things, for we know that this is the way life goes. The person who doesn't want to have any trouble will find more things that trouble him than others will.

TRUE FREEDOM AND FALSE FREEDOM

So if the Son sets you free,
you will be absolutely free.

JOHN 8:36

❖

HERE ARE TWO KINDS of freedom. The first is a false freedom of false disciples. These people want freedom for satisfying their desires. They become Christians for that reason, just as the people in this passage became followers of Christ because they heard his followers were devout, good, patient, and gentle people, not thirsting for revenge. His followers freely gave to the poor and were generous. They also heard that his followers worshiped a merciful God, not an angry one. When they heard all of this, they liked the idea that believers would give to them and serve them. So they said, "I will gladly have others give to me, serve me, and forgive me. The Lord God will also forgive my sins and help me get to heaven." They were glad to be on the receiving end of all this.

However, people like this are scoundrels and don't want to leave their life of sin and idolatry or give anything to anyone. They want to live lives of sexual immorality and self-gratification as they did before coming to Christ. Yet they still want to be considered Christians. These are false disciples who only want freedom for their physical desires. They praise the gospel, and at first, follow it earnestly. Soon after, they do what they want, following their evil lusts and desires. They become worse and more indecent than before. They are more smug, wild, and greedy. They even steal more than others do.

The second type of freedom is the true freedom of genuine disciples. Those who stick to God's Word and endure, suffer, and tolerate what they must are the ones who will be set free. They will become stronger as time goes on.

GOD'S MYSTERIOUS WAYS

Just as you don't know how the breath of life enters the
limbs of a child within its mother's womb, you also don't
understand how God, who made everything, works.

ECCLESIASTES 11:5

❖

OD LEADS AND DIRECTS his people in mysterious ways. In the Bible, we read, "Your road went through the sea. Your path went through raging water, but your footprints could not be seen" (Psalm 77:19). Christ himself told Peter, "You don't know now what I'm doing. You will understand later" (John 13:7). Christ seems to be saying, "You want to see me and want me to do what seems good and right to you. But I will act in a way that will make you think I'm a fool rather than God. You will see my back, not my face. You won't understand what I'm doing or why I'm doing it. Then I'll be able to mold you and remold you the way I would like. My methods may appear as foolish to you as if they were from the devil himself."

We need to learn how God guides his people as they grow and develop. I, too, have often tried to dictate to our Lord God a certain way in which I expected him to run things. I have often said, "Oh Lord, would you please do it this way and make it come out that way?" But God did just the opposite, even though I said to myself, "This is a good suggestion that will bring honor to God and expand his kingdom." Undoubtedly, God must have laughed at my so-called wisdom and said, "All right, I know that you are an intelligent, educated person, but I never needed a Peter, a Luther, or anyone else to teach, inform, rule, or guide me. I am not a God who will allow himself to be taught or directed by others. Rather, I am the one who leads, rules, and teaches people."

THE SPIRIT IN US

Don't you know that your body is a temple that belongs to the Holy Spirit? The Holy Spirit, whom you received from God, lives in you. You don't belong to yourselves.

1 CORINTHIANS 6:19

❖

E SHOULDN'T DOUBT that the Holy Spirit lives in us, but we should certainly recognize that we are a temple of the Holy Spirit, as Paul says in 1 Corinthians 6:19. If someone feels a love for God's Word and gladly hears, speaks, thinks, teaches, and writes about Christ, you should know that this doesn't come from a person's will or reason but from the Holy Spirit. It's impossible for this to happen without the Holy Spirit. On the other hand, where there is hatred and contempt for the Word, you should know that the devil, the ruler of this world, blinds the hearts of the people and holds them captive, so that the light of the gospel, the glory of Christ, can't shine on them. We see this today in the masses who are not moved by the Word but despise it as if it has nothing to do with them.

But those who have any kind of love and desire for the Word should gratefully acknowledge that these attitudes are poured into them by the Holy Spirit. For we are not born with these attitudes and cannot acquire them through the law. This transformation rests completely and absolutely in the hand of the Almighty. So when we eagerly listen to preaching about Jesus Christ, the Son of God—who for our sakes became a human being and subjected himself to the law to save us—then God sends the Holy Spirit into our hearts through this preaching. Therefore, it's very useful for believers to remember that they have the Holy Spirit.

TRUSTING CHRIST INSTEAD OF PEOPLE

Jesus, however, was wary of these believers.
He understood people.

JOHN 2:24

❖

O ONE UNDERSTANDS how difficult it was when I first realized that I had to believe and teach an idea that was contrary to the teachings of the church fathers. This was especially shocking to me when many outstanding, reasonable, and educated people shared their views. The church fathers include many holy people, such as Ambrose, Jerome, and Augustine. Despite that, my dear Lord and Savior Jesus Christ must be worth more to me than all the holy people on earth—yes, even more than all the angels in heaven. When I read Augustine's books and discovered that he had also been in error, I was greatly troubled. Whenever this happens, it's very difficult for me to calm my own heart and differ with people who are so greatly respected.

But I dare not accept something just because a respected person says it. A person can be holy and God-fearing and still be in error. That's why I don't want to rely on people. As this passage says, the Lord Christ didn't rely on people either. Furthermore, in the book of Matthew, Jesus earnestly warns us to beware of false prophets, who will come and not only claim to be Christians, but will also "do wonderful things to deceive, if possible, even those whom God has chosen" (Matthew 24:24).

Rather than trusting the church fathers and their writings, we should crawl under the wings of our mother hen, the Lord Christ, and look to him alone. The heavenly Father said, "This is my Son, whom I love and with whom I am pleased. Listen to him" (Matthew 17:5). God wants us to listen to Christ alone.

HIDING FROM GOD

[Adam] answered, "I heard you in the garden.
I was afraid because I was naked, so I hid."

GENESIS 3:10

❖

E NEED TO REALIZE that hiding from God is the essence of sin. Unless God immediately sends help and calls the sinner back, he will keep on trying to hide from God. And because the sinner tries to justify himself with lies, he piles one sin on top of another. In the end he will reach the point of open hypocrisy and deep despair. As a result, one sin leads to another, until the weight of his sin pulls him down into the pit. Ultimately, the sinner accuses God of causing the sin rather than placing the blame on himself.

Adam should have said, "Lord, I've sinned!" But he didn't do this. Instead he blamed God, saying, in effect, "Lord, you sinned. I would have enjoyed a holy life in paradise in spite of eating the apple if you hadn't said anything." Adam's thoughts and feelings were revealed when he implied that he wouldn't have hidden if God's voice hadn't frightened him. Even though all people are guilty of sin, they don't acknowledge it. Rather, they place the blame on their creator. This will only increase the burden of sin to infinite proportions unless God shows his mercy and comes to help.

Adam believed that his wicked and foolish thoughts were the highest wisdom. He was so overcome by his fear that he was barely aware of what he was saying or doing. As he tried to excuse himself, he actually condemned himself over and over and increased his burden of sin proportionately. At any rate, we must not think that these things happened to Adam alone. Every one of us does the same. Our human nature allows us to do nothing else, especially after we have committed a sin. We all prefer to put the blame on God rather than to admit that we are sinners.

PRAYING FROM THE HEART

*These people honor me with their lips, but their hearts
are far from me. Their worship of me is pointless,
because their teachings are rules made by humans.*

MATTHEW 15:8–9

❖

VERYONE WHO FEELS BURDENED should pray the Lord's Prayer. Even those who don't know the meaning of the words may pray it from their heart. That type of prayer is the best because the heart is saying more than the lips.

On the other hand, another person stands in church, turning the pages, and counting the prayer beads— almost rattling. Meanwhile, his heart is far from what his lips are praying. That is not prayer. For God describes these kinds of people through the prophet Isaiah, "These people worship me with their mouths and honor me with their lips. But their hearts are far from me" (Isaiah 29:13). We also find some religious people who blabber the prayers for each day without any inner feeling. Then they say without shame, "O, I feel happy. I have now paid back our Lord." They think they have satisfied God through their prayers.

Although some might praise them for their efforts, God will say, "These people honor me with their lips, but their hearts are far from me" (Matthew 15:8). What's frightening is that these people rely on these kinds of prayers and never send up any other prayer to God. So those who pray the least appear to pray the most. And those who pray the most appear to pray the least.

Good and Bad Times

When times are good, be happy. But when times are bad,
consider this: God has made the one time as well as the
other so that mortals cannot predict their future.

ECCLESIASTES 7:14

❖

HEN YOU ARE GIVEN a good day, here's what
you should do: be happy. In other words,
enjoy the present. Forget your troubles. Lay
your plans aside. But keep your emotions in check. Let
your wisdom come from God. Commit to him both
your past and your future.

So be happy in the present, but do so in a way that
you don't forget about the bad times. In other words,
you should be ready for times of sorrow. Enjoy the present, but don't start thinking that life will always stay
that way. Beware of becoming overconfident. Don't look
forward exclusively to good things. You also need to be
prepared for bad times. Always try to remain even-tem-
pered and open to whatever happens. In contrast, foolish people cling to the joys of the moment. They
become completely absorbed in them as if these good
times were going to last forever. Then, God uses bad
times to remove their improper attitudes and arrogance.

So, we should be happy in such a way that we don't
immerse ourselves in the present. We should always
keep a part of our heart reserved for God, for he is the
one who will help us get through the bad times. Then,
when trouble comes, we will be less bothered because
we have anticipated it.

JESUS IS THE WAY

Thomas said to him, "Lord, we don't know where you're going. So how can we know the way?" Jesus answered him, "I am the way, the truth, and the life."

JOHN 14:5–6

❖

THOMAS THOUGHT IT WAS STRANGE that Christ was saying, "You know the way to the place where I am going," when Jesus had said nothing about where he was going. Thomas was thinking in simple and concrete terms. He was envisioning a road that a person takes from one city to another or a path that a person walks on. The disciples were saying, "We don't know the way. We don't even know through which city gate you're planning to leave. How can we know the way?"

Christ replied to their worldly thoughts, "Here's what I mean: You know the way. In other words, you know the person who is the way—me. For you see me and know that I am the Christ, your Lord and Savior. You are my disciples, for you have heard my message and have seen my miracles. Since you know me, you also know the way and everything else you need to know."

This is remarkable. All our teaching and faith should center and depend on Christ. Setting aside all of our wisdom and skill, we should know nothing except the crucified Christ (1 Corinthians 2:2). From God's perspective, the highest wisdom and knowledge above all other knowledge and wisdom is to truly know this person Christ. We come to God through Christ alone.

Keep on Believing

[Joseph's brothers] were frightened, because they had been brought to Joseph's house. They thought, ". . . They're going to attack us, overpower us, take our donkeys, and make us slaves."

GENESIS 43:18

❖

OSEPH'S BROTHERS DIDN'T know what was going to happen to them. They certainly didn't expect this ruler of Egypt, who was actually their brother Joseph, to be kind and sympathetic to them. They didn't expect this man to make them rich and promote them to positions of honor. It wasn't time for them to recognize the wonderful things God was doing for them.

In the meantime, they were sleeping and snoring, paying no attention to God's promise. They thought they were going to be severely punished. Yet, everything they thought, said, and did was happening as if they were in a dream. Later on, when Joseph told them, "I am Joseph, the brother you sold" (Genesis 45:4), they would wake up and see that everything they were so afraid of was nothing but a dream.

We, too, live as if we were sleepwalking. No one can tell that we're asleep by looking at us. But we aren't awake. If we truly believe God's Word, a time will come when we will finally wake up and open our eyes. But when facing difficult situations, our hearts might not be able to be as strong and confident as God's Word requires. Then, at the very least, we should keep on believing in a weak sort of way, as Joseph's brothers did here. We shouldn't start complaining against God or grow tired of praying and calling out to him. In difficult times, we may not be able to believe God as strongly, praise him as wholeheartedly, and pray to him as sincerely as we do in good times. But at least we should believe and pray as much as we are able.

LOVING OUR NEIGHBORS

All of Moses' Teachings are summarized in a single
statement, "Love your neighbor as you love yourself."
GALATIANS 5:14

❖

FTER HAVING HEARD and accepted the true
teaching about faith, the apostle Paul seriously admonishes Christians to practice
genuine good works. This is because these remnants of
sin remain in those who are justified. These remnants
resist faith and divert us from doing true good works.
Human reason and the corrupt nature resist the Spirit
in believers and control unbelievers. Reason is naturally
inclined towards hypocritical superstition. It wants to
measure God according to its own thoughts rather than
according to his Word. It does works of its own
choosing more enthusiastically than the ones God
commanded. That's why faithful teachers must teach
and impress on people true love and truly good works
just as much as they teach faith.

No one should think he fully understands this command: "Love your neighbor." Certainly this is very short
and very easy as far as the words are concerned. But
where are the teachers and learners who actually practice this in life? These words, "Through love serve one
another" and "Love your neighbor as yourself," are eternal words. No one can think about, urge, and practice
them enough.

It's remarkable that believers will immediately have
a troubled conscience if they fail to do something trivial. But these same people feel nothing at all when they
neglect love and when their heart isn't sincere and
brotherly toward their neighbor. Unfortunately, this
happens every day. For they don't regard God's command to love as highly as their own superstitions.

SPIRITUAL AND PHYSICAL LIFE

Flesh and blood give birth to flesh and blood,
but the Spirit gives birth to things that are spiritual.

JOHN 3:6

❖

E CAN'T FEEL THE NEW BIRTH or the spiritual life with our five senses. We can't see it. The spiritual life will endure, while the physical life will one day end. Our lives on earth will eventually become like dust, which is blown away and never seen or felt again. Then, only the spiritual life will remain. We will come alive once again and will be raised from the dead.

We can't see or understand this spiritual birth. We must simply believe it. What is born of the Spirit is spiritual, and the primary benefit of this new birth is the forgiveness of sins and eternal life. Nevertheless, Christians still have an external existence. While they live here on earth, they are nurtured by a mother and father, eat and drink, wear clothes and shoes, have a house and garden, and own money and property. They view all of this as if they were guests who were traveling through this land to another city—their true destination. When they arrive there, they will no longer care about the places where they stayed along the way. During the journey, they were always thinking, "Today, I am a guest. Tomorrow, I will continue my trip." In the same way, a Christian also thinks, "Today, I am guest on this earth. I eat and drink here. I live honorably and modestly in this life. But tomorrow, I'll proceed on my way to an eternal life in the kingdom of heaven, where I am a citizen." So Christians also journey through this life. When they come to the end of this life, they will let go of everything physical and enter a spiritual life that will never end.

No Bragging Allowed

Who says that you are any better than other people? What do you have that wasn't given to you? If you were given what you have, why are you bragging as if it weren't a gift?

1 CORINTHIANS 4:7

❖

OD IS LOVING AND KIND by nature. Therefore, he cannot keep himself from giving us abundant gifts. He gives us homes and families, healthy bodies, wisdom, skills and talents, and knowledge of the Scriptures. Unfortunately, we cannot keep ourselves from taking credit for these gifts and bragging about them. Without God's gifts, our lives would be miserable. But even with God's gifts, our lives end up being miserable because we are still experiencing the effects of original sin. The whole human race is thoroughly infected with original sin. Unbelievers don't understand the seriousness of it, so they act as if it doesn't matter.

We see this problem not only in ourselves, but in others as well. We brag about our material possessions, even though these are rated as the least valuable of God's abundant gifts. Consequently, the wealthy, regardless of whether they are nobles, merchants, or farmers, consider other people to be mere pests. Even more serious abuses exist with the more important gifts, such as wisdom and justice. The fact that God gives his gifts to everyone results in the following predicament: God cannot tolerate bragging, and we cannot keep from doing it.

This was how the world sinned before the flood. Among Cain's descendants were some of the finest and most intelligent people in the world. But in God's eyes they were very evil because they had become filled with pride about the gifts God had given them. Then, they despised God who gave them their gifts in the first place. The world doesn't understand why this is wrong and therefore, doesn't condemn this behavior. But God condemns it.

TERRIFIED BY PRAYER

This is how you should pray:
Our Father in heaven, let your name be kept holy.

MATTHEW 6:9

❖

HE LORD'S PRAYER TEACHES you to recognize your great misery and corruption before God. In other words, if you think about what you are praying, you will soon notice you're blaspheming God. You will become terrified by your own prayer. For you certainly haven't kept God's name holy. And whoever isn't keeping God's name holy is dishonoring his name. Moreover, dishonoring God's name is a serious sin, and you would deserve the punishment of eternal fire if God were to judge you. Where, then, will you turn? Your own prayer punishes you and works against you. It accuses and deplores you. You're stuck, lying there. Who will help you?

After you have sincerely repented and are humbled by recognizing the miserable position you're in, then the comforting teaching will come and lift you up again. The Lord's Prayer teaches you not to despair, but instead to ask for God's kindness and help. For you must firmly believe that he will hear you because he is the one who taught you to pray this way. The result of your prayer will be that God won't credit your sin to you or deal with you harshly. God approves of only those who seriously confess that they have dishonored his name and sincerely want to keep it holy at all times. However, it isn't possible for people to be saved if they trust in their conscience and don't think they're dishonoring God's name, for these people are still too confident, secure, arrogant, and irreverent. They're not the kind of people Christ speaks about in Matthew: "Come to me, all who are tired from carrying heavy loads, and I will give you rest" (Matthew 11:28). They don't understand the Lord's Prayer and don't know what they are praying.

THE PROBLEM WITH PROSPERITY

*Listen to this message which I, the LORD, have spoken
against you Israelites. . . . I have known no one else but
you. That is why I am going to punish you for all your sins.*

AMOS 3:1–2

❖

N THIS BOOK, the prophet Amos rebukes and
warns the people of Israel to look inward
and repent of their godlessness. By doing so,
Israel could be aware of God's coming judgment.
However, the message of Amos was widely ignored and
scorned by the Israelites. The world generally hates
God's Word as well as the messengers of the Word. But
worse yet, Amos prophesied during Jeroboam's reign,
when the kingdom of Israel was at its peak, and everything was going well. Though godless, Jeroboam was a
famous and brave king who won many military victories. Through these victories, "he restored Israel's
boundaries from the border of Hamath to the Dead
Sea" (2 Kings 14:25). As a result, he became deluded by
the prosperity of his kingdom.

When things are going well, godless people tend to
become foolish and end up destroying themselves
(Proverbs 1:32). They don't think they need God, and,
in their blindness, they continue to behave in an
ungodly way. They keep on doing this until they face
God's judgment and perish. The Word is proclaimed to
them uselessly, which is what we see happening in the
book of Amos. So, Amos prophesied at an unfortunate
time, but also at a very appropriate time.

We can learn a lot from this. When times are bad, we
should remind ourselves about God's goodness and
mercy. In good times, however, we should remember to
fear God.

Show Us the Father

I have been with all of you for a long time. Don't you know me yet, Philip? The person who has seen me has seen the Father. So how can you say, "Show us the Father"?

JOHN 14:9

❖

WE SHOULD CAREFULLY GUARD against separating Christ and God. This is what Philip was doing here. He ignored Christ and looked for God in heaven. He was thinking, "I hear Christ talking to me. But how do I know what God in heaven thinks about me or has decided to do with me?" What else is this than unbelief and a secret denial of God? Christ had to correct Philip in order to tear him away from such a misconception. He said, "Philip, why are you trying to separate the Father from me? With your thoughts, you're climbing up into the clouds and leaving me here on earth talking uselessly. Don't you hear what I'm saying? Whoever sees me, sees the Father too. Don't you believe that I am in the Father and the Father is in me?"

Those are loving yet serious words from the Lord, for he can't tolerate us fluttering around in uncertainty. Christ wants us firmly tied to him and his Word so that we don't search for God anywhere else except in him.

A devout hermit named Anthony noticed that some of the young and inexperienced monks wanted to be smart and figure out God's secrets. But Anthony warned his brothers that if they saw someone climbing heavenward and planting one foot in heaven, they should immediately pull that person down. For if he set his other foot in heaven too, he would come crashing down headfirst. These are appropriate words for those who like to speculate about lofty matters. Those people would like to drill a hole into heaven to peek in and see God himself and everything he is doing. In the meantime, they ignore Christ. Protect yourself from ideas that go beyond God's Word and that separate Christ from God.

OCTOBER 25

THE FAR-REACHING EFFECTS OF SIN

*Joseph's brothers realized what their father's death could
mean. So they thought, "What if Joseph holds a grudge
against us? What if he decides to pay us back?"*

GENESIS 50:15

❖

 HE BIBLE TELLS US HOW easy it was for Simeon,
Levi, and Joseph's other brothers to sin. But
it also tells us how difficult it was for them
to be reconciled with Joseph again and be healed. This
is the reason why many people who don't hear the message of God's kindness are driven to despair. Some even
commit suicide by drowning or hanging themselves.
They can't handle the power of sin they feel working
inside them. When sin is "lying outside your door"
(Genesis 4:7), people neglect it. Then, it takes hold, and
one offense leads to the next—each more outrageous
than the last. But when sin is stirred to life, the precious
blood of God's Son is the costly medicine needed to
remove it.

Stay away from sin if you can. But if you have fallen
into sin, you must learn how to get up again and regain
a firm faith. These very struggles show us what it means
to really believe.

We need to realize that sin is a horrible evil. This
doesn't seem to be true when we're committing sin. We
enjoy it while we are doing it. But after God's laws make
us aware of our sin, we realize that sin is hell itself and
far more powerful than heaven or earth. After that, we
can't understand God's kindness to us without great
effort. But a heart burdened by sin can say, "Even
though I have committed many sins, 'God sent his Son
into the world, not to condemn the world, but to save
the world' " (John 3:17). Without this comfort, we
would have no remedy or defense against sin and its
sting.

FIGHTING AGAINST SIN

What your spiritual nature wants is contrary to what your corrupt nature wants. They are opposed to each other.

GALATIANS 5:17

❖

ELIEVERS CAN BE DEEPLY comforted by Paul's teaching. They have both the corrupt nature and the Spirit in the same body in such a way that the Spirit reigns and the corrupt nature is subordinate. Righteousness rules, and sin serves. Not everyone is familiar with this teaching. If you think that believers must be completely flawless, and yet you feel deeply flawed, then you will be consumed by sorrow and will despair. Whoever recognizes and makes use of this teaching will discover that even the worst will work out for the best. For when your corrupt nature entices you to sin, you will be motivated to seek forgiveness of sins through Christ. You will want to grasp the righteousness of faith, which you wouldn't normally regard or desire.

Meanwhile, Christians should keep the wickedness of their corrupt nature in mind so that they are encouraged and motivated to believe and call on Christ. At such an opportunity, Christians become skillful artists and wonderful creators. They can create joy from sorrow, comfort from fear, righteousness from sin, and life from death when they restrain their corrupt nature in this way, make it their servant, and subject it to the Spirit.

If you are aware of the desires of the corrupt nature, you shouldn't despair of your salvation. Though you will be aware of these desires, you must not give in to them. The more you grow in Christ, the more you will sense this conflict. Anger or sexual desire may still be stirred up in you, but you must not allow them to rule. Sin may arouse these desires, but you must not give in to them.

GOD WANTS YOUR HEART

*God loved the world this way: He gave his only Son
so that everyone who believes in him will not die
but will have eternal life.*

JOHN 3:16

❖

O WHOM DOES GOD give his beloved Son?
God gives him to the world—the lost multitude who never deserved it. They could only
expect to remain lost and condemned without him.
God gave his Son to the lost so that they might be
saved. Then, what should you do for this loving God in
return? Nothing! Don't go on pilgrimages. Don't do
this or that good work. Instead, simply believe in Christ
alone. Then you will be able to get rid of your old
nature and cling to him. Your faith, of course, should
be the kind that produces good works.

You cannot take hold of this gift—the Son of God—
with your hand. The Son of God cannot be contained
in a jar. He is only grasped with the heart and by faith.
When this gift comes into your heart, when you believe
in Christ with your whole heart, then you won't be the
same person. Even if you once were a thief, an adulterer, or a murderer, you will become a new person, for
you have the Light in your heart.

What the Lord Christ wants first and foremost is
your heart—a heart that believes in him alone. God
wants your best, not your mouth or your hand, but
your heart. He wants you to be righteous on the inside.
When you believe in Christ, your heart becomes clean.
Peter says that faith cleanses hearts (Acts 15:9). That
same faith doesn't permit you to be arrogant or proud.
For when the heart is cleansed, the hands, eyes, feet,
and all other members are also cleansed. You will act
differently than before. Faith won't permit you to be a
sinner, fornicator, or adulterer any longer. So your
entire life will reflect what's in your heart.

RESIDENTS IN A FOREIGN LAND

The LORD said to Abram, "Leave your land,
your relatives, and your father's home.
Go to the land that I will show you."

GENESIS 12:1

❖

E OUGHT TO ADMIRE Abraham because he allowed God to reprimand him. Even though he was afraid of God's anger, he admitted that he had been worshiping idols and had not trusted God. Then, he started a journey without knowing where he was going. Abraham left his familiar homeland to look for an unfamiliar foreign country. While faith convinced him that he would get there, outward appearances made this seem uncertain. As a matter of fact, according to the Bible, he never had a permanent place to live after that. Even David praises this lifestyle, using it as an example when he says, "I am a foreign resident with you, a stranger like all my ancestors" (Psalm 39:12).

Someone might say, "What? Wasn't David a king? Wasn't Abraham a very wealthy man, even though he moved from place to place?" Although all of this is true, David and Abraham didn't have much because they treated their possessions as if they didn't belong to them. As Paul said, "Those who use the things in this world should do so but not depend on them" (1 Corinthians 7:31).

Faithful people have always lived this way. They take care of their home and family, participate in society and government, raise children, and have occupations in agriculture, commerce, and industry. All the while, they realize that they, like their ancestors, are temporary residents of a foreign land. This world is merely a hotel that they will have to soon leave. Because they know this, they don't allow themselves to become too attached to the things of this world. They take care of their physical needs with their left hand while raising their right hand toward their eternal home.

PRAYING WITH CONFIDENCE

So I tell you to ask, and you will receive. Search, and you will find. Knock, and the door will be opened for you.

LUKE 11:9

✥

GOOD PRAYER THAT IS HEARD by God has two prerequisites. First, we must consider God's promise that he will hear us. By reminding him of his promise, we can dare to pray confidently. For if God hadn't asked us to pray and hadn't promised to hear us, then all people praying their requests together wouldn't be able to receive even the smallest item.

So no one receives anything from God because of the quality of the prayer, but only because of God's goodness. God anticipates all of our requests and desires. With his promise, he prompts us to pray and desire these things so that we will learn how much he cares for us. He cares for us so much that he is prepared to give us even more than we are ready to receive or to ask for. Because he is offering us so much, we can pray with confidence.

Second, we must not doubt what the true and faithful God promises to do. He promises to hear our prayers—yes, he even commands us to pray. He promises this so that we might firmly believe that our prayers will be answered. As Christ says, "That's why I tell you to have faith that you have already received whatever you pray for, and it will be yours" (Mark 11:24; Matthew 21:22). Christ also says, "So I tell you to ask, and you will receive. Search, and you will find. Knock, and the door will be opened for you. Everyone who asks will receive. The one who searches will find, and for the person who knocks, the door will be opened" (Luke 11:9–10). By trusting in these promises and obeying these commands, we can pray with confidence.

Letting Evil Flow Past

Then I saw that all hard work and skillful effort
come from rivalry. Even this is pointless.
⌊It's like⌋ trying to catch the wind.

ECCLESIASTES 4:4

❖

N THIS PASSAGE, the writer of Ecclesiastes is saying, "I saw people who were extremely capable at their jobs, but they didn't accomplish anything the way they wanted to because it was not within their power. Their hostile neighbors hindered their efforts."

It's biblical and comforting to know that we shouldn't worry about all the problems in the world. Human concerns and trouble are everywhere. When I was a new preacher, I tried to solve everyone's problems. But people rightfully told me, "You're too inexperienced to reform rascals." The same advice could be given in any job situation. Every occupation has its own problems. Therefore, you should live in the present, enjoy what you have, and just let all the evil flow past you. This is how to defy the world.

In short, if you want to live peacefully, remember that much of what happens in this world will seem pointless. Don't be sad when something bad happens in your life. Instead, enjoy the blessings you still have. If you have been officially given the responsibility for making something better, then do what you can and leave the rest up to God. But if you want to voluntarily take on more responsibility, trying to straighten out everything that is crooked, cure every evil, and throw the devil out of this world, then you'll only cause yourself a lot of pain and sorrow. It's like trying to stop the flow of a swift river. You can't control what people do in this world. Rather, the one who created all things is the one who controls them.

FINDING THE TRUE GOD

While claiming to be wise, they became fools. They exchanged the glory of the immortal God for statues that looked like mortal humans, birds, animals, and snakes.

ROMANS 1:22–23

❖

 UMAN REASON CAN'T quite identify God correctly. Reason knows that there is a God, but it can't figure out which god is the true God. This is exactly what happened to the Jewish leaders while Christ was on earth. John the Baptizer plainly told them that Christ was present. They knew that Christ was living among them and walking among the people. But they couldn't tell which person it was. Hardly any of them could believe that Jesus of Nazareth was the Christ.

In a similar way, human reason plays "blindman's bluff" with God. Reason always makes foolish mistakes and keeps on missing the mark. It calls something god that isn't really God and can't quite identify the real God. If reason didn't have any awareness of God's existence, it wouldn't attempt to identify God. If reason knew exactly who God was, it wouldn't mistakenly identify something else as god. Reason just blurts out, calls something god, and gives divine honor to its own concept of god. By doing so, it misses the true God and instead finds the devil—or its own idea of god, which is ruled by the devil.

There's a big difference between knowing there is a God who exists and knowing who that God is. All of creation teaches us that there is a God. This is already written on all of our hearts. But only the Holy Spirit can teach us who that God is.

DRIED-UP BRANCHES

Whoever doesn't live in me is thrown away like a branch and dries up. Branches like this are gathered, thrown into a fire, and burned.

JOHN 15:6

❖

HEN I WAS A MONK, I read the mass daily. I weakened myself with prayer and fasting so much that I couldn't have kept it up for much longer. Yet all of my efforts couldn't help me in the smallest temptation. I could never say to God, "I have done all this. Look at it, and be merciful to me." What did I achieve with all this striving? Nothing. I merely tormented myself, ruined my health, and wasted my time. Now I'm forced to listen to Christ's judgment on my works. He says, "You did all this without me. That's why it amounts to nothing. Your works don't belong in my kingdom. They can't help you or anyone else obtain eternal life."

So in this passage, Christ has passed a terrifying judgment over all works—no matter how great, glorious, and beautiful they might appear. If these works are performed apart from Christ, they amount to nothing. They may appear to be great in the eyes of the world, for the world considers them excellent and precious. But in Christ's kingdom and before God, they are truly nothing. They don't grow out of him, nor do they remain in him. They won't pass God's test. As Christ says, they will be tossed into the fire as if they were rotten, withered branches—branches without any sap or strength. So let others carve from these branches and see what they can create apart from Christ. Let them try to fashion a new birth from their good works. Let them try to create a tree from its fruit. No matter what they do, all of their works will add up to a big zero.

BALANCING FEAR AND JOY

Serve the LORD with fear,
and rejoice with trembling.

PSALM 2:11

❖

HEN I WAS A YOUNG MAN, I hated this verse because I didn't want to hear that I should fear God. I didn't realize that fear should always be combined with joy and hope. I didn't understand the difference between what we do and what Christ does for us. Everything we do is corrupt, just as all of creation is spoiled. So we shouldn't become overconfident. We need to be afraid of God's judgment. But what Christ does for us is holy and perfect, and we should cling to his mercy.

So we should fear God in a way that doesn't entirely exclude joy. It should be a genuine joy—a joy that can't be kept bottled up in our hearts. Someone who truly believes that he has been reconciled to God because of Christ will have a smile on his face, a twinkle in his eyes, and a song of praise on his lips. The Holy Spirit tells us to serve our heavenly King with inward and outward joy, combined with reverence. If we don't, we'll become overconfident. We'll start acting like animals and sink into lustful human pleasures. If we make sure we don't become overconfident, then God won't be offended by our happiness. In fact, he's offended by sadness and demands joy. That's why people who were in mourning were not allowed to bring God sacrifices, and why the offerings in Malachi were unacceptable to God (Malachi 2:13). We have to mix joy with fear and mix fear with hope.

This psalm warns us not to become either proud or despondent. Falling into despair is as offensive to God as being overconfident. God doesn't want us to be down in the dumps or high up in the clouds. He wants us to be somewhere in the middle.

Avoid Arrogance

If we live by our spiritual nature, then our lives need to conform to our spiritual nature. We can't allow ourselves to act arrogantly and to provoke or envy each other.

GALATIANS 5:25–26

❖

HEN YOU ARE PRAISED, you should know that it is not you who are being praised but Christ, to whom all praise and honor belong. The fact that you may teach in a godly way and live a holy life are not your gifts but God's. So it's not you being praised but God in you. If you acknowledge this, you won't get out of line. You won't become proud because of this praise. For "what do you have that wasn't given to you?" (1 Corinthians 4:7). Instead, you will give God the glory. You will also not allow yourself to give up your calling because of abuse, disgrace, and persecution. God covers our glory with shame by his special grace. He covers it with the world's bitter hatred, persecution, and blasphemy. Furthermore, we face contempt and ingratitude from our own followers—peasants, townspeople, and nobles. Though hidden and inward, their animosity towards and persecution of the gospel is more harmful than the enemies who persecute openly. God allows this so that we don't become proud of our gifts. This millstone must be hung around our necks so that we will not be infected by the plague of honoring ourselves.

Certainly, many of our own followers honor us because we are in official positions as preachers. But for every one who honors us, there are a hundred who hate, despise, and persecute us. The blasphemy and persecution from our opponents, combined with the contempt, ingratitude, and secret hatred from our own followers, is such a lovely sight that delights us so much we easily forget all about personal glory. As a result, we rejoice in the Lord and stay in line.

ASKING FOR FORGIVENESS

*This is why people are condemned: The light came into
the world. Yet, people loved the dark rather than
the light because their actions were evil.*

JOHN 3:19

❖

UPPOSE YOU'RE A HOMEOWNER and something
in your home is damaged. You become
angry about it but soon discover that "No
One" did it. Even though nobody admits to it, the damages remain, and it bothers you. Every so often, a servant is caught in the act of damaging property but still
denies doing it. If the servant would only confess, the
master could easily forgive him.

The devil and death have brought "No One" into the
world. People today are so bad, evil, and full of sin that
they place their own guilt on other people's shoulders. If
they would only admit their sin, they could be forgiven
and would find that God is merciful. God wouldn't deny
us anything if we would only crawl to his cross. But we
don't do it, and in the process we pile seven other sins on
top of one sin. Yes, we multiply our sins to no end and
beyond all measure!

The devil does the same. He denies everything and
makes many sins out of one sin. If a child were to say,
"O father, I have done wrong. Forgive me," he would be
forgiven. But the child stubbornly says "no" and refuses to admit any wrongdoing. He adds a lie to the sin
and to the damage he has already caused. Once again,
more sins spring from the first sin. On the other hand,
if he were to confess the sin and say, "I have done it,"
he would remain in the light and would be like an
angel.

ESSENTIALS OF THE BIBLE

You know the commandments: Never commit adultery.
Never murder. Never steal. Never give false testimony.
Honor your father and your mother.

LUKE 18:20

❖

 OD HAS SO ORDERED matters so that a Christian who might not be able to read the Bible should still learn the Ten Commandments, the Apostle's Creed, and the Lord's Prayer. The essentials of Scripture and everything else a Christian needs to know are summed up in these three. They are written so briefly and clearly that no one has an excuse. No one should complain that it's too much or too difficult. In essence, a person only has to know three things to be saved.

First, he must know what he should and shouldn't do. Second, when he sees that he isn't able to do good or refrain from doing evil in his own strength, he must know where he can find the strength. Third, he must know where he should look for this strength. It's similar to being sick. To begin with, a sick person needs to know what his illness is and what he can and cannot do. After that, he needs to know where he can find the medicine that will make him well. Finally, he must want this medicine, obtain it, or have someone bring it to him.

So the Ten Commandments teach a person to recognize his illness. They help him see what he cannot do or refrain from doing. They help him see himself as a sinner. Then, the Apostle's Creed shows him where he can find the medicine—the grace—to help him become faithful so that he can keep the commandments. The Apostle's Creed points out that God and his mercy is offered in Christ. Finally, the Lord's Prayer teaches a believer how to desire and obtain all this through orderly and humble prayer. In this way, he will receive the cure and be saved.

BELIEVERS WILL LIVE BY FAITH

Look at the proud person. He is not right in himself. But the righteous person will live because of his faithfulness.

HABAKKUK 2:4

❖

ABAKKUK WROTE DOWN the words from God on a tablet, which included this brilliant statement: "The righteous person will live because of his faithfulness." This means that if someone wants to be righteous and live a righteous life, he must believe in God's promise. This truth can't be changed. As a result, the ungodly person will die in his unbelief. So we must believe the writing on the tablet if we want to live now and forever. We must believe that Christ will come with his kingdom. But when things appear otherwise, when we are troubled in this world, we must not lose our way. God's Word holds things before us that are beyond our senses and higher than our understanding. We feel troubled because we look at our current condition. By faith, we need to get beyond these feelings. Even when surrounded by trouble, we must be confident that the kingdom will come and be established in a glorious way.

In this passage we see a clear example of how the prophets in the Old Testament preached and emphasized faith in Christ, just as much as we do in the New Testament. We see that Habakkuk was so bold and that he condemned all other works. He attributed life exclusively to faith. Habakkuk states very plainly that the unbeliever won't succeed on his own. Let him pray and work himself to death. His efforts are already judged. They won't be worth anything, won't achieve anything, and won't help him at all. Meanwhile, believers will live by faith.

FRIENDS OF GOD

I don't call you servants anymore. . . . But I've called you friends because I've made known to you everything that I've heard from my Father.

JOHN 15:15

❖

HRIST STRESSES THE WORD *friend* and highlights the difference between a servant and a friend in this passage. Jesus is saying, "I don't call you servants, as you were under the law before I came. For a servant doesn't know what his master is thinking or wants to do. A servant doesn't share ownership in a master's properties but is given an hourly wage for his service. You aren't servants, as the false believers are. They serve me for personal gain, not from a heart of love. But you are my friends, for I have given to you everything that I have received from my Father."

Take note of whom Jesus calls his friends and why he calls them his friends. We can tell who are his friends by whether or not they receive good things from him. This is illustrated by the parable in Luke 10:30–37. A wounded man had fallen among murderers, and the Samaritan was the one who showed him mercy. The Samaritan treated the wounded man like a friend. We usually reverse it and call people "friends" who do good to us. However, Christ shows us how we become God's friends—it's by receiving good things from Christ. We can't give him anything, and we can't earn the right to be called his friends.

As Jesus says in the next verse, "You didn't choose me" (John 15:16). Jesus initiated friendship with us by receiving us. He's the one who made friends out of his enemies. So we ought to thank God and admit that it's only because of his kindness and goodness we are his friends.

LOVING AND HATING

I have hated the mob of evildoers
and will not sit with wicked people.

PSALM 26:5

❖

 E SHOULD HAVE NOTHING to do with evildoers and wicked people. David said, "I hate them with all my heart" (Psalm 139:22). The author of Psalm 1 praises believers who avoid them: "Blessed is the person who does not follow the advice of wicked people, take the path of sinners, or join the company of mockers" (Psalm 1:1). If you spend too much time with false teachers, you will eventually share in their false doctrine, lies, and errors. If you play with tar, you're going to get dirty.

But doesn't our Lord Jesus Christ command us to love our enemies in Matthew 5:44? So why does David brag that he hates the mob of evildoers and won't sit with wicked people? Shouldn't a person do good things for them and by doing so make them feel guilty and ashamed? Yes, we should hate them, but only in regard to their false teachings. Otherwise, we must be ready to serve our enemies so that we might be able to convert some of them. We need to love them as people, but hate what they teach. So we are forced to choose between hating them or hating God, who wants and commands us to cling to his Word alone. Our hatred is a sacred animosity that flows from love. So love is subject to faith, and faith must be in charge of love.

When the Word of God is at stake, love ends and hate begins. But if only personal things are at stake, such as our property, honor, or body, we should show respect and serve others. God gives us these gifts to help others. We can risk them in order to serve. However, we cannot risk God's Word because it belongs to the Lord our God.

SEAL OF APPROVAL

Work for the food that lasts into eternal life. This is the food the Son of Man will give you. After all, the Father has placed his seal of approval on him.

JOHN 6:27

❖

HE WORDS OF JESUS in this passage seem foolish, crazy, and unintelligible to those who are clever and educated. The Jewish people must have thought of Christ as senseless, crazy, and foolish.

How did it look? How did it sound? This poor, simple man comes on the scene and tells intelligent people that he can give them food that will last forever. He sounds like a charlatan in the marketplace who tells the crowd he is selling a cure-all that will prevent illness, gunshots, wounds, and even death. Everyone would laugh at his claim. Here Christ, a beggar, who doesn't own a square foot of land, is talking about giving away eternal food. If a great king had claimed this, the people might have considered it. But Christ is saying, "I can do what no one in the entire world can do. I will give you a new kind of food that will last forever." Even I would have said, "Where did this fool come from? Have you ever heard a greater fool in your life? A beggar who doesn't have a penny will give us more than all the powerful rulers on the earth. He wants to give us eternal riches, and yet he doesn't own anything himself."

These words of Christ require faith. So this message is aimed only at believers. The world doesn't understand these words, for it doesn't know anything about this type of food. Christians, those who are familiar with God's Word and are convinced of its truth, know Christ through faith alone. They remain loyal to Christ. They believe he is the one on whom "the Father has placed his seal of approval."

CONTENT IN YOUR CALLING

Brothers and sisters, you should remain in whatever circumstances you were in when God called you. God is with you in those circumstances.

1 CORINTHIANS 7:24

❖

E ALL HAVE A CALLING in life. We serve God when we wholeheartedly take care of these responsibilities. An official who governs well serves God. A mother who cares for her children, a father who goes to work, and a student who studies diligently are all servants of God.

Many overlook this God-pleasing lifestyle because they consider simple, day-to-day work insignificant. They look instead for other work that seems more difficult and end up becoming disobedient to God.

Doing what God requires is a sign of superior wisdom. God requires that you work hard at your calling without worrying about what anyone else is doing. Yet few people do this. A poet who reflected on what people are like once said, "The farmer would like to be a shopkeeper, and the shopkeeper a farmer." As the saying goes, "The grass is always greener on the other side of the fence."

Few people are satisfied with their lives. The person in the pew wants to be a member of the clergy. The student wishes he were the teacher. The citizen thinks he should be mayor. Few people are content with their calling. However, there is no other way to serve God except simply living by faith, sticking to your calling, and maintaining a clear conscience.

EFFORTLESS PRAYER

*When you pray, don't ramble like heathens
who think they'll be heard if they talk a lot.*

MATTHEW 6:7

❖

ELIEVERS DON'T VIEW PRAYER as hard work, but as a responsibility that's easy to fulfill. They pray in faith because they know God has promised to hear them. They pray from the heart, revealing their agony and needs. They pray with groans and sighs, as Paul says, "The Spirit intercedes along with our groans that cannot be expressed in words" (Romans 8:26). The Spirit knows that God is listening to him and that excessive rambling isn't necessary.

Elijah, Elisha, David, and others in the Old Testament used few words when they prayed and came straight to the point. The fathers in the early church said it well, "Nothing will be accomplished by long-winded prayers." In fact, the church fathers recommended short, whispered expressions of sorrow and prayers consisting of only a word or two. This kind of praying can be done anytime, even when reading, writing, or doing other tasks.

However, people who think of prayer as bothersome, difficult work will never find any joy or satisfaction in their prayer life. Their only source of pleasure will be their continual rambling. If you try to pray, but you have no faith and you feel no sense of need, your heart won't be in it. And if your heart isn't in your prayers, but you still feel obligated to pray, then prayer becomes boring and difficult. This becomes obvious when you look at physical work. If a job is done reluctantly, it will be boring and annoying. But if a person's heart is in his work, he isn't even aware of the difficulty of his task. So, whoever has an inner joy when he prays isn't aware of the hard work and trouble involved. God doesn't want long, drawn-out prayers. Instead, he wants sincere prayers that flow out of a faithful heart.

Spiritual Poverty

Listen, my dear brothers and sisters! Didn't God choose poor people in the world to become rich in faith and to receive the kingdom that he promised to those who love him?

JAMES 2:5

❖

 OU MAY WONDER, "What? Do all Christians have to live in complete poverty and not own anything? Do we have to get rid of all of our honor, prestige, and power? What are prosperous people, such as business owners and government officials, supposed to do? Should they sell all their possessions and give up their authority in order to buy heaven from the poor?" The answer is no. Scripture doesn't say that you can buy heaven from the poor. But it does say that you should be counted among the poor and also be spiritually poor. Jesus said, "Blessed are those who recognize they are spiritually helpless" (Matthew 5:3).

The little word *spiritually* shows that self-imposed poverty won't bring God's blessing. It's not intrinsically evil to have money, own possessions and land, or employ workers. These are all gifts from God, and the way God has ordered our society. No one is blessed simply because he is a beggar and owns nothing. Jesus was talking about being spiritually poor, or spiritually helpless.

The world can't keep on going without money, respect for authority, land ownership, and servants. A lord or prince can't be poor and fulfill his responsibilities in life. In order to carry out his official duties, he must have the necessary resources. So the idea that we must live in poverty is incorrect. The world couldn't keep going if we were all beggars and owned nothing. We couldn't support our families and servants if we didn't have any money. To sum up, being financially poor isn't the answer. So, be satisfied with whatever God gives you, whether it's poverty or prosperity. But be sure of this: Each and every one of us must become spiritually poor in the sight of God.

CHRIST'S VICTORY

I've told you this so that my peace will be with you.
In the world you'll have trouble. But cheer up!
I have overcome the world.

JOHN 16:33

❖

E SHOULD LEARN TO REMIND ourselves of Christ's victory. In Christ, we already have everything that we need. We only live to spread this message of victory to other people. With our word and example, we tell them about the victory that Christ secured for us and gave to us. Christ, our victor, accomplished everything. We don't need to add anything to it. We don't need to wipe away our own sins, or try to conquer death and the devil. Everything has already been done for us. We're not fighting the real battle. We're only suffering now in order to share in Christ's victory. All of our suffering combined, even all the suffering and blood of the martyrs and saints, wouldn't give us the victory. It's not accomplished by what we do. Some people claim that we ought to be able to conquer sin, death, and hell on our own. By saying this, they insult Christ. But our struggles and fighting come way too late. The battle must be won beforehand if we are to have any comfort and peace. Christ says, "I have already won. Accept my victory. Sing about it and glorify it. Take comfort in it."

We know from the past, when believers were severely tested, the Holy Spirit reminded them of Christ's victory and strengthened them so that they could endure everything. They could even face martyrdom, relying on Christ's victory. May God help us also to hold on to Christ's victory during our troubles and when we're dying. Even though we don't understand these words of Christ completely, we can still believe in them in times of trouble and reassure ourselves: "My Lord and Savior spoke these words to my heart. In Christ I have a victor over the world, death, and the devil. It doesn't matter how small and weak I am. Amen."

DANGEROUS PRAISE

*O Lord, open my lips,
and my mouth will tell about your praise.*

PSALM 51:15

❖

Y ASKING THE LORD to open his lips, David showed how difficult it is to offer thanks to God. This is something God demands of us (Psalm 50:14). Talking about the Lord and thanking him publicly require an extreme amount of courage and strength because the devil is constantly trying to stop people from doing this. If we could see all of Satan's traps, we would know why David prayed for the Spirit's strength and asked the Lord himself to open David's lips. He wanted to tell the devil, the world, kings, princes, and everyone about the Lord.

Many things can keep our lips shut: the fear of danger, the hope of gaining something, or even the advice of friends. The devil uses these ways to stop us from offering thanks to God, as I have often experienced in my life. And yet, at important times, when God's honor was threatened, God stood by me and opened my mouth in spite of the obstacles. The Spirit urges us on, just as Peter says, "We cannot stop talking about what we've seen and heard" (Acts 4:20). The Spirit prays to God for us with many groans (Romans 8:26). Then, the Lord opens our lips to announce his praise.

Whenever Scripture talks about praising God publicly, it's talking about something extremely dangerous. This is because announcing his praise is nothing other than opposing the devil, the world, our own corrupt nature, and everything evil. For how can you praise God without first declaring that the world is guilty and condemned? Anyone who condemns the world is asking to be hated and puts himself in a very dangerous situation.

HOLDING HIGH THE CROSS

It's unthinkable that I could ever brag about anything except the cross of our Lord Jesus Christ. By his cross my relationship to the world and its relationship to me have been crucified.

GALATIANS 6:14

❖

AUL IS SAYING HERE, "I am foolish, a sinner, and weak. I boast in my suffering. I brag that I am without the law, without works, without the righteousness that comes from the law, and finally, without anything except Christ. I want it to be this way. I am happy that I am viewed as unwise, evil, and guilty of all crimes." As Paul says to the Corinthians, "So I will brag even more about my weaknesses in order that Christ's power will live in me" (2 Corinthians 12:9). For the cross of Christ has condemned everything that the world calls good, including wisdom and righteousness. As Scripture says, "I will destroy the wisdom of the wise. I will reject the intelligence of intelligent people" (1 Corinthians 1:19). Christ says, "Blessed are you when people insult you, persecute you, lie, and say all kinds of evil things about you because of me" (Matthew 5:11). So this not only means being crucified with Christ and sharing in his cross and suffering, but also bragging about it and going along joyfully with the apostles, who are considered worthy of suffering dishonor for speaking about Jesus (Acts 5:41).

But some seek honor, riches, and pleasure for the name of Jesus and flee contempt, poverty, and suffering. Do they brag about the cross of Christ? No. Rather, they glory in the world while using the name of Christ for appearances. They end up making a mockery of it.

DIFFICULT TO UNDERSTAND

They asked, "Isn't this man Jesus, Joseph's son?
Don't we know his father and mother?
How can he say now, 'I came from heaven'?"

JOHN 6:42

❖

HIS PASSAGE SHOWS HOW the Israelites complained about what Jesus taught. They
thought it was ridiculous, foolish, and offensive for him to claim that he came from heaven and
could give eternal life. After all, they knew his father,
Joseph, and his mother, Mary. They complained
because they thought he was either telling an outrageous lie or he was a complete fool. Why would he try
to convince them that he had come down from heaven
when his parents lived near Capernaum?

John writes this as a warning to everyone. When it
comes to God's Word and how God deals with us, we
shouldn't worry whether or not it makes sense. If you
want to be a Christian and understand the teachings of
the Christian faith, you shouldn't judge the Christian
doctrines with your mind to find out whether or not
they sound correct. Instead, you should immediately
say, "I'm not asking how it all makes sense. All I need
to know is whether it is God's Word or not. If God said
it, then that decides it." Often, I have warned you not to
argue about lofty, spiritual matters or try to figure them
out. For as soon as you try to make sense of it and put
it in terms you can understand, you slip and fall.

Origen and other church fathers had that experience.
They made the mistake of reaching too high. They tried
to combine reason and worldly righteousness with the
doctrines of the Christian faith. These teachings tran-
scend our reason.

HANDLING SECULAR MATTERS

Abraham took some sheep and cattle and gave them to Abimelech, and the two of them made an agreement. . . . that place is called Beersheba, because both of them swore an oath there.

GENESIS 21:27–31

❖

BRAHAM MADE A BINDING agreement with King Abimelech. This incident shouldn't be passed off as purely secular and superficial. Instead, we should carefully note what Abraham did here because it can bring us comfort. Some people think that Christians shouldn't get involved in public matters. But this story goes against that mistaken notion. God didn't establish the church to get rid of the family and government. He wants the church to support them. That's why Abraham, the father of the promise and king of all earthly kings, doesn't refuse to take an oath and enter into a binding secular agreement with this king.

No one should use Christianity as an excuse for not wanting to have a job or hold public office, as certain religious people do. They're only trying to avoid serving others. But by avoiding this, they're ignoring God's command to love him and to love other people. In the end, they will receive what they deserve for their hypocritical behavior.

We should carefully consider God's laws and Abraham's example. Abraham didn't concern himself only with religious matters. He was a prophet of God, but he also dealt with matters relating to the government and his own household. So we need rulers in the world, as well as in the church. The church doesn't have the right to do away with the family structure or the government. Rather, the church should affirm and support these institutions.

FORGIVE AND YOU WILL BE FORGIVEN

If you forgive the failures of others, your heavenly Father will also forgive you. But if you don't forgive others, your Father will not forgive your failures.

MATTHEW 6:14–15

❖

OME PEOPLE WONDER why Christ would attach such a condition to this part of the Lord's Prayer: "If you forgive the failures of others, your heavenly Father will also forgive you." He didn't attach similar conditions to other parts of the prayer. He could've said, "Give us our daily bread today, as we give it to our children." Or, "Don't allow us to be tempted, and we won't tempt anyone else either." Or, "Rescue us from evil, just as we try to help others."

None of the other parts of this prayer have a condition tacked on to it, except this one. People are left with the impression that we earn forgiveness for our sins by forgiving others. What does this mean for the doctrine that forgiveness of sins comes only through Christ and is received through faith?

Jesus phrases the prayer so that God's forgiveness is linked to our own willingness to forgive others in order to make mutual love a Christian duty. We should always forgive others. After faith in Christ, loving and forgiving others should be our primary concern. We shouldn't cause other people pain. Instead, we should remember to forgive others, even when they have caused us suffering, as we often experience in this life. If we are unwilling to forgive, we can be certain that we won't be forgiven ourselves. If we are full of resentment and hostility, that prayer will be spoiled and all of the requests in that prayer will be rejected. We must establish a strong and durable bond of love with other Christians that will keep us united. When we come before God in prayer, we shouldn't be divided into various splinter groups. Instead, we should be guided by love, tolerate differences of opinion, and preserve unity.

CHRIST'S MISSION ON EARTH

Therefore, your minds must be clear and ready for action.
Place your confidence completely in what God's kindness
will bring you when Jesus Christ appears again.

1 PETER 1:13

❖

HE GOSPEL TELLS US who Christ is. Through it, we learn that he is our Savior. He delivers us from sin and death, helps us out of all misfortune, reconciles us to the Father, makes us godly, and saves us apart from our own works. Anyone who doesn't acknowledge Christ in this way will fail. For even if you already know that he is God's Son, that he died, rose again, and sits at the right hand of the Father, you still haven't known Christ in the right way. This knowledge doesn't help you. You must also know and believe that he has done all of this for your sake—in order to help you. Some have contemplated only Christ's pain and suffering and mistakenly think he is now sitting in heaven with nothing to do, enjoying himself. As a result, faith cannot come alive, and their hearts remain barren.

We should not think the Lord Christ belongs to himself alone. We must preach that he also belongs to us. Otherwise, why would it have been necessary for him to come to earth and shed his blood? As Jesus said, "God sent his Son into the world, not to condemn the world, but to save the world" (John 3:17). So Jesus must have accomplished what the Father sent him to do. God sent to earth not only Christ's divine nature, but also his human nature. As soon as he was baptized, he began what he had been sent to the world to accomplish. God sent him to proclaim the truth and win us over so that all who believe in him would be saved.

DEATH'S STING

*Sin gives death its sting, and God's standards give
sin its power. Thank God that he gives us the
victory through our Lord Jesus Christ.*

1 CORINTHIANS 15:56-57

HIS IS A BEAUTIFUL PASSAGE for Christians. It
shows us how, through Christ's victory, we
can get rid of death's sting. It shows us how
we can get rid of the power of the law, which drives that
sting into us and kills us. Ultimately, the sting will be
completely removed from us. Paul closes with an
appropriate song, which we can also sing, "Thank God
that he gives us the victory." With this song, we can continually celebrate Easter, praising God for this victory.
We didn't win this victory or achieve it in battle, for it's
too great and lofty. But this victory was given to us out
of God's kindness. He had mercy on our misery, and he
knew no one else could help us. So he sent his Son into
battle. Christ secured the victory. He defeated the enemies—sin, death, and hell. He gave us this victory so
that we can call it our own, just as if we had won it.

Now we must take it seriously and not live in con-
tradiction to God, as do those who presume to conquer
sin and death by themselves. Also, we don't want to be
found ungrateful, as apathetic Christians will often be.
We should rather hold this victory in our hearts with
firm faith and strengthen ourselves with it. Keep this
message of Christ's victory in mind. Sing about it, and
travel along joyfully until that day when you experience
this victory in your own body.

THE SOURCE OF LIFE

Jesus told them, "I can guarantee this truth: If you don't eat the flesh of the Son of Man and drink his blood, you don't have the source of life in you."

JOHN 6:53

❖

O MATTER WHAT ANYONE SAYS, this passage is clear. If Jesus had phrased this in the affirmative, "Whoever eats my flesh has life," then somebody could have challenged it by saying, "Those who don't eat it will also be saved." Some scoundrels also say, "Your teaching is correct, but ours is also correct. The Lord didn't mean to exclude other ways." They create many ways to receive eternal life, including praying to the saints, worshiping the virgin Mary, or living in a monastery. But none of these ways can achieve eternal life. Christ excludes all other ways. They are all unacceptable.

Take a look at this from another angle. If I were to say, "Wittenberg beer quenches thirst. Annaberg beer also quenches thirst," then I don't exclude other beers. But it would be very different if I were to say, "If you don't drink Wittenberg beer, no other beer will quench your thirst." In the same way, Christ doesn't speak in the affirmative here. He excludes everything else when he says, "If you don't eat the flesh of the Son of Man and drink his blood, you don't have the source of life in you." If we despise his flesh, nothing else will prove helpful. I may call on Saint Mary or Saint Peter, but they cannot help me. It's out of the question. In a word, all other ways are rejected.

Life, grace, and salvation come to us by faith alone and not by good works. They become ours by believing and by eating and drinking the body and blood of Christ.

DOING WHAT YOU CAN

Rebekah . . . said to him, "Watch out! Your brother Esau is comforting himself by planning to kill you. So now, Son, obey me. Quick! Run away to my brother Laban in Haran."

GENESIS 27:42–43

❖

EBEKAH SHOWS HER WISDOM in sending Jacob away to avoid Esau's anger. She didn't test God by saying, "The one who blessed you will also care for you," and let it go at that. To be sure, whatever God wants will indeed happen, but he uses people and things to accomplish what he wants. Rebekah believed that the worship of God and the blessing entrusted to Jacob would be protected. So she made use of what God had provided to find a way for Jacob to avoid danger.

Those who assume God will take care of everything and don't think it's important to make use of what's available should carefully note this example. These type of people sometimes don't take any action because they believe that if something is meant to happen, then it will happen with or without their help. They even put themselves in unnecessary danger, expecting God to protect them because of his promises.

But these kinds of thoughts are sinful because God wants you to use what you have available and make the best of your opportunities. He wants to accomplish his will through you. For example, he gave you a father and mother, even though he could have created you and fed you without them. This means that in your everyday life, you have the responsibility to work. You plow, plant, and harvest, but God is the one who provides the outcome.

If you stopped giving a baby milk, reasoning that the baby could live without food if he were meant to live, then you would be fooling yourself and sinning. God has given mothers breasts to nurse their babies. He could easily feed children without milk if he chose to. But God wants you to use the resources he has provided.

OUR CHILDREN WILL BE BLESSED

Hallelujah! Blessed is the person who fears the LORD and is
happy to obey his commands. His descendants will grow strong
on the earth. The family of a decent person will be blessed.

PSALM 112:1–2

❖

HY WILL THE DESCENDANTS of God-fearing people grow strong on the earth? They will grow
strong because they have God's blessing. God
will bless their children and grandchildren. Even if they
don't have a penny right now, they will get what they
need at the right time. Even if the whole world is hungry,
they will have enough. In another psalm we read, "Even
in times of famine they will be satisfied" (Psalm 37:19).
David said, "I have never seen a righteous person abandoned or his descendants begging for food" (Psalm
37:25). Even when times get bad, the descendants of a
God-fearing person will always have what they need.

Which situation would you prefer? Do you want to
have a lot of money and property but be so greedy that
you never use the cash, constantly look for more
money, hoard what you have, and never find happiness? Or, would you rather have no money but be so
happy and peaceful that you trust in God and never
doubt that he will provide for you?

Greedy people have the feeling that they can't use
what they have. A person who has ten thousand dollars
might say, "I have to keep this for my children, but what
will I use to buy food?" He acts like a poor person
because he doesn't want to use what he has. Christians,
on the other hand, don't hoard things this way. They
store their treasures with God in heaven (Matthew 6:20;
Luke 12:33–34). Christians say, "Dear Lord, I know that
you have so much that you'll never run out of anything.
So I will never be in need. I want you to be my cabinet
and pantry. You are my treasure. When I have you, I
have enough."

THE SOURCE OF BLESSING

*[Abram] brought back everything they had, including
women and soldiers. He also brought back his
relative Lot and his possessions.*

GENESIS 14:16

❖

OT AND HIS PEOPLE were captured and carried
off by enemies, but Abram rescued them.
After suffering this great defeat, Lot had his
land and possessions restored to him through Abram's
efforts. This was far more than he had hoped. Similarly,
people in the world today receive good things because
Christians are living faithfully on the earth. So we
should be encouraged and comforted when we see
God's blessings. It proves that the church is still present
on earth and that God's people, though small in number, haven't disappeared completely. It's for the sake of
Christians that God shows his undeserved kindness to
everyone in the world.

Unbelievers do just the opposite. They think they are
responsible for the blessings they receive, attributing all
good things to their own wisdom and efforts. In their
misplaced self-confidence, they indulge in their pleasures, getting drunk and gorging themselves as arrogantly as did the people of Sodom. In the end, they will
receive the punishment they deserve, while God's people will remain securely in his care.

Furthermore, this passage makes us aware that
devout Christians will always suffer in this world. Their
lives are filled with problems, but it's precisely these
problems that help them to become more holy and
righteous. All things, even problems and troubles, work
together for the good of those who love God—those
whom he has called (Romans 8:28). Suffering kills the
corrupt nature, strengthens faith, and allows the gifts of
the Holy Spirit to multiply.

PHYSICAL AND SPIRITUAL BLESSINGS

Faith enabled Abraham to become a father, even though he was old and Sarah had never been able to have children. Abraham trusted that God would keep his promise.

HEBREWS 11:11

❖

THE BIBLE CLEARLY SHOWS that promises of physical blessings also include spiritual blessings. We weren't created for an existence like that of cattle and donkeys. Instead, we were created for eternity. When God gives us a promise, he doesn't limit himself to our physical needs. He isn't concerned only about our stomachs. He also wants to keep our souls from being destroyed and wants to give us eternal life.

Consequently, promises concerning external and physical matters are like the shell of a nut. But the real essence, or inner kernel, is Christ and eternal life. God, who makes the promises, isn't speaking to donkeys and cattle, as Paul points out, "God's concern isn't for oxen" (1 Corinthians 9:9). Rather, he's concerned about intelligent human beings created in his image to live with him for eternity.

Clearly, the promises of physical blessings are like the nuts and apples we use to get the attention of our children. God gets our attention with physical blessings so that we will learn to appreciate the eternal blessings. This is how God encourages us to expect eternal life. God's purpose in giving us food and water isn't merely that we would eat and drink without thinking, as horses and donkeys do. Rather, he gives us physical blessings so that we will realize that he is loving and kind. This will help us to believe he will take care of all our needs. Even if God only gave you a piece of straw, he would want you to acknowledge him as the eternal God whose kindness is overflowing. If you still believe in him, you will have eternal life. Even though Abraham didn't see all of these promises fulfilled in his own lifetime, he still believed God. That's why he was given eternal life.

NOVEMBER 26

SHOVING ASIDE GOD'S KINDNESS

*I don't reject God's kindness. If we receive God's approval
by obeying laws, then Christ's death was pointless.*

GALATIANS 2:21

❖

ANTING TO RECEIVE God's approval by our own works through the law is so wrong that the apostle Paul calls this throwing God's kindness away. It shows not only ingratitude—which is extremely bad in itself—but also shows contempt because we should eagerly seek God's kindness. Instead, we shove aside his kindness, which we receive free of charge. This is a serious error. Consider Paul's argument, "If we receive God's approval by obeying laws, then Christ's death was pointless." Paul confidently declares that either Christ's death was pointless, which is the highest blasphemy against God, or Christ's death was essential, and through the law we can have nothing but sin.

Some teachers categorize various kinds of righteousness using distinctions they have made up in their heads. If these teachers try to bring these ideas to theology, they should be kept far away from the Holy Scriptures. For these people say one kind is moral righteousness, another is righteousness of faith, and they describe others I don't even know about. Let civil government have its kind of righteousness, the philosophers have theirs, and each person have his own. But we must understand righteousness the way the Bible explains it. The apostle clearly says that there is no other righteousness than through faith in Jesus Christ. All other works, even those according to the most holy laws of God, do not offer righteousness. Not only that, they are actually sins.

Our sins are so great and so far away from righteousness that it was necessary for the Son of God to die so that righteousness could be given to us. When discussing theology, don't call anything righteousness that is apart from faith in Christ.

GOD'S PROMISES ARE CERTAIN

Then Abram believed the LORD, and the LORD
regarded that faith to be his approval of Abram.

GENESIS 15:6

❖

E MUST RECOGNIZE that God's promises and commands are distinctly different. God's promises require faith. God's commands demand action. God's promises are absolute and will certainly happen because God himself carries them out. On the other hand, his commands are never fully obeyed. People don't live up to God's standards because they are pathetic sinners. Fortunately, God's approval doesn't depend on our efforts to obey his commands. We can never live up to God's standards. Instead, God's approval depends on his promise, which is firmly established and cannot be changed. The promise will certainly happen when we believe it. Therefore, it's undeniably true that faith is what secures God's approval because faith alone accepts the promise.

Our own efforts to obey God's commands don't earn us God's approval. Still, we must teach God's commands and try to obey them in order to become aware of how desperate our situation is. We need to realize just how much we need God's mercy and goodwill. We didn't make this theology up, and it didn't grow inside our heads, as our opponents keep yelling and screaming. Paul teaches it by quoting Moses, who says that Abraham believed God and that God regarded that faith to be his approval. In other words, Abraham received God's approval because he believed the promise.

All of God's promises are based on Christ. If we didn't have Christ as our mediator, God would have nothing to do with us. Abraham believed in the promised Christ who was still to come. We believe in the Christ who has already come. We all receive God's approval because of this same faith.

GOD IS OUR REFUGE

A prayer by Moses, the man of God.
O Lord, you have been our refuge
throughout every generation.

PSALM 90:1

❖

OSES BEGINS THIS PSALM with comforting words for people who fear death. They have learned to trust in God's mercy because of this fear. They are glad they have life. They recognize they're sinners and don't ignore their sins or laugh them off. They are teachable and willing to be comforted. When I was a monk, I often had to set down the Bible when I came to this psalm. I didn't understand the harsh language in the later verses. Back then, I didn't understand that this psalm wasn't meant for those who are already frightened by their sins. Moses is primarily preaching to the indifferent and arrogant masses of humanity who aren't concerned about God's anger, their impending deaths, or their own misfortune.

Look at the title of this psalm, and you will see it's called a prayer. The most important requirement of a true, sincere prayer is that a person firmly believes that he has eternal life and that God is merciful. It's only because God is merciful that a person can be sure that the Lord will protect him from eternal death. If this weren't true, why would Moses call God our refuge? Therefore, these words assure us that God is able to give us eternal life.

Although Moses was aware of his sin and God's anger, he dared to say, "Lord, even though you are rightfully angry with us because of our sins, you have never abandoned us. You have always preserved your faithful people on earth in spite of our sins. You have continued to be a refuge and safe harbor for those who, through you, confidently expect eternal life." The most important requirement of prayer is firmly holding on to God and believing that he is merciful and compassionate—someone who wants to help you.

Praying Sincerely

Don't be like hypocrites. They like to stand in synagogues and
on street corners to pray so that everyone can see them. . . .
When you pray, go to your room and close the door.

MATTHEW 6:5–6

❖

N THIS PASSAGE, Jesus emphasizes that our prayers must be sincere. Christ teaches us the right way to pray so that our prayers won't be hypocritical. Instead of standing on street corners reciting long prayers, it would be more appropriate if we would pray at home in private. Most of all, Christ wants to make it clear that we need to get rid of improper motives. We shouldn't pray in order to be recognized or to gain something from others.

This doesn't mean that you should never pray in public. Christians aren't restricted to certain places where they may or may not pray. Locations, like street corners, marketplaces, outdoor areas, and churches, are certainly not off limits for prayer. You can pray anywhere.

But you shouldn't show off when you pray or use prayer to gain admiration or profit. Christ doesn't denounce blowing trumpets or ringing bells to attract attention for good causes. But he does rule out impure motives in prayer when he says emphatically, "So that everyone can see them."

Going into a private room and locking the door isn't required when you pray. However, you might want to be alone to pour out your wants and needs to God with words and gestures that you wouldn't feel comfortable having others see. Although you can pray in your heart without saying anything aloud, words and gestures help kindle the spirit. So the Christian's entire life should be devoted to God—spreading his Word and praising his kingdom. Whatever a Christian does must be grounded in sincere prayer.

GOD USES WEAK PEOPLE

Isaac answered, "She's my sister." He was afraid to say "my wife." He thought that the men of that place would kill him to get Rebekah, because she was an attractive woman.

GENESIS 26:7

❖

THE THEOLOGIANS ARGUE about whether Isaac was sinning when he lied and said that Rebekah was his sister. In his weakness, he thought, "I'll say she's my sister, or else they might kill me." That almost sounds like, "Go ahead. Take my wife and disgrace her, as long as I don't get hurt. If I say she's my wife, you'll only feel like you can't have her unless you kill me first." Isn't that a foolish, silly, and unworthy attitude for such an important man? Shouldn't he just have said, "She's my wife. I don't care whether you kill me or not?" But the passage says that Isaac was afraid. What a shame that someone as important as he was should be so afraid of death!

This story was written to comfort God's people. It shows how merciful and kind God really is. Even though we are sinful and weak, the Lord will be patient with our weaknesses, as long as we stay away from those who deny, hate, or curse God. I don't want to excuse our ancestors in the faith, as some people do. It's comforting to hear that even good people in the Bible slipped and did wrong. I don't hold up their actions as if they were good. Similarly, I don't excuse Peter for denying Jesus. I don't excuse the apostles for deserting Jesus or for any other foolish thing they did.

Among his little flock, there are some poor, miserable, and weak souls. Jesus is the king of the weak as well as the strong. He hates arrogant people and opposes the stubborn. He punishes hypocrites and people who are overconfident. But he doesn't want to discourage or crush those who are scared, sad, or worried. He doesn't want to extinguish the flickering light (Isaiah 42:3).

COMMANDED TO PRAY

If you ask the Father for anything in my name,
he will give it to you. So far you haven't
asked for anything in my name.

JOHN 16:23–24

❖

N THIS PASSAGE, Christ shows us how to defend against the obstacles thrown at us by the devil and our corrupt nature. These threaten to tear us away from prayer. Christ tells us, "If you ask the Father for anything in my name, he will give it to you." First, Christ commands us to pray. Then, he admonishes us for not asking. He repeats his command and drives it home to show that he's serious. He demands prayer as true worship and as the real work of Christians.

Study what Christ commands in this passage and put it into practice. Don't consider prayer as something that you do voluntarily, as if it wouldn't be a sin if you neglected to pray. Don't act as if it's enough for others to pray. But now you know that Christ earnestly commands prayer. If you don't pray, you risk the greatest disgrace and the highest penalty. Christ's command here is similar to the commandment that prohibits worshiping any other gods and blaspheming God's name. Those who never pray should know that they aren't Christians and don't belong in God's kingdom. Now don't you think that God has good reason to be angry with idolaters, murderers, thieves, blasphemers, and others who despise his Word? Don't you think he's right to punish these sins? Why, then, aren't you afraid of God's anger when you disrespect his command and confidently act as if you aren't obligated to pray?

So this passage should serve as a strong encouragement to pray diligently. Prayer is our comfort, strength, and salvation. It's our first line of defense against all of our enemies.

GOD WAITS FOR THE RIGHT TIME

Then Pharaoh sent for Joseph, and immediately he was brought from the dungeon. After he had shaved and changed his clothes, he came in front of Pharaoh.

GENESIS 41:14

❖

BRAHAM, ISAAC, JACOB, and Joseph were humble people. They waited patiently for God's help. God was with Joseph in prison. The Lord knew the exact time he wanted to free Joseph. Joseph had no idea how he was going to become free, but he sat in the dark and didn't worry about it. He put himself totally in God's hands.

Joseph had exceptional faith, and God came and rescued him in a miraculous way: "They hurt his feet with shackles, and cut into his neck with an iron collar. The LORD's promise tested him through fiery trials until his prediction came true. The king sent someone to release him. The ruler of nations set him free." (Psalm 105:18–20). Oh, what a wonderful freedom that was! While in prison, Joseph would have loved to have someone intercede for him. Whether his defender was his father, the chief cupbearer, or his former master, he would have jumped at the opportunity. He would have even accepted help from his master's wife if she felt sorry for her sin. But God chose none of these methods. God wanted the king to proclaim Joseph's freedom. This made it a public and spectacular event, especially since Joseph was elevated to a position second only to the king.

We must learn to trust the Lord and wait for him, just as Joseph did. His faith enabled him to wait patiently for a long time, even though he had no idea when he would be released. Joseph's example should encourage us to resolve: "I know my sinful nature is going to complain, but I will try to restrain it." Biblical examples, like Joseph's, set the hearts of faithful people on fire and inspire them to faith, hope, and love.

LOVE YOUR NEIGHBOR

The second most important commandment is this:
"Love your neighbor as you love yourself." No other
commandment is greater than these.

MARK 12:31

❖

HEN YOU'RE WONDERING whom you should show love to, there's no living creature better than your neighbor to show love to. Your neighbor is not a devil, lion, bear, or wolf. He is not made of stone or wood, but he is a living being who is much like you. There is nothing living on the earth more lovable, kind, useful, good, comforting, or more necessary. He was even created for friendly conversation and for social life. There is nothing in the whole world more worthy of our love than our neighbor.

But it's the remarkable craft of the devil that he not only severely darkens our hearts and tears this superior object of our love from our hearts. But he also persuades our hearts of the opposite opinion so that we think our neighbor is more worthy of bitter hatred than of love. This is easy for the devil to do. He simply nags us: "See, this person has such and such a fault. He abused you. He hurt you. . . ." Then this object of love quickly becomes contemptible to us so that we no longer recognize our neighbor as one who should be loved but rather as an enemy worthy of intense hatred. In this way, Satan can amazingly change the love in our heart so that, instead of loving our neighbor, we become capable of demeaning, hating, and persecuting him. Then all that remains of this commandment, "Love your neighbor as you love yourself," are the bare and empty letters and syllables.

THE WORD MAKES US CLEAN

*You are already clean
because of what I have told you.*

JOHN 15:3

❖

N THIS PASSAGE, Christ is offering us a remedy for the poison of arrogance, which is overestimating your own holiness. Jesus says this so no one will think that his own suffering, apart from Christ, can attain forgiveness of sins or make that person a fruitful branch in the sight of God. Here's what usually happens. Someone does many good works and endures much suffering. That person becomes aware of producing fruit. In other words, he is aware of achieving something through preaching or some other method. Then, that sweet poison begins to make the person think, "Oh, I have now done something that will make God notice me and be merciful to me." In this way, little wild branches begin growing alongside the true branches. These wild branches steal the sap and energy from the true branches so that they don't flourish. That is why the gardener must be alert. He always has to restrain such arrogance and presumption by constant application of the Word.

Christ is saying here, "You aren't clean because of what you do, what you suffer, or the fruit you produce. You wouldn't have done any of these things if you hadn't already been pruned and been made into good and true branches. Only God's Word can make you clean. It must be present at all times. The Father sends various kinds of suffering, danger, anxiety, need, and temptation to you so that you may hang on to God's Word tightly and so that it may powerfully work in you. In this way, he humbles and teaches you that you can't make yourself clean. Your suffering doesn't make you clean before God. Yet it drives you to reach for and hold on to God's Word more tightly and firmly. This is how God exercises your faith.

NO FEAR OF DEATH

Abraham lived 175 years. Then he took his last breath, and died at a very old age. After a long and full life, he joined his ancestors in death.

GENESIS 25:7–8

❖

THIS PASSAGE TEACHES us that the death of one of God's people is a dignified event and precious in God's sight. These departing souls don't suffer in the same way unbelievers do. Instead, they pass away calmly.

The world hates God's people, looks down on them, and rejects them. Although their deaths appear to be sad, depressing events to the world, in reality, believers give up this life as if they were slipping into a restful, gentle sleep. When they lie down to die, death descends on their minds and bodies like a liberating slumber. The trials of life have taught them to be humble and peaceful. Death doesn't terrify them. They're able to say, "My Lord and my God, I am ready to die if that's what seems best to you." But unbelievers are full of panic and anxiety at even the thought of their impending death.

This should be a lesson to us. It should encourage us to surrender to God when he calls us out of this miserable existence. We should freely declare, "I don't wish to live a moment longer than what you intend for me. Lord Jesus, you may come for me whenever you want." Abraham, the man of God, died at a very old age, having lived a full and satisfying life. But where did Abraham go? Moses tells us, "he joined his ancestors." Do people still exist after this life? This passage makes it sound as though Abraham migrated from one group of people to another, from one place to another. This passage is outstanding evidence of the resurrection and eternal life.

INVISIBLE GUARDIANS

*The Messenger of the LORD camps around those
who fear him, and he rescues them.*

PSALM 34:7

❖

O CHRISTIAN SHOULD THINK that he is alone when he is dying. Instead, he should know that many eyes are on him. First, if a person believes God's words and clings to the sacraments, he knows that God himself and Christ are present. Second, angels, saints, and all Christians are also looking on.

If a Christian can picture this and not doubt it, then he can die with confidence. Whoever doubts this must not understand the sacrament of the Body of Christ in which communion, help, love, comfort, and support in times of need are pointed out, promised, and pledged. For if you believe in the signs and words of God, then God keeps an eye on you, as the Lord says in the Psalms, "I will advise you as my eyes watch over you" (Psalm 32:8). If God looks upon you, then all of the angels, saints, and other beings will look in the same direction. And if you remain in faith, they all hold you with their hands. When your soul leaves your body, they will be there to receive it. You will not perish.

This is confirmed by the story of Elisha and his servant when enemies surrounded them. Elisha said, "Don't be afraid. We have more forces on our side than they have on theirs." The servant could see no one else, but then "The LORD opened the servant's eyes and let him see. The mountain around Elisha was full of fiery horses and chariots" (2 Kings 6:16–17). Similarly, everyone who trusts God is also surrounded, even though he can't see it. The words of Psalm 34:7 fit well here, "The Messenger of the LORD camps around those who fear him, and he rescues them."

LIVING IN HOPE

May God, the source of hope, fill you with joy and peace
through your faith in him. Then you will overflow with
hope by the power of the Holy Spirit.

ROMANS 15:13

❖

HE ONLY REASON WE are living on earth is to
help other people. Otherwise, it would be
best if God choked us and let us die as soon
as we were baptized and had begun to believe. But he
allows us to live here so that we will bring other people
to faith, just as he has done for us. Meanwhile, because
we are still on earth, we must live with a confident hope.
Although we know that we possess God's treasures
through faith—for faith gives us the new birth, our
standing as God's children, and the inheritance that
comes with it—we don't see it yet. It's still in the future,
like something put off to the side, hidden from our eyes.

Peter calls this a living hope (1 Peter 1:3). We have
God's treasures, but they are still concealed. They can
only be grasped with the heart and through faith. John
writes about this in his letter, "Now we are God's children. What we will be isn't completely clear yet. We do
know that when Christ appears we will be like him
because we will see him as he is" (1 John 3:2). For this
life and the future life are separate and cannot coexist
with each other. We can't eat, drink, sleep, wake up, and
go through the other activities of this life and also be in
heaven at the same time. We can't enter eternal life
without dying and having this life pass away. So while
we are here, and until that day God wants us to see the
treasures we possess, we must keep on living in hope.

WE WILL BE REWARDED

Blessed are you when people insult you, persecute you, lie, and say all kinds of evil things about you because of me. Rejoice and be glad because you have a great reward in heaven!

MATTHEW 5:11-12

❖

 F IT'S IMPOSSIBLE TO RECEIVE God's undeserved kindness except through faith in Christ, why does the Bible include so many passages about God rewarding people for the good things they've done? These passages are intended to comfort Christians. When you become a Christian, you will find forgiveness both for past sins and the ones you commit every day. But you'll have to work hard and suffer a lot as a result of your faith and baptism. Jesus makes it clear that the devil, the world, and your corrupt nature will attack you from every direction and make you feel hemmed in on all sides.

If you were left in this predicament without anything to comfort you, you would give up in despair and say, "Who wants to be a Christian, or speak about Christ, or do good works? Look at what happens to Christians. The world walks all over them, slanders and humiliates them. It plays all kinds of cruel tricks on them. In the end, they lose their honor, property, and life. Christ calls them helpless, sorrowful, hungry, meek, afflicted, and persecuted! Is that all he can say? Will this last forever and never change?"

At that point, Christ strengthens and comforts us by saying, "You are God's children. He is going to take care of you. Even though you have to suffer in the world now for being God's children, don't let that suffering frighten you. Don't let what you experience tire you out or wear you down. Every one of you must continue to do your duty. This is painful, but it won't do you any real harm. The kingdom of heaven is yours, and you will be richly rewarded."

EVERYDAY MIRACLES

The LORD's deeds are spectacular.
They should be studied by all who enjoy them.

PSALM 111:2

❖

HAT THE LORD DOES is spectacular. But in this passage, the psalmist points out that only a few devout people notice what God has done. Most people don't praise God or thank him. They never say, "The LORD's deeds are spectacular." Though they are completely surrounded by his gifts, they have gotten used to them. They take advantage of what God has given them, rooting around in God's gifts like a hog in a bag of feed. They say, "What's so special about the fact that the sun shines, fire gives warmth, the ocean provides fish, the earth yields grain, cows have calves, women give birth to children, and hens lay eggs? These things happen every day!"

Is something insignificant just because it happens every day? If the sun wouldn't shine for ten days, suddenly it would be a great thing when it began shining again. If fire only existed in one place on the earth, I think it would be more precious than gold or silver. If there were only one well in the world, I would imagine that a drop of water would be worth more than a thousand dollars.

God showers people with rich and wonderful blessings. But how ungrateful and blind people are! They don't recognize these blessings as amazing miracles from God, so they don't admire them, give thanks for them, or act happy about them. However, if a clown can walk on a tightrope or train monkeys, people are ready to admire and praise him for it. The psalmist points out that the Lord's deeds are spectacular, but these deeds are only appreciated in the eyes of God's faithful followers.

BELIEVING IN THE TRIUNE GOD

In the beginning the Word already existed.
The Word was with God, and the Word was God.

JOHN 1:1

❖

HE FOLLOWING ILLUSTRATION is overly simplistic, but it makes the birth of the Son of God a little easier to understand. As a human son receives his body and his very being from his father, so the Son of God, born of the Father, receives his divine essence and nature from the eternal Father. But this or any other illustration can never adequately describe how the divine majesty can be given to another, as when the Father gives his entire divine essence to the Son. A human father can't give his entire being to his son. This is where the comparison breaks down.

However, as far as the divine being is concerned, all of God's divine essence and nature passes into the Son. Yet the Son, who remains in the divine being together with the Father, is one God together with the Father. Likewise, the Holy Spirit has the same divine nature and majesty as the Father and the Son.

You must simply believe this. No matter how clever, sharp, or intelligent a person may be, the human mind will never be able to fully comprehend it. If human wisdom were able to grasp this, then God wouldn't have needed to reveal it from heaven or announce it through Holy Scripture. So you should say, "Even though I can't completely comprehend it, I believe and confess that there is one eternal God, who is also three distinct persons. Holy Scripture is God's Word and says that this is the way it is. I will live by what it says."

THE WORD IS GOD

In the beginning the Word already existed. The Word was with God, and the Word was God. He was already with God in the beginning. Everything came into existence through him.

JOHN 1:1–3

❖

OHN WROTE ABOUT the majesty and divine nature of our dear Lord and Savior Jesus Christ in a profound way. John said that Christ, in his divine essence, is the Word of the eternal Father. If the Word existed from the beginning before anything was created, then it must follow that this Word is God. We can easily draw this conclusion: Whatever had its existence before the creation of the world must be God because only the Creator can exist separate from creation. Everything that exists is either Creator or creation—either God or creature. Through John, the Holy Spirit stated that "In the beginning the Word already existed" and "Everything came into existence through him." For this reason, we can never think of the Word as something created. The Word is eternal. No one can deny or disprove the conclusion that this Word is God.

This passage establishes that Christ is God. On the basis of this fact, we believe and know with certainty that Mary gave birth to our Lord and Savior and that he is true and natural God, born in eternity by the Father. This is why he can't be considered an angel. Instead, he is the Lord and Creator of angels and of all other creatures, as Paul states, "He created all things in heaven and on earth, visible and invisible" (Colossians 1:16).

Now, we know that Holy Scripture is God's Word and will last forever (1 Peter 1:25). Scripture clearly states that the Word existed in the beginning before anything was created and that the Word made everything. So, it follows that believers can't hold any other opinion or come to any other conclusion: The Word was not created or made, but already existed from eternity.

CREATOR OF THE UNIVERSE

Everything came into existence through him.
Not one thing that exists was made without him.

JOHN 1:3

❖

HIS PASSAGE IS A CLEAR, concise statement about Christ's divinity. John included all creatures when he said that everything was made by the Word. Whoever uses the term *everything* hasn't left anything out. In other words, John was asserting that the Word existed before all creatures and that the Word was a coworker with the Father. He was an equal Creator of everything along with the Father.

Everything that exists has been made through the Word. The Word is the Creator of all creatures. There is no difference between the Word and the Father regarding the divine essence. The Word is the true God because he shares the divine essence with God the Father. The Word existed in the beginning and was with God. He demonstrated this when he created the universe. He made heaven and earth, angels, and all creatures. Christ declared, "My Father is working right now, and so am I" (John 5:17). So this passage clearly asserts that he is the coequal Creator: "Everything came into existence through him. Not one thing that exists was made without him" (John 1:3). "He is the image of the invisible God, the firstborn of all creation. He created all things in heaven and on earth, visible and invisible" (Colossians 1:15–16). "God made his Son responsible for everything. His Son is the one through whom God made the universe" (Hebrews 1:2).

This passage affirms that the Father created everything through his Son. This keeps us from having doubts about who the Son is. We can know and believe that our dear Lord and Savior, born of the virgin Mary, is also the real, true, natural God and Creator together with the Father and the Holy Spirit.

GOD BECAME A MAN

The Word became human and lived among us.
We saw his glory.

JOHN 1:14

❖

HE WORD BECAME HUMAN. We can never fully grasp this teaching concerning our salvation and eternal life using human reason. Nevertheless, we must believe it, and we must cling tightly to what Scripture says about it. The Bible says that Christ, our Lord, is true and natural God, and true and natural man. The Bible says that in his divine essence and nature Christ is coequal with the Father. The heretics have cast doubts on both the divine nature and the human nature of Christ. During the lifetime of the apostles, some heretics claimed that Christ was not God. Centuries later, others claimed that Christ was not human. Some of our contemporaries teach similar things. They claim that because he was conceived solely by the Holy Spirit, Christ could not have been a human being like we are. He could not have had the same kind of body that we do. They insist that because he was a man from heaven, his body must have been from heaven too.

That's why I urgently warn believers to beware of religious splinter groups. If Christ isn't true and natural God, born in eternity of the Father, and if he isn't the Creator of all creatures, then we are doomed. What good is Christ's suffering and death to us if he was only a human like you and me? If he were just a human, he couldn't have overpowered the devil, death, or sin. He would've been too weak for them and would've never been able to help us. We must have a Savior who is true God and Lord over sin, death, hell, and the devil. Christ is eternal in nature, lacks nothing in his being, and is perfect in every way.

GOD IS ABLE AND WILLING

Mary said, "My soul praises the Lord's greatness! My spirit finds its joy in God, my Savior, because he has looked favorably on me, his humble servant."

LUKE 1:46–48

❖

 ARY PRAISED GOD for his power, knowledge, and desire to perform many amazing and great works. This song of praise strengthens our faith, comforts those who are humble, and terrifies all the powerful people on earth. She didn't sing it for herself alone. She wanted all of us to sing this song with her.

The great works God has done won't comfort you unless you believe that God is capable of doing them. More importantly, you must believe that God is willing to do them. However, believing that he is willing to do them for others but not for you is inadequate, too. If you only believe this much, you will put yourself beyond the reach of what God wants to do for you. This is what people who don't fear God do, as well as what people who have weak faith do. Those with weak faith have lost hope in God and, because of their hardships, have fallen into despair.

Believing that God is willing to help other people but unwilling to help you shows that your faith is dead. It's like believing in a fairy tale. You shouldn't waver or have any doubts about God's intentions toward you. You must train yourself to firmly believe that he is able to do great things for you and that he is willing to do them. This kind of faith is alive and real. It will spread throughout every aspect of your life and transform you. If you are powerful, it will make you afraid. If you are humble, it will give you comfort. The more powerful you are, the more afraid you will be. The more humble you are, the more comfort you will receive.

Loving God for Who He Is

Mary said, "My soul praises the Lord's greatness! My spirit finds its joy in God, my Savior, because he has looked favorably on me, his humble servant."

LUKE 1:46–48

❖

ARY HAD TOTAL CONFIDENCE that God was her Savior, even though she couldn't tell that this was true by seeing or feeling it. Mary was able to fully trust God because the Lord had placed this faith inside of her.

Mary put things in the right order in this verse. First, she called God her Lord. Next, she called him her Savior. Then, she proclaimed what God had done. By doing this, she teaches us to love and praise God for who he is. She shows us the right place to start. We shouldn't begin our prayers by selfishly asking what God can do for us. Mary's example teaches us to love and praise God for no other reason than his goodness. We should find joy and pleasure in who he is. This is an exalted, pure, and tender way of loving and praising God. It shows us Mary's extraordinary and tender spirit.

By contrast, some people are only parasites, always expecting to get things from God. They don't love or praise God because he is good. They're only concerned about how good God is to them, how much they feel his goodness, and how many good things they receive from him. The moment he hides his face and withdraws his goodness, leaving them in misery without anything, they stop loving and praising him. They no longer love and praise the goodness that they now can't see or feel. By doing this, they prove that they don't find joy in God, their Savior. They don't love or praise the goodness when it's hidden in God. They find much more joy in their salvation than in their Savior, in the gift than in the Giver, and in the creature than in the Creator.

TRUE HUMILITY

Mary said, "My soul praises the Lord's greatness!
My spirit finds its joy in God, my Savior, because he has
looked favorably on me, his humble servant."

LUKE 1:46–48

❖

GOOD DEAL OF PRIDE lurks behind the outward show of humility we see in the world today. People put themselves down, but don't want others to look down on them. They decline honors, but they really want more honors to follow them. They appear to avoid prominence, but they still want to be praised and don't want to deal with unimportant matters.

Yet in this passage, Mary says little about herself except that she was a servant. She was content to remain in her lowly position the rest of her life. She never gave any thought about her own glory or honor. She wasn't even aware of her own humility. Humility is so fragile and sensitive that it's not capable of looking at itself. Only God can look at it, as we read in Psalm 113:5–9.

If someone were able to look at his own humility, he would conclude that he deserves to be saved because he knows that God saves humble people. That's why God reserves the right to look at humility for himself. He hides it from us by making us look at unimportant things and by keeping us busy with them so that we forget to look at ourselves. That's the reason we have to endure so much suffering, death, and all the other kinds of hardships here on earth. Pain and difficulties force us to get rid of the envy within us.

By using the word *humble*, Mary shows us that she served God with an attitude of a despised, unimportant, lowly servant. She had no idea that her humility was so highly regarded by God.

WHAT THE ALMIGHTY HAS DONE

*Mary said, ". . . From now on, all people
will call me blessed because the Almighty has
done great things to me. His name is holy."*

LUKE 1:46–49

❖

 HAT'S THE PROPER WAY to speak about Mary? If you think about the words in this passage, they will teach you to say, "Blessed virgin, mother of God, you were unimportant and ignored by people. However, because God is kind, he looked favorably on you and performed great things in you. You didn't deserve any of those things, and you could never have earned them. Nevertheless, God's rich and unlimited kindness rested on you. You were blessed the first moment you found such a God, and you will be blessed forever."

To show Mary the proper respect, you must always think of her in relation to God—standing far beneath him. Mary said that God looked favorably on her for being a humble servant. Don't think about all the honors people have heaped on Mary. These people don't see that they are drowning out Mary's own words in this passage. Their eloquent words make the mother of God sound like a liar and diminish God's grace. To the degree that they say she earned or deserved what God did for her, they lower the value of God's kindness and make the truths in this passage more difficult to understand.

You should marvel at God's unlimited kindness. He generously and tenderly cared for, embraced, and blessed such a despised, insignificant person as Mary. If you think about her in this light, you will be inspired to love and praise God for his undeserved kindness. You will be encouraged to look for everything that is good from him alone. From what happened to Mary, you can learn that God doesn't reject humble, poor, insignificant people. He tenderly cares for them. This will strengthen your faith, love, and hope.

CHRIST'S BIRTH AND HIS KINGDOM

*At that time the Emperor Augustus ordered a census of
the Roman Empire. This was the first census taken
while Quirinius was governor of Syria.*

LUKE 2:1–2

❖

T'S INTERESTING THAT LUKE makes a point of saying this census was the very first one. A new census was conducted from time to time, but taxes were demanded every year. The religious leaders challenged Christ about these taxes in Matthew 22:17. When Christ was arrested, they even falsely accused him of telling people not to pay taxes to the Romans. The Israelites paid their taxes unwillingly and hated the taxation and laws of the Roman emperor. They claimed that because they were God's people, they ought to be free from the emperor. They argued over whether they should have to pay tribute money at all. But they had to pay it anyway because they couldn't defend themselves by force. They wanted to pull Christ into the middle of this dispute and hand him over to the Roman authorities. So this census was nothing more than a common duty in all lands. Every year, a tribute was due from every person.

Notice how Luke chooses his words precisely. The birth of Christ occurred during the reign of the emperor Augustus and when Quirinius was governor of Syria—the Roman district that included Israel at that time. The fact that Christ was born during the first census shows that his kingdom wasn't political and his reign wasn't over secular rulers. Instead, he subjected himself and his parents to these rulers.

If Christ had wanted to show that he wouldn't be subject to others, he could have been born before this census. The timing of Christ's birth, which was by God's design and intention, shows us that he didn't want to reign in the world.

LYING IN A MANGER

She gave birth to her firstborn son. She wrapped
him in strips of cloth and laid him in a manger
because there wasn't any room for them in the inn.

LUKE 2:7

❖

 VERYONE SHOULD USE the gospel to evaluate himself. How near or far are you from Christ? How are you doing in faith and love? Many become inflamed with dreamy devotion when they hear about how impoverished Christ was when he was born. They grow furious at the people of Bethlehem and criticize their blindness and ingratitude. They think that if they had been there, they would have served the Lord and his mother. They wouldn't have allowed them to be so miserable. But these people don't even notice their own neighbors who are nearby and need their help. They ignore them and leave them as they are. Who on earth doesn't have miserable, sick, blundering, or sinful people around them? Why don't they show their love to these people? Why don't they do for their neighbors what Christ did for them?

Don't deceive yourself by thinking you would have treated Christ well when you don't presently do anything for your neighbor. If you had been at Bethlehem, you would have paid just as little attention to him as everyone else did. You only want to serve him because you know who he is. Let's say that he were to come, lay in the manger, and let you know that he is the one you now know so much about. Of course you would want to do something to help. But before that, you wouldn't have done anything.

Similarly, if could see your neighbor now as he will be in the future, and if he were lying in front of you, then you would certainly take care of him. But because you only see him for what he is now, you ignore him. You fail to recognize Christ in your neighbor.

THE GLORY OF THE LORD

An angel from the Lord suddenly appeared to them.
The glory of the Lord filled the area with light,
and they were terrified.

LUKE 2:9

❖

IRST OF ALL, THE EVENT described in this passage wasn't merely one person telling another some good news. But an angel came from heaven and announced the birth of Christ to the shepherds. No human being knew anything about it. Second, notice that Christ was born at midnight. This shows that the world was dark at his coming and human reason on its own can't recognize Christ. Heaven must reveal it. Third, the bright light, which surrounded the shepherds, shows that something completely different than the light of reason is needed.

Luke says, "The glory of the Lord filled the area with light." He calls this light the glory of the Lord. Why? He does this to emphasize the mystery and show us the nature of the gospel. It is a heavenly light that teaches Christ alone.

This light from heaven shines around us through the apostles and their followers who now preach the gospel. The angel in this story is like all of the preachers of the gospel, and the shepherds are like all listeners. Accordingly, the gospel comes from heaven and doesn't tolerate any other teaching added to it, for human teaching is earthly light and human glory. It lifts up human glory and praise and makes people arrogantly rely on their own efforts. But the gospel teaches everyone to trust in Christ. So rely completely on God's kindness and goodness. Glorify Christ and be bold in him.

CHRIST IS BORN FOR YOU

The angel said to them, "Don't be afraid! I have good news for you, a message that will fill everyone with joy. Today your Savior, Christ the Lord, was born in David's city."

LUKE 2:10–11

❖

 O MATTER WHERE YOU'RE reading in the Bible, faith is the first mystery you should recognize. Faith is not believing that the story you're reading is true as written. That does nothing for anyone. Even unbelievers can believe this Bible story about Jesus' birth is true. Faith is not a natural work apart from God's grace, as the Scripture clearly teaches. Rather the right kind of faith, the kind that flows from grace and that God's Word demands, is firmly believing that Christ was born for you. His birth is yours and occurred for your benefit.

For the gospel teaches that Christ was born for our benefit and that everything he did and suffered was for us. As the angel says here, "I have good news for you, a message that will fill everyone with joy. Today your Savior, Christ the Lord, was born in David's city." With these words, you can clearly see that he was born for all of us.

He doesn't say, "a Savior was born," but rather "your Savior, Christ the Lord, was born." In the same way, he doesn't say, "I have good news," rather "I have good news for you." For you! "I have good news for you, a message that will fill everyone with joy." This joy is for everyone who has this kind of faith.

JOYFUL NEWS

The angel said to them, "Don't be afraid! I have good news
for you, a message that will fill everyone with joy. Today
your Savior, Christ the Lord, was born in David's city."

LUKE 2:10–11

❖

THE ANGEL HERE IS MAKING an announcement.
He doesn't say, "I would like to preach to
you," but simply "I have good news for
you." In other words, he is saying, "I am an evangelist,
my words are the gospel." So the gospel is a good, joyful message, which will become the main message of
the New Testament. What is the gospel? Listen to the
angel. He says, "I have good news for you, a message
that will fill everyone with joy." The gospel speaks of a
great joy. Where do we find it? Listen again, "Today
your Savior, Christ the Lord, was born in David's city."

So the gospel is a joyful message about Christ our
Savior. Whoever preaches correctly preaches the gospel
and nothing but joy. How can our hearts have a greater
joy than knowing that Christ is given to us to be our
own? The angel doesn't merely say "Christ was born,"
but also indicates that his birth is for us by saying,
"your Savior."

So the nature of the gospel isn't just teaching the
story and life of Christ but also personalizing it and
offering it to all who believe. What would it help me if
Christ were born a thousand times and this was sung to
me every day with wonderful music, if I didn't understand that his death was for me and that I should make
it my own? No matter how badly it's preached, my
heart hears the gospel with joy. It penetrates all the way
through and sounds wonderful. If there were something else to preach, then both the evangelical angel
and the angelic evangelist would have mentioned it.

GOD HONORS THE LOWLY

Suddenly, a large army of angels appeared with the angel. They were praising God by saying, "Glory to God in the highest heaven, and on earth peace to those who have his good will!"

LUKE 2:13–14

❖

HILE CHRIST'S BIRTH goes unnoticed on earth, it's being highly honored in heaven—a thousand times more highly. Suppose a single angel came from heaven and praised you and what you have done. Isn't it true you would prefer this to all of the world's praise and honor? You would wonder if you could endure the humility and contempt that it would require to deserve it. What kind of honor is this that all the angels in heaven can't contain themselves for joy? They burst forth and let the poor shepherds in the fields hear them preaching, praising, singing, and pouring out their joy beyond measure. What did all the joy and honor of those in Bethlehem—even of all the kings of the earth—compare to this joy and honor?

Notice how lavishly God honors those who are despised by the world. Here you see that God's eyes are turned toward the low places, for God sits above the angels and looks down to the depths. The angels were not sent to princes or powerful people, but rather to the uneducated, lowliest people on earth. Didn't they want to speak to the high priests, the highly educated men in Jerusalem, who had much to say about God and angels? No, the ones worthy of receiving such great honor from heaven were the poor shepherds, who were considered nobodies by the world.

God completely ignores what is high. Still, we race around madly to reach useless heights on earth in order to be honored in heaven. But God's eyes are only turned to the depths. So all we end up doing is stepping out of God's line of sight.

Faith of the Shepherds

The angels left them and went back to heaven. The shepherds said to each other, "Let's go to Bethlehem and see what the Lord has told us about."

LUKE 2:15

❖

F THESE SHEPHERDS hadn't believed the angels, they wouldn't have gone to Bethlehem. Neither would they have had done any of what is recorded in Luke. But when an unbeliever says, "Yes, I would certainly believe the message if an angel from heaven announced it to me," he doesn't know what he is saying. For whoever doesn't receive the Word on its own account will never receive it no matter who preaches it—even if all the angels come and preach it to him. Moreover, whoever believes the message on account of the one preaching it isn't believing the Word. Neither does he believe in God through the Word. Instead, he believes in the preacher. As a result, his faith doesn't endure.

But whoever believes the Word overlooks the one who is preaching it. He doesn't honor the Word because of the person. On the contrary, he honors the person because of the Word. He never places the person higher than the Word. If the preacher is ruined, falls from faith, or begins preaching a different message, the believer would rather let go of the preacher than give up the Word. He would stick with the Word regardless of the person involved or the situation.

This is the true difference between genuine and human faith. Human faith is always attached to the person. It believes, trusts, and honors the Word because of the one who speaks it. On the other hand, genuine faith clings to the Word, which is God himself. Genuine faith believes, trusts, and honors the Word because of what it is, not who said it. Faith so strongly senses the Word is true that no one can tear it away—not even the same preacher who first brought it.

JOSEPH AND MARY

Jesus' father and mother were amazed
at what was said about him.

LUKE 2:33

❖

HAT ARE THE AMAZING WORDS that were said? Who said them about Jesus? Of course, the amazing words were Simeon's. He took the baby Jesus in his arms and said, "Now Lord, you are allowing your servant to leave in peace as you promised. My eyes have seen your salvation, which you have prepared for all people to see. He is a light that will reveal ₍salvation₎ to the nations and bring glory to your people Israel" (Luke 2:29–32). Mary and Joseph were amazed that the baby was going to be a light to the whole world, a Savior to all people, and the glory of Israel. They were also amazed that Simeon himself thought so much of the child that he would gladly die after seeing him.

Now, it was remarkable for such a great man to praise this child in a public and holy place, for Jesus was only a poor, unimportant baby. His mother was poor and humble, and his father Joseph wasn't wealthy. How could such a child be looked upon as the Savior of all people, the light to the nations, and the glory of Israel? Today, now that we know the entire story, it doesn't seem so amazing. But back then, no one knew anything about it, and it sounded very strange. The poor child was so very different from the great and mighty person whom Simeon spoke about. But Joseph and Mary believed him anyway, and that is why they were amazed. If they hadn't believed, they would have disregarded Simeon's words. What he said would have seemed false and useless rather than amazing. So the simple fact that Joseph and Mary were amazed shows us their great faith.

ANNA'S EXAMPLE

Anna never left the temple courtyard
but worshiped day and night by fasting and praying.

LUKE 2:37

❖

OMEONE MIGHT SAY about this passage, "In Anna's story, we see Scripture praising good works, such as fasting, praying, and going to the temple. Doesn't this keep us from rejecting good works?" Here's our answer: Who rejected good works? We only reject the false works that appear to be good works. Fasting, praying, and going to church are good works if they are done in the right spirit.

But the problem begins when blind fools jump into Scripture, clomp around in it with boots and spurs, and only look at the works and outward example of people in the Bible. They want to learn about being holy and so immediately try to follow their example. This only leads to people becoming hypocrites because they forget that the Scriptures speak much more about the person than his works. For example, the Bible praises Abel's sacrifice, but it praises the kind of person he was even more. These hypocrites, however, skip right over the person and only take note of what they do. All they grasp is the works—they miss the faith. They eat the husk and throw out the grain, as the prophet Hosea says, "They have turned to other gods and love to eat raisin cakes" (Hosea 3:1).

If you wish to fast and pray as holy Anna did, that will be fine. But see to it that you first follow the example of her as a person and then afterwards follow the example of her works.

THE FAITH OF THE WISE MEN

*The star they had seen rising led them until it stopped
over the place where the child was. They were
overwhelmed with joy to see the star.*

MATTHEW 2:9–10

❖

THE WISE MEN STRUGGLED to continue believing
the words of the prophets when they were
led to such an inappropriate setting for a
royal birth. God comforted and strengthened them
with the star. It was closer to them now than it was at
the beginning. It guided them. When they started out,
it was far away from them, and they didn't know where
they would find the king.

Christians experience something similar when they
successfully endure trials. Near the end, God feels close
to them. He becomes so clearly recognizable that they
not only forget about their affliction but also desire
more of it so that they can become stronger. They are no
longer bothered by the circumstances of Christ's life.
They know by experience that anyone who wants to find
Christ must realize that it will seem as if he is only finding disgrace. The wise men would've felt ashamed if they
had slipped and said what they were probably thinking
in their hearts, "Oh my, what have we here! I can't wait
to take another journey and look for new kings!" They
felt like they were being led down a blind alley.

Our foolish nature often feels this way when trying
to follow God's words. Since the wise men became so
happy when they saw the star, we can infer that they
faced these doubts and were deeply depressed. Their joy
indicates that their hearts had been greatly disturbed.
They struggled with their doubts, and there was certainly enough reason for doubt in this situation. So
Christ really means it when he says, "Whoever doesn't
lose his faith in me is indeed blessed" (Matthew 11:6).

USING WHAT GOD HAS PROVIDED

God warned them in a dream not to go back to Herod.
So they left for their country by another road.

MATTHEW 2:12

❖

 HY DOES GOD WARN the wise men not to return to Herod? Even if Herod had found out, God could have easily protected Jesus from him and the entire world. The reason God did it this way was so we would learn not to test God. We should never look down on what we can conveniently accomplish with the help of what God has created.

Certainly, you should believe in God and say, "I will trust God. Everything will turn out all right." You should trust him as much as if you didn't want to work and were saying, "I will trust God. What is supposed to grow will grow anyway." But if this is all you do, what's the use of all that God has created? According to Genesis 1, God created everything in the world and established how human beings should use and work with all of it. He's not going to revoke that created order or make a special one just for you.

So in areas where God's Word gives you no command, you should continue to make use of your strength, your possessions, your friends, and everything else that God has given you. You should remain in the created order God established in Genesis 1, for he didn't give it to you for nothing. He will not make wine into water or turn bread into stones just for you. Rather, you should accept everything God has provided and use it just as he created it to be used, unless God's Word tells you to do otherwise.

Numbering Our Days

Teach us to number each of our days
so that we may grow in wisdom.

PSALM 90:12

❖

NTIL I REALIZED HOW seriously and urgently Moses prayed in this passage, I didn't understand that we should ask God to teach us to number our days. I thought everyone was just as afraid of death as I was. However, out of ten thousand people, only ten might believe that numbering their days is important. The rest of the masses of people live as if God doesn't exist and death doesn't occur.

But this isn't the worst part. Some people who are about to die imagine that they'll go on living. Others, overwhelmed by misery, still dream of happiness. Still others, who are in extreme danger, foolishly think they're totally secure. Their delusion is the saddest part of all.

So Moses appropriately teaches us to pray that we might number our days. We aren't supposed to ask God exactly how much time we have left. Rather, we must pray that we may become aware of how miserable and short our lives are. Death and God's eternal anger threaten us every second.

Occasionally, we'll find people who really are concerned about the shortness of life. They are preoccupied with thoughts of their impending death, even though they didn't pray for this knowledge. But most people aren't aware that their days are numbered. They live as if the present moment will last forever. So for most of us, praying the way Moses suggests in this passage is indispensable.

THE BEGINNING, MIDDLE, AND END

Faith convinces us that God created the world through
his Word. This means what can be seen was made
by something that could not be seen.

HEBREWS 11:3

❖

NO CREATURE CAN ASSIST in its own creation or sustain itself. Similarly, we didn't create ourselves, and we can't keep ourselves alive for a single moment by our own strength. God alone is responsible for our growth and development. Without him, we would have died a long time ago. If our Creator, who continues to work, and his coworker Christ were to stop their work, everything would break down in an instant. This truth inspires us to confess, "I believe in God the Father Almighty, Maker of heaven and earth." If God hadn't been sustaining us all along, we would have died long ago—even in infancy or at birth.

The writer of Hebrews also teaches us about how God creates and sustains us: "Faith convinces us that God created the world through his Word. This means what can be seen was made by something that could not be seen." In other words, the author of Hebrews is saying that through Christ, the Father continually makes the invisible become visible. He makes what is nonexistent come into existence. A hundred years ago none of us could be seen. People who will be born ten or twenty years from now can't be seen either. They haven't been born and don't exist yet. But when they are born, they will become visible and real.

Christ is the one who creates something visible from the invisible. Through him, heaven and earth were created out of nothing. Christ the Lord was present when everything was created. He wasn't merely a spectator, but equal to the Creator. He was the Father's coworker. He will continue to rule and will sustain everything until the end of the world. He is the beginning, the middle, and the end for everything and everyone.

INDEX TO OTHER EDITIONS

Date	American Edition (English) volume:page		Saint Louis Edition (German) volume:column
Jan 1	22:275		7:1849

Date	American Edition	Saint Louis Edition	Date	American Edition	Saint Louis Edition
Jan 1	22:275	7:1849	Feb 11	23:42	7:2235
Jan 2	5:157	2:320	Feb 12	30:269	9:1453
Jan 3	43:24	3:160	Feb 13	7:130	2:1324
Jan 4	26:136	9:186	Feb 14	27:166	8:1369
Jan 5	42:88	14:1416	Feb 15	51:267	9:891
Jan 6	42:13	11:581	Feb 16	1:137	1:167
Jan 7	42:12	11:580	Feb 17	24:385	8:702
Jan 8	52:95	11:212	Feb 18	42:45	7:782
Jan 9	30:35	9:994	Feb 19	24: 142	8:426
Jan 10	26:380	9:500	Feb 20	4:21	1:1392
Jan 11	24:193	8:483	Feb 21	24:264	8:567
Jan 12	42:22	7:757	Feb 22	6:148	2:805
Jan 13	24:12	8:271	Feb 23	27:73	9:687
Jan 14	52:29	11:142	Feb 24	51:348	12:1977
Jan 15	30:263	9:1447	Feb 25	27:57	9:669
Jan 16	30:126	9:1091	Feb 26	30:232	9:1412
Jan 17	28:177	8:1229	Feb 27	28:104	8:1143
Jan 18	26:356	9:470	Feb 28	42:21	7:756
Jan 19	24:48	8:315	Mar 1	12:274	5:437
Jan 20	12:318	5:493	Mar 2	5:56	2:193
Jan 21	4:364	2:64	Mar 3	22:382	7:1977
Jan 22	30:108	9:1072	Mar 4	6:360	2:1090
Jan 23	30:235	9:1416	Mar 5	24:119	8:398
Jan 24	12:328	5:507	Mar 6	28:124	8:1167
Jan 25	26:232	9:308	Mar 7	12:188	5:298
Jan 26	42:76	7:817	Mar 8	6:133	2:785
Jan 27	30:142	9:1108	Mar 9	42:19	7:753
Jan 28	6:360	2:1091	Mar 10	3:311	1:1296
Jan 29	23:23	7:2213	Mar 11	24:251	8:551
Jan 30	53:66	10:231	Mar 12	15:25	5:1397
Jan 31	7:126	2:1318	Mar 13	2:103	1:556
Feb 1	21:235	7:609	Mar 14	24:202	8:494
Feb 2	24:249	8:548	Mar 15	26:341	9:452
Feb 3	26:114	9:158	Mar 16	4:296	1:1739
Feb 4	23:28	7:2219	Mar 17	52:79	11:194
Feb 5	4:93	1:1484	Mar 18	30:94	9:1056
Feb 6	9:74	3:1430	Mar 19	4:122	1:1522
Feb 7	30:322	9:1515	Mar 20	21:189	7:556
Feb 8	6:158	2:817	Mar 21	30:140	9:1106
Feb 9	27:355	8:1595	Mar 22	4:181	1:1596
Feb 10	5:232	2:414	Mar 23	43:235	20:2211

INDEX TO OTHER EDITIONS

SUBJECT INDEX

Cross
hold it high (Nov 16)
(see also Suffering, Trials)

Death
the dead will be raised (Jan 17,
  Oct 1)
believers need not fear (Feb 27,
  Apr 16, May 23, Nov 21,
  Dec 6, Dec 7)
gateway to eternal life (Jun 21)
destroyed by Jesus (Jun 30,
  Sep 29, Nov 21)
numbering our days (Dec 30)

Devil (see Satan)

Discipleship
evidence of true disciples
  (May 14, Aug 26)

Discipline
God disciplines his children
  (Jun 7, Aug 10, Aug 21,
  Aug 22)

Eternal Life
is certain (May 23)
hidden in death (Jun 21)
has already begun (Jul 5, Oct 21,
  Nov 26)

Faith
faith and good works (Jan 1,
  Feb 2, Feb 10, Mar 1, Apr 18,
  Jun 27, Aug 6, Nov 22)
saved through faith alone (Jan 4,
  Apr 19, Oct 28)
true faith (Jan 18, Apr 14,
  Aug 4, Aug 20, Sep 28,
  Nov 17, Dec 25)
looking at Christ alone (Jan 18,
  Nov 28)
given by God (Jan 29, Jun 24)

bears fruit (Feb 21, May 9,
  Jun 4)
living by faith (Mar 13, Mar 15,
  Sep 19, Nov 7)
the only way to see God (Jun 23)
fellowship with God (Sep 22,
  Sep 26)
of Joseph and Mary (Dec 26)
of the wise men (Dec 28)

Family
when problems arise in (Jan 28,
  Jun 15)

Fear
fearing God (Jan 9, Nov 3)
fearing death (Feb 27, Apr 16,
  May 23, Nov 21, Dec 6,
  Dec 7)

Forgiveness
forgiving others (Apr 25,
  Nov 19)
from God (May 7)
accomplished by Christ (Jun 17,
  Jul 28)
asking for (Nov 5)

Freedom
in Christ (Jul 6, Jul 14)
from sin (Aug 2)
to serve (Sep 3)
true vs. false (Oct 11)

God
loves us (Jan 6, Oct 2)
name is holy (Jan 12, May 24)
as our guardian (Mar 4)
has plans for our lives (Mar 24,
  Apr 2, Oct 12, Nov 11)
cares for his children (Apr 12,
  Jun 5)
known through his Son (May 10,

May 31, Jul 7, Jul 25, Oct 18,
Oct 25)
there is only one (May 19,
Dec 11)
disciplines his children (Jun 7,
Aug 10, Aug 21, Aug 22)
goodness of (Jul 11)
calls those who stray to return
(Aug 29)
chose us (Sep 1)
has mercy on us (Oct 9, Dec 1)
is our refuge (Nov 29)
can do all things (Dec 15,
Dec 18)
honors the lowly (Dec 24)

God's Word (see Scripture)

Golden Rule (Feb 1)

Good Works
cannot save us (Jan 1, Jul 23,
Jul 30, Nov 2)
good works and faith (Jan 1,
Feb 2, Feb 10, Mar 1, Apr 18,
Jun 27, Aug 6, Nov 22)
the fruit of a faithful life (Jun 4,
Aug 5, Dec 27)

Gospel/Gospels
one true message (Mar 29,
Sep 7, Sep 16)
gospel vs. law (Apr 22)
teaches us to trust in Christ
(Dec 21)
joyful news (Dec 23)

Government
attitude toward (Jul 1, Jul 4)

Grace (see Kindness of God)

Guidance
of God (Mar 24, Apr 2, Oct 12,
Nov 11)

Harmony
among believers (Mar 18,
Jun 15)

Holiness (see Righteousness)

Holy Spirit
helps in times of trial (Jan 10)
is our helper (Aug 16)
lives within us (Oct 13)

Humility
in sharing our faith (Jan 22)
in our daily walk (Feb 3,
Aug 15)
when God has honored us
(Feb 24, May 20, Jun 25,
Aug 31, Dec 17)
regarding sin (Mar 10, Jun 6)

Jesus Christ (see Christ)

Joy
joy and sorrow (Jun 18)
balancing fear and joy (Nov 3)
in the gospel message (Dec 23)

Judging
beware of judging others (Apr 25)
do not judge by appearances
(Apr 28)

Judgment of God
refusing God's help (Mar 3)

Kindness of God
freeing us from sin's penalty
(Jan 24)
helping us to obey (Sep 27)
don't shove it aside (Nov 27)